THE PHOTOGRAPH

Eamonn Sweeney was born in 1968 in Sligo.
His acclaimed first novel, *Waiting for the Healer*, was
published by Picador in 1997. He now lives in Cork.

Also by Eamonn Sweeney

Waiting for the Healer

EAMONN SWEENEY

THE PHOTOGRAPH

PICADOR

First published 2000 by Picador

This edition published 2001 by Picador
an imprint of Macmillan Publishers Ltd
25 Eccleston Place, London SW1W 9NF
Basingstoke and Oxford
Associated companies throughout the world
www.macmillan.com

ISBN 0 330 48084 7

9 8 7 6 5 4 3 2 1

A CIP catalogue record for this book is available from
the British Library.

Typeset by SetSystems Ltd, Saffron Walden, Essex
Printed and bound in Great Britain by
Mackays of Chatham plc, Chatham, Kent

To Antonia

Thanks to my family for their support, and to Colm Tóibín and Pat McCabe for assistance and advice. Thanks to my agent Pat Kavanagh for her faith, and to Peter Straus and Becky Senior for their help with the book. Part of this novel was written at the Yaddo Artists Community, New York. My gratitude to the people at Yaddo for their hospitality, Cathy Clarke and Joe Caldwell particularly. With love to Antonia, without whom this or any other book would not be possible. And in memory of Martin Healy. The like of him will never be again.

Prologue / A box of black and whites

McKeon was back in the *Herald* newsroom. The name of the place was the same, but the building had changed. New technology had put the workforce into a former small shoe shop. There were no printers any more. McKeon was glad his father had died before he could see the Coosars and Linotype machines dispatched to some elephants' graveyard of the newspaper industry.

The building was different, but the young lad with the cheap suit and polished cracked leather shoes reminded McKeon of himself at the same age. Keen, clueless and learning. All three had been in his voice when McKeon rang him that evening.

—Listen, it's Seamus McKeon here. I wonder if there's any way you could let me have a root through the *Herald* photo files? For research purposes.

—The editor said not to speak to anyone from the nationals or television.

—If you want to get out of here, you'll have to speak to people from the nationals. You're from the town yourself, aren't you?

—Yeah, Colmcille Park.

—Same as myself. You're a bright lad, you don't want

to be there all your life. Sort me out on this and I'll line up some work for you when you get to Dublin.

—I'm not going to Dublin.

—You're not going to Dublin yet.

Two hours later the youngster handed over his keys to McKeon.

There were envelopes upon envelopes, binders upon binders, boxes upon boxes of black and whites taken by the *Herald*'s first ever photographer, alcoholic Gerry McDonagh who had hardly been able to stand up on the night in 1965 when he had taken the picture McKeon was looking for.

A classic *Herald* picture. Men standing in a crooked line and trying to look sober. McKeon was one of them. That was why it never appeared in the paper. The editor didn't want any of his reporters thinking they were a local personality. McDonagh kept a print all the same, and tucked it into a brown envelope just like the ones McKeon was leafing through now.

—We'll hang on to that. For when you get to be famous, young McKeon, McDonagh had said.

He had taken it the night the Majestic Ballroom opened in Rathbawn. Shy women with immense hair milled around the mineral bar as Gerry tried to manoeuvre the quartet into position. In the background, Dickie Rock was singing,

—From the candy store on the corner, to the chapel on the hill.

One of McKeon's arms was severed by the left edge of the photo. Beside him, Henry Caslin smiled his famous smile and dominated the picture to such an extent that he seemed like a hologram floating above the surface. His right arm was around the shoulder of Father Gerry Lee, who appeared to shrink away from the camera. Beside Father Lee, Jimmy Mimnagh's eyes were going both ways with drink but one of them managed to gaze at Caslin as if he was afraid the man would bolt from the building and never be seen again.

McKeon kept searching for this photograph. As if the answer to what had happened to the four of them could be found there. He started to remember.

HENRY

The National School children knocked great crack out of tormenting Tommy Caslin.

It helped that he was a man who generally rose to the bait before it had even hit the water. He would be at the front door of his shop when the kids were coming home from school, and the minute he saw them would start waving his arms and shouting.

—Who stole the sheep? Who stole the fucking sheep? Young Finneran, ask your father who stole the sheep. The young McGlynns know who stole the sheep. Who stole the sheep?

The kids would echo Tommy's shouts until his voice started to sink. After a final plaintive

—Who stole the sheep?

he would turn on his heel and walk slowly back into his shop.

Young Henry and Eugene Caslin went to National School in Aughabeg for a couple of years before switching to Kiltymore, which lay four miles out of the country. They walked there and back. Henry had asked to be sent to Kiltymore.

People didn't like explaining what had driven Tommy to shout at the children of the village. When it came to retelling the War Of Independence, they preferred talking about the young Kennedy lad who was killed by the Black and Tans. His body was dragged to the doorstep of every house in Aughabeg. In the middle of the thirties, the war had ended barely a dozen years, not nearly enough time to look straight at it.

The Tans never caught up on the leaders of the local flying column, Peter Finneran, Joe McGlynn, Terry Galvin and Tommy Caslin. Caslin's family owned a small shop in the village; the other three lads came from small farms in the hills where the land was so bad the snipe had to wear wellingtons.

When war nears an end soldiers count their losses. McGlynn's farmhouse had been burned down by the Tans. Galvin's fiancée had left for Chicago and a job in the stockyards after he refused to leave the IRA. At a meeting in Duignan's pub, Galvin pointed out that the forces of the Empire seemed to be in retreat. The Tans were rarely to be seen, and he had it on good authority that the Brits were planning an unconditional surrender. He also mentioned that in three years of fighting, the Aughabeg flying column had always behaved impeccably towards soldiers and citizens alike.

—But I just think it'd be a poor thing if this war ended, and we ended up worse off than when we came into it.

Finneran and McGlynn nodded their agreement. If Caslin had been a suspicious man, he might have wondered how his fellow commanders seemed already familiar with Galvin's spur-of-the-moment plan.

—That Protestant fucker above in Kingsley House has six hundred head of beasts on his land, and he's nearly better off now than when this all started. It's hardly fair, considering Joe's family had their house burned from over their heads and their cattle killed.

—Both of them, said McGlynn.

—I reckon that hoor is an informer to the Tans. And I reckon it would serve him right if he wakes up some morning in the same state that Joe's father found himself in last March, said Finneran.

It was agreed that Kingsley would be divested of his animals. The four commanders would sell the beasts to a friendly dealer who would provide financial restitution commensurate with their service in the war. Terry Galvin would get beef cattle, Joe McGlynn dairy cattle, Tommy Caslin sheep and Peter Finneran poultry and goats.

The animals were easy rounded up. A few belts of a rifle across the puss sorted out any estate workers who took their job too seriously. McGlynn decided that while they were at it the volunteers might as well teach Kingsley a lesson. He led the men who set fire to the house, and when Kingsley charged out in his dressing gown, McGlynn shot him twice in the greying seventy-two-year-old head.

Spirits were high on the way home. In rare moments of sobriety, Tommy would remember that night as the last when he had been truly happy. The beasts were driven to the isolated hill farms. Tommy's sheep were penned on the land of Finneran's father. They would be driven to Cavan at five o'clock the next morning. The commanders split up to grab a couple of hours' sleep before starting the journey.

Galvin fell into step with Tommy as he was walking back to the village. He suggested a knock on the window of Duignan's for a late drink.

—Don't we deserve one. As volunteers.

Beatrice Duignan wasn't happy to be woken at three in the morning. But better woken than waked. She knew what had gone on from the orange light in the sky above Kingsley House. A similar light hovered over the village of Drumbo, which the Tans had razed in retaliation. McGlynn had worked out that Drumbo was a mile and a half nearer to Kingsley House than Aughabeg was. It was also on a less ambush-friendly road.

The whiskey-drinking in Duignan's was led by Galvin. He was more experienced. Tommy had not taken a drink before the war, but had since begun to sup bottles of stout in order to quell dreams of capture by the Tans, torture and castration.

He woke face down in a pool of whiskey at the counter. The woman of the house looked amused.

—I was going to bring you back to life, but young Galvin said leave you to sleep it off.

—What time is it?

—Twelve o'clock. You had a fair oul rest.

Even before reaching Finneran's farm, Tommy knew what had happened. The sight of them sitting together in the kitchen and the look they gave him confirmed his suspicions.

—Lads, how are things? How did it go with the beasts?

—It went grand, Tommy, only we have terrible bad news for you, said Finneran who was looking into the fire now.

—What bad news?

—There's supposed to have been tinkers around last night, and we reckon it was them that stole the sheep, said McGlynn who looked straight into Tommy's face.

—Did they steal anything apart from my sheep?

—Not a thing, said McGlynn and began toasting a piece of bread.

Tommy jumped at Finneran and knocked him to the ground. He was about to draw out with the boot when he felt the cold metal of a Webley revolver against his cheek.

—If you don't get out, Caslin, I'll blow the fucking head off you. You know I will, said McGlynn.

He knew McGlynn would. Finneran gave him a parting shot at the door.

—You ever try and do anything like this and we'll kill you in your bed. That's no lie.

What hurt most was that McGlynn and Finneran had made no effort to make him believe their lie.

It was after the war before Tommy realised the value of the animals they had stolen. Joe McGlynn bought a meat factory. Peter Finneran moved to the county town of Rathbawn and bought a hotel. Terry Galvin set up a chain of bakeries which made him the richest man in the county. Every month he would arrive at Caslin's shop and buy a mouldy apple or a bit of stale soda bread before telling Tommy

—I never knew what was going to happen that night. Only for I chanced home from the pub when I did, they would have had my cattle gone and all. It's a disgrace what happened to you. I still feel guilty I wasn't able to wake you up that night.

The smile on Tommy's face would make his old friend marvel at the gullibility of the man who had saved his life in the famous Kiltymore ambush. He was not to know that on the day of Galvin's funeral, Tommy would shuffle to the edge of the grave and hawk a black spit on the polished pine surface of the coffin.

Galvin died a rich man, as did McGlynn and Finneran, who had by then passed on their wealth to their sons. People forgot how the families had come by their money in the first place, and made knowing comments about the value of hard work and thrift. While his old friends prospered, Tommy took to the drink in a way that made his wife despair of the future awaiting their own two sons.

The first time Henry stood in Duignan's was the day his grandfather on his mother's side died. On her way to

Caslin's, the postmistress met him battering a handball up against the gable wall of the abandoned RIC barracks. She told him it might help if he fetched his father home.

The pub seemed infinitely large to Henry. He was disturbed by the smell, the compound odour of the living-room couch after his father had slept there, the empty bottles he found in the kitchen in the morning and shit in a field on a warm day. The light in the bar was of a kind that did not exist outside, and it seemed to swallow up the figures at the counter. He did not fully recognise his father until he was close enough to tweak his elbow and whisper

—Daddy, could you come home? Granny King is dead. Miss O'Grady says you should come home.

He had not often looked his father in the eye. Tommy tended to avoid straight-on gazes, but drink had made him careless enough this day to turn round and press his face right up against Henry's. The eyes were soft and dead, wet round the rim, and did not look attached to their owner. Little red lines ran through them like bloody caterpillars. Henry had a sudden urge to run but checked it.

Beatrice Duignan left a bottle of stout and a double whiskey at the counter. Tommy turned around and grabbed them quickly before facing Henry again. Henry stayed where he was. He knew this was not a good place to be. It made him determined to stay there as a test. He was good at tests. His father put him sitting on a bar stool.

—You'll have a pint of Guinness, son.

—I will not, Daddy. I'm too young.

—What age are you?

—Nine.

—Ah, nine. Ah, Jesus, the years fucking fly. Ah, Beatrice, they fucking fly. Where did they go at all at all.

Big round stones of tears fell down Tommy's face, some dissolving into the redness of his cheeks, others falling on his hands, teeming over the wrist to fall into the shaking glass of whiskey.

Three more hours and six drinks went by before Tommy left Duignan's. Henry stayed there with people buying him minerals before they became disenchanted by his obvious disdain.

—He's a mighty snotty young fella, considering whose son he is.

—Ah, but the mother was always a right oul bitch.

Each time his father finished a drink, Henry would ask him to come home. Tommy would smile, order another one and say

—Do you know what, Beatrice, work is the curse of the drinking classes. That's a good one, work is the curse of the drinking classes.

When Beatrice told Tommy he would get no more drink, he raised his walking stick threateningly, pitched forwards and got sick on the floor. Henry tried to get hold of him but was brushed aside as the two other customers hefted his father out on to the street, where he lay on his side frantically trying to attract the landlady's attention.

—No problem, Tommy, of course you're not barred. Don't worry about it, said Beatrice.

—It's hardly like this is different from any other day, said one of the other drinkers, and winked at Henry.

Henry kept a hand on the side of his father's leg and steered him in the direction of the front door when they arrived at the house, before slipping away to avoid seeing his mother's face. He would never take a drink in his life.

In later years, Henry was never sure whether his conviction that he was special had come because of or despite his circumstances. But he knew it was that conviction which made him insist on going to school in Kiltymore. Away from his own village he could become who he wanted to be.

His teacher noticed this driven quality from a young age. Henry was of average intelligence but his desire to learn was phenomenal. Other kids lost interest at some point, and began to chew their chalk or doodle idly on their slates. Henry sat bolt upright all day, and beads of sweat would decorate his forehead when he could not work out a problem or remember a line from a poem or the date of a battle. Often he would stay behind after school to find out just how well he was doing.

—I don't want to rest on my laurels, Missus Boyle.

Most impressive of all was the way he managed to behave like this without alienating his schoolmates. Anyone who tried to brand him a lick found it was they who became the odd ones out. He had the knack of being successful without arousing the envy of others. He made them feel they were part of his success. He had just succeeded by accident. It could have been them, which was how his classmates felt when Missus Boyle announced that her prize pupil had won a scholarship to the diocesan college, which would pay for his tuition and boarding fees.

Henry had got where he wanted to be. Out in the world on his own.

When he turned seventeen, both his final year in secondary school and a Second World War, which Ireland affected to find unimportant, were coming to an end. He had not once been a cause of concern to any of his teachers, before it came to their attention that now he was never seen in the evening without a posse of other lads trailing after him. The suspicion had to be that he was distributing cigarettes, pornographic magazines or corrupting works of banned literature. His form tutor, Father Murray, called him in for a wee chat.

—Master Caslin, I'd be glad if you could let me know exactly what you're up to, and why you're surrounded by a group of lads every evening when prep ends.

—They'd be mainly my friends, Father.

—Come, on man, I'm talking to you man to man. As one adult to another.

—Well you see, Father, it's all to do with sweets. The tuck shop closes at the end of the school day and a lot of the lads, the younger lads especially, have a fierce sweet tooth. They'd be craving for toffees and crisps and things for the remainder of the evening.

—And you're the supplier.

—I am of course, Father. Supply and demand, it's supposed to be one of the big rules of business. Maybe the biggest one. I read that in a book I got out of the library, one about economics.

—How do you get these sweets?

—I spend most of my pocket money on them when we go down the town at the weekend. Then I add a few pence on to the price and sell them to the lads when the supply is small and the demand is big.

—Do you think that's an honourable way to carry on with your school chums?

—Oh, it is, Father, that's how business works. And I want to be a businessman when I leave school.

—We were hoping you might go on for the teaching. What sort of a businessman do you want to be?

—A successful one, Father.

Two weeks later Father Murray received a letter from Henry which asked if he could arrange a meeting with Father Tobin, the school Principal. The cheek of him.

The heat of the day made the paper of the Sacred Heart picture on the wall of the Principal's office rumple up like a disturbed bedsheet. Henry put his heart and soul into a confident handshake. Father Tobin knew there was a tremor somewhere underneath the grasp, but he gave the young man credit for hiding it so well.

— Young Master Caslin. I hear you have a proposal for us. I don't suppose you want to tell us what subjects we should teach, or how much we should charge in fees next year?

— Indeed I don't, Father.

— Maybe you want to tell us what food we should have in the dining halls, or how many weeks' holidays there should be during the year.

— That's not it at all, Father.

This young lad is hard shook, thought Father Tobin.

— What would it be, then? You have a minute to tell me. I haven't the time to be talking to every young whipper-snapper who thinks he can run the college better than I can.

— Begging your pardon, Father, but I'd never think anything like that. It's only about the tuck shop. I heard it's losing money for the college.

— Who told you it was losing money?

A blush from the attendant Father Murray eliminated the necessity for an answer.

— A sort of a little bird told me, Father. I heard the man who ran it is going away for a while because of his health, and I'd like it if you gave me the chance to run it.

— Why would we do that? You're a student, not an adult.

— I know about shopkeeping from home, Father. And I know about business and economics from the library. I'd have the tuck shop making money in a shot.

— Is that what you have been wasting my time with?

— With respect, Father, I'm not wasting your time. If that shop isn't making money within a month, I'll cut the grass on the football pitch every week until I leave this school.

When Henry arrived in Gray's Confectioner's, Martin Gray's first impulse was to regard him as a potential shoplifter. The little teenager was hopping nervously from one foot to the other, and showed no sign of buying.

—Hello Mister Gray, my name's Henry Caslin. I'm a student above at the college, and I'm after being put in charge of running the tuck shop. Father Murray says you sell us a lot of the sweets there.

—You're hardly running the tuck shop now. Sure you're only a gossan. Buy something or get out, it isn't a library I'm running.

Caslin bit his lip, and from his pocket produced a neatly rolled letter bound with a piece of red ribbon. Gray read it. Father Tobin had put this young lad in charge of running the tuck shop all right. It must be some make of project.

—I'm wondering, Mister Gray, could you see your way to halving the price of the sweets that you sell to the tuck shop?

—. . . . .

—It's only that the tuck shop is losing money hand over fist, and I have a sort of an idea of how to stop that. But it'd need you to be supplying us a lot cheaper.

—You have some fucking cheek coming into this shop here and asking me a thing like that. And the fucking size of you. I'll speak to Father Tobin and he'll put your tail fairly quickly between your legs.

—I told Father Tobin what I was going to do, and I told him as well that you're charging us a higher wholesale price than any of the other sweetshops in the town.

—I charge a fair price. And fair or not, I can charge what I like. Ye'd be rightly gone if I didn't supply ye.

—I sort of did a check-up, and I think you should see your way towards halving the price. There's a few hundred boys up there in the college. It's a captive market, and you do great business there. You should make a gesture of goodwill.

—Goodwill, me arse.

—I checked a couple of the smaller wholesalers. They'd supply us at a much lower price. I just thought it would be fair to give you first refusal before you lost an order this big.

By the time Gray had charged out from behind the counter, Henry had glided out the door.

The shopkeeper cut his prices by forty per cent, the tuck shop made a lot more money for the college and Henry took most of the credit, although he let Father Tobin keep some. Profits soared, but the prices of the tuck-shop items actually increased. There was not a word against Henry from his fellow students about this. He had pointed out that it was not his triumph but theirs, because he had shown the college authorities that the students could do the job better than them. Everyone should be proud of the success of the tuck shop.

Henry won the Most Popular Student award in his final year, and landed a job as a clerical officer with CIE in a small town called Carnamodda, which was four counties and one province away. He told himself it would be his platform to make a big name in the world.

Ten years later he was still there. All the while telling himself this was not the job he was cut out for. On his twenty-seventh birthday the other lads in the boarding house had a party for him and Missus Farry, the landlady, told him he was doing well for such a young lad. After ten years they had made him Deputy Stationmaster.

He did not think he was doing well or going anywhere, but the work was hard. The Irish railway boom had imploded, and dead rural stations stood round the country like obsolete watchtowers from a lost civilisation. Six trains stopped in Carnamodda each weekday, four on Sunday. Henry noted the arrival of goods and sometimes brought the boxes containing those goods to shops in the town. Grady's Drapery was a black building with rows of mainly dark clothes sheltering behind a dusty front window. A piece of metal at the top of the door screeched when you entered and immediately summoned one of the assistants, young women who scooted around the floor, lighting up the joint like fireflies and coaxing even the shyest of bachelors into spending a few bob.

The metal wailed, heels appeared behind a shoe stand, a blue outfit rustled and someone stood in front of Henry. When he looked up he felt as if he'd suddenly been pinned against an electric fence with volt after volt bringing his heart to the verge of explosion.

—Hello, how are you doing? Can I help you?

—Well now . . . the boxes . . . they're here . . . they're for here . . . they're there.

—Is this the delivery off the train?

—It is. It's just in.

—I'll take it then. Thanks very much.

—My name is Henry Caslin.

—My name is Mary Flynn. Thanks. It's a warm oul day to be carting these yokes around.

—Hard work never hurt anyone.

—It's hardly hard work all the same. Have ye a farm at home?

—We have a shop. What part are you from yourself?

—Toorgraney. You hardly know it.

—I played football in it one time to raise funds for the Yugoslavian Church.

—Were ye bet?

—We won. I'm from Aughabeg. I work up at the railway station.

—I know. We'll be seeing you again, I hope.

He had never taken a drink because he saw what it had done to his father. And more importantly to his mother, who had no choice in the matter. That was the big reason. The small reason was that he feared losing control. Drink destroyed your ability to make rational decisions. Now he found there was something else that had the same effect. For a man who hadn't passed much remarks on the Romantic poets in school, it was a bit of a frightener.

His whole week began to revolve around the five-minute walk to Grady's and the ten-minute chat that followed. Mary Flynn always dealt with him. The sound of her skirt swishing and her high heels scuffing along the lino became the language of love. He committed her words to memory so he could parse them, hold them up at every angle against the light, try to locate their core.

One or more of the other girls from Grady's always found an opportunity to join in the conversation between Henry and Mary. They tended to be very giggly, which Henry didn't mind. He'd seen few enough giggles around his own place, and enjoyed their novelty. Mary seemed to mind a good deal. He noticed her frown, and how she never seemed as commanding when the other girls arrived. The interlopers words explained why.

—I'd better be going, Mary.

—Hurry back next week, now. Mary'll be pining the whole time for you.

—Shut up, you.

—I'll see you next week, Mary.

—Make sure to, now, or we'll never hear the last of it.

—Will you be quiet.

—Good luck now, Mary.

—Will you be going dancing this weekend, Henry? I

believe you might be interested in the company if you go to the temperance hall.

—Don't mind them here, Henry, they'd have your head annoyed if you paid any heed to them.

For the first time in his life Henry thought it mightn't matter if he didn't become the most famous man in the county. It might be enough to be happy with Mary Flynn. Then he realised that only the most famous man in the county would deserve her. He had double reason to make something of himself.

Luck was on his side, too. Mary's brother David landed a job with the ESB in Carnamodda and lodged in the same house as Henry. Mary visited him there. David saved his money and bought a Ford Prefect.

Eight people usually wedged into the car on a Saturday night. They would leave Carnamodda in search of dances farther afield. Sometimes the door would open mid-journey as a sardined back-seater moved too vigorously. David always drove. Henry was always there. Bertie Moran from the creamery. Assumpta Colgan, the usherette from the Star cinema. Mary came occasionally at first, and soon never missed a night.

Henry arranged that there were always eight. Four lads and four girls. So there would be no one left out at the dances. This was not out of selfishness on his part. Everyone wanted to dance with Henry. Even in the little villages where dances came around as often as leap years, women would glance shyly at him and the ladies' choice became a stampede.

All because he was able to dance. Other men disdained to do it properly, hanging slyly and drunkenly around the chairs at the edge of the hall before venturing forward to stand on the feet of their partners. But Henry loved to dance, and knew the figure of a man he was in the bespoke suit made by the Protestant outfitters in Market Street which he paid for with the money he had not drunk. Seeing the curl of the lip as he was measured, Henry fixed Mister Craig with a look, held himself upright and reminded himself whose country it was not.

The dance bands were smooth and shiny and sophisticated, calling out the steps and tempo to which Henry moved with grace and precision. When he and Mary danced together, people stopped dead and watched them move in unison like Siamese twins on elastic before they parted for the company of other members of the eight.

The dancehalls bothered Henry. The way the time was called for you. The fact that the landlady knew what tunes the band played and wondered why they hadn't changed since her time. The way the rigidity of the music sucked the spring from your step in those draughty halls where the dance-band members perched tired and nervous behind their music stands. When you got home you could never remember what any of them looked like.

—Mary, who are we going to see next week?

—Brosna.

—Who are we going to see? Which band?

—I don't know, to be honest with you. It's Brosna we're going to.

—What's Brosna hall like?

—Like everywhere else. Cold and damp.

—We'll have a good night, all the same.

—Do you hear that, Mary. He's calling ye we now.

—Shut up, you.

—See you Saturday night.

Brosna hall wasn't like every other place. It was colder, it was damper, it was smaller, and when the band came on they looked like they wanted to cry. One of the trumpet-players sneezed so much that eventually he laid his instrument down gently, climbed off the stage and walked slowly through the hall into the dark Brosna night.

The saxophonist was the musician Henry would remember. The rare solo he played as the gouty lumps of water slithered down the walls. Mary always insisted she'd noticed the wonderful difference in the way Henry had looked at her from the start of the night.

—I was tired, Mary. I wanted to be in me bed.

—That wasn't how you looked at me. You looked at me the right way.

—I didn't mean to if I did.

—But I hoped that was how you were looking at me. Maybe that was it.

—Sure I've looked at you the right way since the second I saw you.

—Shut up, you.

The solo was Blue Moon. A ladies' choice. And although Mary had already danced more than her fair share with Henry, she came over and took his arm.

—Blue moon. You saw me standing alone.

When their eyes met Henry felt as if he was looking through Mary. At her heart and her soul. They moved slower than ever before. Mary felt the saxophone was a silk glove being rubbed gently across the inside of her mind.

—Without a dream in my heart. Without a love of my own.

Henry's new white shirt throbbed in time with his heart. The smell of soap from his neck surrounded Mary and made her legs shake.

—And then I saw blue moon had turned to gold. The song was over. Henry tried to say something. Mary put her finger to her lips and nodded her head to show the question would never need to be asked.

They did not say one word on the way home. In the

jumble of bodies on the back seat, their fingers intertwined. He looked at her once. She didn't notice him doing this. He wondered did he look as crazily happy as she did.

David Flynn dropped everyone else off first. There was just himself, Henry and Mary left when he got to the boarding house. Normally he would have continued on around by the mart and left Mary off at her digs. This night he killed the engine and walked to the front door, leaving a few words behind like a spatter of snowflakes.

—Lock the door when you're getting out.

When Mary Flynn kissed Henry Caslin, he thought how he had never really been kissed before and didn't mind that most of Mary's mouth ended up on the side of his cheek or just under his eyes.

When Henry Caslin kissed Mary Flynn, she thought he kissed like someone out of the films, and tried to remember how Rita Hayworth and Marilyn Monroe did it.

—Would you mind if I called round and walked you to Second Mass in the morning?

—I'd love it.

Henry thought of how the word love had sounded in her mouth. That night he dreamed that he had scored the winning goal for the county team in the All-Ireland final, and was not disappointed when he woke up.

People marvelled at their courtship. For two years they did a line together and did not have one row. They were said to be cut out for each other. But sometimes Mary held Henry's head in her lap and felt the stifled energy pouring through him. He was kicking against the bars of a cage because he wanted to be someone. Henry said it was for her. She knew part of it was.

On Sundays they would go for a spin and look at something made beautiful by its physical irregularity. A waterfall, a lake, mountains, cliffs, an island you could drive across to at low tide. Mary would sit with the landlady in the kitchen while Henry fastidiously got himself ready and talked to David from the bathroom.

It was David who discovered the music. He was messing around with an old radio when its sound drowned out Henry's conversation. The sound of the new music people were going mad for in England, and that was even heard in Ireland the odd time, though not in the dancehalls but in the bedrooms of well-off town youngsters who had record players and sent abroad for discs. It arrived in Carnamodda on freak foreign waves travelling through a sky without clouds.

—You shake my nerves and you rattle my brain. Too much love drives a man insane.

David turned the music up. Mary and Missus Farry stopped talking. All that could be heard in the house was this music, and Henry's footsteps on the stairs.

—Goodness, gracious, great balls of fire.

Henry stopped on the stairs like a wounded western bad guy about to tumble over and take the banisters with him. Mary tapped her feet and moved her upper body in a slow and puzzled manner. Henry began to move the same way.

—You're fine, so fine, gonna tell the word that you're mine, mine, mine.

When the music stopped Henry threw the keys of his Hillman Minx to Mary and they continued her driving lessons. She was a quick learner, though there were still gaps in her knowledge.

—I'm not able to reverse, Henry. And home is the other way.

—Keep going this way. We'll find some driveway or something and you can go round in a circle. It'll be good practice for you.

They drove on. On a few occasions there was a hint of

enough ground on the right to turn in, but Mary's confidence failed her. She asked Henry to take the wheel, but he just laughed and told her to keep going.

—The world is round, you won't drive off the edge of it.

For some reason he seemed to be in massive good humour.

There was enough room in front of the big building up ahead to turn a hundred cars. Mary was happy now. So was Henry. He hummed the tune that had been on the radio in the boarding house and she joined in.

—Mary, switch off the engine. We'll get out of the car.

Still humming the song.

—Do you know what this place is?

Kilbricken parish hall. Kilbricken had been the poorest place in the county, and now there wasn't a sinner left in it. A man from the area had become a building-trade millionaire in Coventry and set all his neighbours up with jobs there. You could smell the emptiness from the houses farther up the road.

—There hasn't been a dance in that hall in ten years, Mary. There's no one left to dance.

Henry put his hands behind Mary's legs and lifted her into his arms.

—We're going to be rich. I'm going to fix up that hall and reopen it, and do you know what I'm going to have in it? New music, new bands, music people can dance rightly to so they enjoy themselves. Mary, I can see the future.

—Great balls of fire.

Henry asked the bishop to bless the Sunshine Ballroom on opening night, and with the maximum of deference let him know that it would not be the same as a parish hall. The Caslin brothers owned it, and priests would not be allowed to hang round the place keeping an eye on the dancers. The bishop knew he had no choice in the matter, but also that Caslin would be a dead man commercially if he fell out with the Church. He banked on him keeping the place respectable out of cuteness.

Eugene Caslin came in as his brother's partner. He was a builder now, and knew the best tradesmen in three counties. They wired the Sunshine, painted it, tidied it and improved it a hundred different ways till it looked like a luxury liner run aground in the dark, soggy fields of Kilbricken. Neon lights beamed out the ballroom's name, and on the opening night the lights of several hundred cars and bikes answered back.

The Regal Showband played on opening night. The Caslins somehow crammed everyone who turned up into the ballroom. There wasn't much room for dancing, but that didn't matter on the night that was in it. So many people would claim to have been there that Henry could have quadrupled the size of the place and still not fitted them all in.

The sound of the crowd when the Regal launched into Come Down The Mountain Katie Daly could have been bottled and sold as the essence of pure joy.

When the night ended, Henry walked outside to say goodbye to the Regal. Some girls were hanging around with the band. Two of them came over to thank Henry for a great night.

—Where did ye come from, girls?
—Carrigfin.
—I didn't know there was two Carrigfins.
—Ah, no, there's only the one.

And it was sixty miles away. He rushed back into the ballroom, scattering couples in a way that would have delighted the sternest of curates. He grabbed Eugene by the shoulders and summoned Mary from her task of checking the receipts at the mineral bar.

—Do you know what we're going to do now? Do you know what we're going to do now?

—We're going to make a fair few bob out of this place.

—We're going to have another place like this in the next county. Even if we have to build it ourselves. Even if we have to take out another loan from the bank. We're going to do that, and then we're going to have another place and another place and another place.

—Stop, Henry. You're gone fierce excited.

—I was talking to two lassies at the door. Do you know where they came from? Carrigfin.

—Jesus Christ Almighty.

In the background the bishop frowned but nobody noticed.

Two years and four ballrooms later, Henry dropped to his knees on the shores of Lough Glass as he and Mary looked at the birds which arrived the same time each winter and left the same time each summer. He knelt right on a damp patch of grass and dirt. On the way back into town, he watched the stain turn dark green and rubbed it like it was a magic lamp.

Pointing out the landmarks around Mary's home place to his father on the morning of the wedding was like saying an official farewell to his childhood.

—And over there, there was a mass rock. The next cross, now, is where the Toorgraney Ambush took place.

—Did they pot many Tans?

—Four.

—Good stuff. Did they do anything in the Civil War?

—No.

—Better again.

At the reception, the Caslins and Flynns moved their heads the same shy way when they talked, and employed the common gestures of people from small villages before falling speechless at the sight of Benny Dixon from the Regal Showband walking into the Park Hotel and embracing Mary before he shook hands with Henry.

The occasion seemed to call for television cameras. All the showband stars turned up because they couldn't afford not to. The youngsters jived and the old folks sang along with the ballads. Tommy Caslin and Mary's father, Brendan, took the stage and accompanied Benny Dixon on Black Velvet Band. Henry sang If I Didn't Have A Dime, Eugene and David mumbled the Hucklebuck. Mary brought the whole place to silence when she did Send Me The Pillow That You Dream On. Her voice was like the perfect piece of Waterford glass the Regal Showband had bought for her and her husband.

Henry and Eddie continued to build, buy and bankroll ballrooms, their empire becoming multicultural, as empires do, until the United Nations would have had its work cut out to beat the Caslin ballrooms for variety.

A bunch of Mayo lads dressed up as African warriors and called themselves the Bushman Showband. The Comanches were a rake of fellas from Cavan who wore feathery headdresses and painted their faces. Kenny Ball and the Jazzmen's big tune was Midnight In Moscow. The Chessmen played the music of The Beach Boys from California. Tom Nolan always sounded like he came from Italy or Greece or somewhere else sunny.

Henry and Mary built a big house in Rathbawn, his county town. People called it The Hacienda. They knew the Caslins would never be short of money. If you'd just opened a ballroom at the time without music, lights or anything at all, a crowd would still have filled it because they loved the places themselves almost as much as they loved the bands who played there.

The country was changing as it hit the mid-point of the sixties. Rumours of jobs in the West and Midlands of

Ireland came true. Men and women and children, who spoke with English accents, filled boats back home, bringing with them money and expectations of entertainment which had nothing to do with old draughty parish halls. For the first time, people had money for frivolity and Henry had exclusive Midlands rights to the commodity. He started bingo sessions in the ballrooms on weekday nights, the thousand-pound first prizes drawing crowds to the Sunshine, the Tropicana, the Kon-Tiki and the Roseland like water to a plughole.

The only worry was the continued reluctance of the courts to grant drinks licences to the Caslin brothers. A tight ship had been run for six years, but still they were not trusted. Henry felt blackguarded, and the words cabaret and singing lounges afflicted him strangely, giving him the same sensation as when he had seen Kilbricken parish hall. But in reverse. Ireland was swinging to the sound of the big showband, and things couldn't get any better than this. Which meant they could only eventually get worse.

But for the moment he was happy. Caslin ballrooms were the home of the stars. A star was in the eye of the beholder. Like a star in the sky. It might really be a satellite or a meteor, but if the onlooker called it a star then that was what it was. The biggest showband star of all was Tom Nolan, who one month was digging the road for Offaly County Council and the next was top of the charts. His manager, Willie Flaherty, had bought most of the copies of his first single and dumped them off the end of a pier, because he knew that topping the hit parade made you a number-one attraction with the promoters. He told Henry this once Tom was comfortably and irreversibly a star.

Tom sang like a turf-cutter impersonating a Spanish hustler who was trying to lure young Irish colleens into the white slave trade. During pleading songs of love, he dropped to his knees with such conviction that his trousers were soaked with blood when he came off stage. He was not the only showband singer excitable young women asked to spit on them, but he was the only one who looked like he relished the idea. The biggest managers in Britain and Ireland wanted to sign him, but he stuck with Willie Flaherty, explaining

—Myself and Willie go back a long way. He's a special friend.

The night Tom opened the Apollo, Eugene booked out an eating house where the company ate steaks and drank whiskey. Henry enjoyed the feeling of power engendered by being the only one sober at these pow wows.

No one twigged the row between Tom and Willie until it became so bad that some people left glasses of whiskey behind them at the table. Their rows were terrible, frequent and mysterious, though everyone had the impression they were always about the same thing. Willie was the bitter one in the arguments, while Tom would just roll his eyes and turn away like a big child who couldn't understand what he'd done wrong. The argument continued after Henry had driven them back to the hotel. Willie stumbled around the lobby with a broken glass, holding his palms outwards, and appealed for assistance from some invisible source. Even Tom looked worried.

They had both left the lobby when Henry came back from the jacks. Willie had obviously cut himself on the glass. A trail of drops led to the stairs. Henry resolved to find Willie, prompted by a vague memory of some pop star who'd died by choking on his own vomit after a feed of drink.

The door of Willie's room was open and the lights were on. Some of his clothes lay in the corridor outside. His white shirt was just over the threshold with a big strip torn off the back as if it had been used to make a bandage.

Henry knocked at the door and looked in. At first he thought they were wrestling. Fighting or messing, or something like that. Henry might even have jumped on the bed and joined them if the covers hadn't fallen off to reveal exactly what Tom was doing to Willie. At first he wondered if he should go to the rescue, but then he heard both boys using the sort of language familiar to him from similar moments with Mary. He deliberately made a lot of noise, slammed the door and vowed that Tom Nolan would never again see the inside of a Caslin ballroom.

A white-faced Tom smoked cigarettes in the lobby the next morning. Willie fiddled with his bandaged right hand. Henry could not look either of them in the eye, and when Willie handed him the new copy of *Spotlight*, left it facedown on the table to show he was having none of this friendship crack.

—I'm sorry about last night, Henry.

—Leave it now, Willie.

—What are you talking to me like that for, Henry?

—I'm not working with you again, Willie. Not with yourself or Tom. And you'll be lucky if there's anyone who'll work with ye again.

—Ah, now, Henry, we're sorry. Sorry for drinking too much. I won't get as drunk again.

—Be honest for once in your fucking life, Willie – you know what this is about.

—I am honest, Henry. Do we ever let you down? We always turn up and do the best show in Ireland. We did half an hour extra last night because it was one of your ballrooms. Don't tell me I'm not honest.

Tom was looking intently at the television, singing along with Andy Pandy and Looby Loo.

—You know full well what this is about.

Willie shrugged his shoulders and threw his arms wide. Henry's new knowledge made the gestures seem saturated in effeminacy. He realised that even a rumour of the truth would make it impossible for anyone to watch Tom Nolan on stage. Oh Golly Gee You're Such A Beautiful Lady would draw sniggers in ballrooms from Buncrana to Bantry.

—I don't know what it has to do with the singing lark.

—It's fucking disgusting, and I can't work with ye any more.

—Don't be daft, man. If you didn't work with people like us any more, I'm telling you, you'd be short a fair few acts.

Henry waved Willie away. The gesture felt wrong. He wished his arm movement had been more rigid. Willie followed him out to the car.

—It's no big deal. Me and Tom have been together for six years. That's the way we are, Henry, it's like the way you are. Don't you know I feel bad about it, it sends me on the spirits. But it's the way I am. Don't do anything bad to Tom. I love him, Henry, I couldn't bear to see him ruined.

When he got home, Henry couldn't believe how Mary reacted to the news.

—I suppose it is wrong, and I wouldn't like anyone I knew to be at it. But it's up to themselves. Some people are born that way.

—Mary, it's not right. And it's against the Church.

—Henry, you know well why I haven't had a child these past two years. The Church is grand, but sometimes it doesn't suit.

Flaherty and Nolan were wrong. He couldn't think of them as Tom and Willie any more. But they were wrong in the sense of being incorrect. Henry knew what it meant to be alone in the dark with a woman. They did not. Maybe they were entitled to make a mistake. He rang Flaherty and asked him to line up Nolan for the opening of the Majestic in Rathbawn next month. No more was said. Henry got back to making out the guest list, which included the names of Jimmy Mimnagh, Chairman of the Urban Council, Father Gerry Lee, the parish priest and Seamus McKeon, the young reporter on the Rathbawn *Herald*.

JIMMY

Jimmy Mimnagh always told people that he had a happy childhood. This was true, up to the point when he was eight years old and his brother Jackie came back from America.

There were seventeen children in the Mimnagh family. Missus Mimnagh regarded the pregnant state as normal, and developed eating idiosyncrasies when she wasn't expecting. She had lost another five children. Jimmy was fourteenth in the family. He had still not seen four of his siblings. Two he never did get to see; one he bumped into at a fund-raising expedition for the Party in Boston and the fourth was Jackie, who came home with his wife that summer. It was the last summer Jackie returned to Glenmone, and at that time he had never even heard of Iwo Jima, the place he would die in ten years later.

Agnes from New York arrived arm in arm with Jackie, the Yankee emigrant who sent home the biggest remittances in the parish, enabling his parents to buy two new copper basins for wash-time and mend the children's cast-offs with better-quality material. She seemed alarmed by the goat in the doorway of the Mimnagh house. Agnes had been Gadocha before she was Mimnagh, Robertson before that and Roth when she was born, though none of this was made known to her latest set of in-laws. The sang-froid with which the children regarded the rats which scooted in the front door and toured the kitchen might have unnerved her, but she did not show much emotion until it was suggested that she sleep in a different bed to Jackie.

A spectacular meteor marked the night of Jackie's homecoming. Jimmy crept out to watch it swoop towards the county town before it eventually fizzled out and became a pinpoint of poignantly dissipated light. When he was about to climb back in the bedroom window, he became aware of voices at the front door. He could hear that his brother was whispering but everything Agnes said was perfectly clear to him, her urban whisper proving far too loud in a tiny village with no night-time traffic.

—. . . . .

—I don't care, Jackie. I want outta here. This place gives me the creeps. You said we could see the country, the Lakes of Kerry, Connemara, Dublin City.

—. . . . .

—I can't stand it, I'm telling you, the dirt, the rats, the way the kids look at me all the time. And that fucking priest, he gives me the creeps. He knows, I bet he does.

—. . . . .

—I know they're your family, Jackie, but you've left this behind. Can't you see they're nothing but poor white trash?

A wet click in the dark announced a Judas kiss.

Jimmy knew what poor and white were. He had never heard the word trash before, but the tone of Agnes's voice made the meaning clearer than any dictionary could have.

When the war which had killed his brother ended, Jimmy left for London. The city was in shite from the Blitz, and many of the men who should have been rebuilding it were fertilising fields on the continent of Europe or slowly being subsumed into the sands of North Africa and Burma. He left home with two suits of clothes in a suitcase tied up with string and the address of a pub on the Holloway Road where he would find neighbours who'd get him a start on the buildings. There were no thoughts of coming back. The money was supposed to be unbelievable, and the work was nothing to someone who'd grown up on a farm.

And he did not intend to stay working on the buildings for ever. There were ways of getting on in England. No matter who you were or where you came from, if you wanted to be educated they would do it. You could learn trades and earn certificates which would get you work anywhere in England at good rates. Trade unions looked after the tradesman. If you wanted to work there was no stopping you, and Jimmy wanted to work. He was as strong as a young bull, and determined that no one would ever include himself and trash in the same sentence again.

He went to college at night to get his City and Guilds certificate in carpentry, dragging his tired body to a damp room in a technical college where the instructor had taken three months to understand his accent. The other lads in the digs laughed at Jimmy. Giving up a night's drinking to get a certificate in something you could learn yourself was pure daft. He persisted. He didn't drink much, and had no interest in the women who his friends were taking to like Hollywood Indians to whiskey. A couple of times they tried to pair him off with girls from home, but he couldn't be bothered making the effort.

London was home to him, and he felt it would stay that way. It had been different at first. The English took getting used to; cities didn't seem suitable for people to live in, and digs were an almighty pain in the arse altogether, although living on your own would be worse again. The change came slowly. He found himself getting used to the rhythm of the city, and when one of the other Irish lodgers complained about the place he would always stick up for it.

As he received his certificate, his instructor told him he'd been the best member of the class.

—Not bad for an Irish git from the bogs, he said in a friendly tone.

The weather was one of the few difficulties remaining. Summers in London were harder to cope with than winters. He was used to mild and damp from home, but not the way the tight knot of buildings in a big city squeezed the heat against you until your head started spinning.

He sat drinking half a bubbly and warm bitter outside the pub, overlooking Hampstead Heath before setting out for a walk. The heat of the sun bounced back off the baked ground and moulded Jimmy's clothes to him. He removed his shirt and wrapped it around his waist, exposing chest muscles turned into a grid of taut hills and hollows by years of work, before sitting under a tree whose leaves dappled and broke the sunlight in a way that made Jimmy lose his sight for a second. When he recovered, he saw a young man peering quizzically down at him.

—Daydreaming?

—I was surely . . . mate, said Jimmy, and wondered why his voice sounded so oddly pleased.

The young man must have been hot as well, because his shirt was off too. Jimmy found himself looking at the mounds of muscle on his chest with a light sprinkling of hair covering them like a wispy curtain.

—You're Irish, aren't you?

The voice was posh. Jimmy knew posh English from the films of Ealing and Elstree. Michael Redgrave and Noël Coward, Anna Neagle and Edith Evans.

—I am, but I've lived here a while.

—Guy Morton, pleased to meet you.

—Jimmy Mimnagh, it's good to make your acquaintance.

—I think a few beers might be in order. This wretched weather is giving me the most terrible thirst.

They drank a lot of beers. Jimmy forgot about the weather and concentrated on Guy's voice and the way he tossed his hair back while laughing at an outlandish building-site story. Twice their giddy giggling locked their legs together.

When they left the pub, Jimmy could have headed for his digs, but instead he walked with Guy to Islington, their laughter seeming to float along in front of them, cushioned by the alcohol which he felt must be making his insides shine. Guy told Jimmy he was an army officer, serving in what had once been Palestine, what was to Jimmy the Holy Land and was becoming Israel. He was staying in a hotel on his leave.

It was a day when anything could happen. Jimmy followed meekly as Guy suggested a drink in his room.

He knew what 'nancy boys' were. Had been warned about them on the sites. Men who'd get up on you given half a chance. Miserable skulking creatures who were more woman than man and spoke in high-pitched shrieks, flinging their limp-wristed hands through the air as they did so.

The grip of Guy's hand was the strongest Jimmy had ever felt. He resisted for ten seconds, and then it was he who pushed Guy down on to the bed.

That night Jimmy worried about the fact that he might never have come across this beauty which had waited in the world for him. He kissed and licked and plunged and dipped and finally surrendered, Guy's careful attentions widening him until he came chaotically.

Guy held Jimmy between times, and playfully stroked his head.

—That was your first time, Jimmy, wasn't it?

—It was. I hope you don't think I'm one of them fellas.

—But you are, Jimmy, and a very beautiful one. Welcome to the rest of your life.

Jimmy woke alone the next morning. In years to come he tried to tell himself that he had been filled with shame and disgust when he looked down at his naked body and the mass of stains on the crumpled tent of sheets. That was a lie. His first emotion was a desire to repeat the night before. He called Guy's name but there was no answer. Only a note.

—Dear Jim,

This may sound like a poor excuse, but I actually do have to rejoin my unit and prepare to head back to Palestine tomorrow. You looked so peaceful and happy while sleeping that I did not have the heart to wake you. I will be back in London in six months. This may be of little interest to you, but there is a pub named the Black Gull in the East End where men like us can be found. Maybe I will meet you again there,

Guy.

The day outside was again torrid. But the sun would have shone for Jimmy even if the day was rainy. He had found love.

Guy Morton had too much drink again a week later. He followed a brown-eyed Israeli boy down a Jerusalem alleyway, and four Irgun bullets left him mercifully dead before lust had time to turn to fear.

Six months came and went, and Jimmy still visited the Black Gull, checking his bruises from the previous week in the mirror beforehand. When they had turned yellow he told himself it was time to make the trip again. They would be replaced.

It was strange how different the men in the Black Gull were to what he had expected. Mainly they were working men like himself, whose conversation and accents were the same as in the pubs of his other life. This should have made him feel at ease, but it did not. The otherness of the life was the point.

The memory of Guy drew him to men in uniform. Mostly sailors in off ships with fresh tattoos soaking into their arms and no time for normal congress. They often begrudged the time spent buying a drink. Jimmy marvelled at the amount of hate present in the back rooms, back alleys and occasional dark upstairs bedrooms where there was so little light he knew he would not recognise the men if he saw them again. The men were quick and anonymous in the dark; anger burned off some and excitement rose off others.

Rough trade they called it, and it was rough sure enough. Fists flying everywhere and beatings from time to time. Eventually he stopped wondering if Guy would come back. He was not sure if Guy would like him now and was not convinced he liked himself. But there was a part of him which enjoyed the Black Gull, and this frightened him into stopping his letters home in case his family might spot the change to his inclination through his handwriting.

A growing edginess began to afflict him after the first few years, spreading like the fog in the streets outside and throwing a shroud over his heart. It was a fear that God would pay him back. Not a fear of Hell, but of what would happen before that inevitability.

It was a quiet night in the bar. He sat and drank on his own, but no one approached him. He wondered if his misery had become visible and was scaring people away. He decided to leave after this drink and hoped he would be able to delude himself that he had stayed on his own out of choice. A warm hand on his leg stalled his departure.

The boy was younger than usual. Perhaps seventeen. He was also nervous but smiled a lot. He didn't suggest a trip to the back room, but a walk outside to look at the stars.

Jimmy cheered up. Perhaps he would even feel close to the boy when the time came. Because the time would come. He could see how keen the boy was to leave.

—Ronnie Fraser.

—Paddy O'Reilly.

Just twenty yards from the pub the boy ducked into a side alley and signalled to Jimmy to follow.

Away from the light.

Ronnie leaned up against the wall at one side of the alleyway and moved his tongue back and forward between his lips as Jimmy staggered towards him.

The first blow to the back of his head puzzled Jimmy. When the second sent his face thudding against the wall he wondered if the H-bomb had gone off or if he was having a brain haemorrhage. His silent wonderings were answered by voices.

—Kill him, fucking kill him.

—Fucking queer bastard, kick the shit out of him.

—Come on lads, let me get a kick at the bleeder.

Someone banged his face against the ground. Jimmy tried to turn to see his attackers. How many of them were there? Were they big or small? Young or old? He never knew, and it would always annoy him. Pain took over his whole body. They kicked his ribs. Blood was coming from somewhere, or perhaps several somewheres, and scooting down his face.

It felt like floating. He seemed to be on his back. The stars were over his head but they were moving too fast. Maybe these were more meteors. He could taste chippings in his mouth. His teeth. Everything seemed to happen very slowly. They beat him with a bin lid, dumped the rubbish from the bin on top of him and continued their kicking until he started to pass out.

His last thought was of the daftness of their behaviour.

How could anyone possibly want to do this to another person? Then he wondered if he was dying.

The doctor in the London Hospital said he might have died had a man not discovered him just a few minutes after the beating. It was a few weeks before Jimmy remembered how he had been found. The man had walked down the lane and pissed against the wall. The heat and smell of the piss lapping around his face brought Jimmy back to moan a plea for help. His rescuer called the ambulance and then disappeared. There weren't many legal reasons to be in the vicinity at that time of night.

After two weeks Jimmy discharged himself, thinking he had booked the bed for himself the day he left Hampstead Heath with Guy Morton. He might as well have used the sticks, the coshes and the bin lids himself.

His attackers had done a good job. His back would be damaged for life and he would remain stooped for the rest of his days. His left leg would stay limp and there was no way of replacing the bitten-off thumb.

—At least there wasn't much chance of them inflicting brain damage on you, Paddy, the doctor joked.

—My name is Jimmy.

They might as well have killed him. He would never again be able to do a day's work. His crisp white shirts hung at an odd angle off the stooped back that was studded with small lumps. Cuchullain the legendary hero had been able to twist round in his skin, facing his head one way and his feet the other. Jimmy looked as if he'd been midway through doing that when the wind changed.

His diligently accrued savings were withdrawn and poured down his throat. It was not that he was trying to kill himself. There were quicker ways. His use for drink was a practical one. It helped to kill the pain. Morphine had been prescribed in the hospital, but he found himself becoming too fond of it. The thought of becoming entangled in another world of unknown consequences scared him, so he took to the jar.

Drink made the world certain. Four whiskies would take away the fears and worries the previous day's drink had put into his head. It took twenty straight whiskies before his stomach would give way. His eyes became the colour of the red curtains hanging at the entrance to the back room of the Black Gull, and when he had sickened himself with London completely he caught the Irish Mail at Euston and hit for home, passing Glenmone on the bus, swearing to himself that he would not return there until he had enough money to drop a casual ten-pound note and pretend it didn't matter to him whether it was picked up or not.

The bus came to the end of the line in the next county. There was a dirty pub next door to the bus station and Jimmy was ankle-deep in sawdust by the time he got to the bar.

—It's good to be back home.

The barman regarded him with suspicion.

—I don't think you're from around here.

—It's good to be back in Ireland. I was beyond in England these last few years.

—I hear it's great.

—It's not. It's fucking shite. And you can't get a decent pint of porter there.

—What do you want?

—I'll buy the pub.

—Of course you will.

It was sorted inside a week. Jimmy still had enough savings to get a loan off the bank. In the late fifties not many people were buying anything in Ireland. The look in the bank manager's eyes when he heard how much a skilled tradesman made in England brought home to Jimmy why there was still such a trail there. Fuck the Brits and their bribery.

His customers were farmers who took their time getting home from the mart. When it rained he let their dogs in beside the fire, mixing the smell of steaming fur with that of unwashed bodies. He preferred the smell of the fur.

The tinkers drank there too, sitting in a circle among themselves and gazing warily at the door until they got drunk enough to turn their attention inwards. Then offence could be taken. Jimmy didn't mind. They could not inflict any extra physical pain on him, and there was not anything valuable in the pub. He watched slash hooks, hayforks and hatchets being wielded in a way which made it seem impossible that the street would not be black with dead when the fight ended. No one got killed, and afterwards Tom Nevin or Martin Connors or Charlie Stokes would apologise and ask if they were still sound for a drink in Mimnagh's.

—Any time. As long as ye take yere fights outside.

He needed their money. And slowly the pub began to draw a crowd. People liked Jimmy behind the bar. In England he had been admired as a young lad going places. In Rathbawn they came to his pub because they knew that no matter how bad they were, the poor twisted drunken fucker running the dirtiest place in town couldn't look down on them.

Some of his clients he even felt fond of. Like Matt, Batt and Pat, the three oul lads who lived up a boreen out the Cavan road and were always last to leave the pub. At four o'clock in the morning they would fall asleep with the guard dog licking their faces. They insisted on being woken. After a couple of weeks, Jimmy took the hint and gave them a seat home.

Brambles and bushes made a curtain in front of the

boreen, whose surface was made up of overlapping pot-holes and jagged rocks. Matt lived in the first house, where a goat ate grass from the flat roof and looked disdainfully at his owner. Pat lived next door with a nonagenarian mother who looked out the window each night as he returned and sometimes came out to strike him for galli-vanting. Batt was farther on again.

He was a man who liked to talk and didn't get much practice, so Jimmy listened to him. The words were slightly out of kilter, and a look of surprise at hearing himself spread over Batt's face as he spoke them. He knew the world through newspapers, even reading English ones when he could get them.

—I think this young Kennedy buck might do something in the next general election over in America.

—They reckon in England they've never had it so good.

—I'd say yon Congress Party will never be out of power beyond in India.

Only twice had Batt ventured outside the county. Both times for funerals. His house was four miles on from Pat's. Jimmy leaped back in fright the first night he helped Batt in the door.

—Jesus Batt, you're infested with rats.

—Ah, no, I am not. It bes like this the whole time.

Everything other than stone in the house had been chewed. The thought of Batt lying there with rats using him as a playground disturbed Jimmy, who resolved to get him out of the house as much as possible. He began bringing him for spins, once going as far as Strandhill where Batt saw the sea for the first time.

—It's big all right Jimmy, but you'd wonder what use is it.

He bought Batt a rake of English papers when possible, got him his dinner in the Imperial Hotel every Friday and transported him to the hospital when Batt fell sick, paying for medicine that had no effect.

By the winter of 1959, Batt looked like a small man forced to change clothes with a far bigger one. He talked about different things.

—You've done a fierce amount for me, Jimmy, and don't think I'm not grateful because I am so I am. I haven't a relation left alive, and I'm going and changing me will to leave everything to yourself. It would have gone to Father Beirne otherwise, but he doesn't know that so there'll be no bad feelings.

—Don't be daft. What would I do with land?

Jimmy smiled as he thought of Batt's patch of overgrown stony ground that hardly fed his one remaining beast, an old donkey in worse shape than his owner. Maybe Batt saw the smile.

—Ah, now, I'm telling you, the man that owns that land is going to be rich. I do see lads up there during the day, digging at things and taking measurements. They asked my permission to go on the land. They do be here every day, and they're serious-looking clients. I'm telling you, there's gold or something on my land. I'll be worth a fortune.

On Paddy's Night, Batt got out of the car and turned deliberately towards Jimmy.

—That's sorted out with the will, now. And there's something else, I have some money saved and it's under the mattress, so when I go, come in and take it. I always said you'd be looked after.

In Mimnagh's the next day Batt took a weakness and was dead before Jimmy got him to the hospital. His solicitor called to the pub the day after to tell Jimmy he'd been left twenty acres of land, some of which was pure stone up in the hills.

—You might as well go up to the house and see if

there's anything you want to take. It's out of the way, but you should do it soon because there's tinkers around and they'd get to the middle of the Sahara Desert if there was something to rob there.

The solicitor faltered near the end of sentence, as he realised the tinkers were only around the place because Jimmy was the only publican in the county who would serve them.

Rats scurried round Jimmy's feet as he looked through the house. No ornaments except a chipped Child of Prague, whose head barely clung to his shoulders. Head-high piles of newspapers were stacked in the corner of every room, white at the top of the bundle, changing to brown and green near the bottom. Thousands of little chewed pellets lay nearby.

He thought of what Batt had said about money under the mattress. It would be disrespectful and underhand to look for it.

But money was money.

The bedroom was the coldest room in the house. Green growths decorated the walls like huge abstract expressionist daubs. The imprint of Batt's little head was still on the pillow. Six rats flitted away when Jimmy lifted the mattress to find a rusty biscuit tin filled with money. Hundreds upon hundreds of notes. Mainly tenners and fivers. A life's worth of money. Enough to set any man up.

Jimmy started laughing. He laughed and he laughed and he laughed. Because what Batt had left was thousands of pieces of worthless paper. The rats had chewed and nibbled at the notes until they were useless and all but unrecognisable as money.

It looked like he was going to be staying in his small pub.

The man from the Dutch mining company called to the pub two months later to explain about the significant quantities of zinc and copper they had found in the hills above Rathbawn, some of it on land formerly owned by Batt.

—We will need to buy that land in order to maximise the profitability of the find.

Jimmy shook his head in disbelief. The Dutchman took this as a refusal to sell, and explained just how much money he was prepared to pay. Jimmy recovered his nerve and began to bargain.

For ten years, before it closed overnight and left just a scar on the hillside as a memorial to the glory days, a job at the mine made the difference between staying in Rathbawn and emigrating. A man who could get you one of those jobs was a powerful man. Powerful enough to take his place on the County and Urban Councils with the Party. Jimmy set up as a developer, bought the Imperial Hotel and heard other people calling him a success. They made him Chairman of the Urban Council, in which capacity he was naturally invited to the opening of the Majestic Ballroom.

FATHER LEE

The village of Ballinkeeny was draped with bunting, and papal flags were flying out of all the shop windows. It was the most important day folk could remember.

It was a singular honour for any village when a young native man was ordained a priest, but it meant even more in a village like Ballinkeeny. A village which an act of opportunistic cartography had left marooned in a land where being a Catholic meant being kept down, and looking out your window at fife and drum bands leading men in bowler hats showing that this was their land. If you wanted to complain about that you could take it up with the B Specials, the auxiliary police force of the Protestant people. Because you were stuck with them. The IRA had not fired a shot in anger these years, the South had forgotten you and the border was becoming less of a scrawl on a map than a tangible boundary to a twilit land of nightmare.

Tears rolled down Martin Lee's face as he hugged his son outside the church. Martin had been trampled by a bull a year ago and had not been the same man since. His neighbours spoke of God's mercy in at least allowing Martin to see his son being ordained.

—Gerry, I'm as proud of you.

Father Gerry Lee would never forget the look on his father's face as he said that.

Neighbours handed him rosary beads and relics for good luck in Rome. It reminded him of his best friend in the seminary, Edward O'Hanlon. They had exchanged keepsakes the day they left. O'Hanlon had given him a piece of cloth touched by the hand of Christ. He had given O'Hanlon a petal from a rose bush which had been growing in the Garden of Gethsemane on the night Our Lord had prayed there and O'Hanlon, emotional, had told him

—If you ever have any problem or there's anything up, tell me. I'll sort it out. I give you my word.

They were shooting the film *Roman Holiday* when Father Lee arrived in the Holy City to attend the Irish College there. Passing by a hotel, he had seen photographers crowding round a tiny, frightened Audrey Hepburn as she attempted to reach her limousine.

When he saw the film years later, he was disappointed by its lightness and frivolity, the way it treated Rome as a backdrop for enjoyment and the forgetting of life. His Rome was a place of seriousness and solemnity, where he grew closer to God than he had ever hoped to.

He saw the catacombs, where the Christians had hidden as they tried against seemingly insurmountable odds to keep alive the small sect which would emerge from under ground to spread throughout the world. The Colosseum startled him with its air of stark authority. It must have seemed impossible to break with the past it had represented. Yet the Christians had prevailed. Though the lions tore them to pieces, they died with a prayer on their lips and both hope and forgiveness in their hearts.

In the Sistine Chapel his heart jumped at the sight of two cardinals moving by, the smell of their power sufficient to knock over the faint-hearted.

Father Edward O'Hanlon passed through Rome on his way back from the missions. He had been given his own parish in Armagh, a signal honour for one so young. Father Lee felt that something of Africa adhered to his old friend, as if his voice and gestures bore witness to formative years among people not wholly civilised.

On their final day in Rome together, they joined the giant serpent of devotion winding towards St Peter's Square. Father Lee had never seen so many people before. He thought of the few thousand huddled below the city almost two millennia ago, and shivered joyfully at the thought of their increase and his presence among their successors.

Pope Pius was too far away to see, but his voice could be heard clearly. Father Lee became lost inside his own head as he contemplated the power and the glory, the mystery and the passion, the faithful and the Vicar of Christ. O'Hanlon was shocked by the beatific look on the face of his friend. It reminded him of the faces of tribesmen in the African jungle at the moment they first became convinced of Christ's existence. Strange for a man who was already a priest.

The heat and the crowds and the power which he was sure was radiating from Pope Pius showed Father Lee the light. He understood that God would never desert him and that, no matter what happened, he would never desert God.

Walking helped him discover Rome and made the place more fascinating still. The Tiber made him think of the history of the place. The story of Romulus and Remus was probably a pagan lie but he wanted to believe it, liked the idea that even a she-wolf could show mercy. He thought of the emperors, from Augustus to Nero to Constantine all the way through to Mussolini, whom many of the Italian priests still held in high regard. Mussolini had kept the communists at bay. The communists who would have won in 1948, had the United States not bought the election for the good people of Italy with the help of the Vatican.

In Spain the communists had raped nuns and slit open the bellies of priests before being defeated by the will of God and General Franco. Father Lee kept a picture of General Franco in his room. It puzzled him that communism had come so close to conquering Italy. The Spaniards were an untamed tribe, but the Italians were a good people who had respect for the Church and made the Irish clergy feel at home. He looked for an answer to this puzzle from a young man in a nearby trattoria, who sometimes engaged him in political and religious disputation when he returned from his walks.

—I am not a communist, Father. I am a democrat and a Catholic. But I can see why some people follow them.

—Why? Communism is inherently evil. The Holy Father himself has said so. There can be no reason for good people to believe in such a creed.

—Not two miles from here people live in such poverty that even you, Father, and you come from Ireland, will not be able to imagine it. Their houses fall apart, their children starve and they live like beasts. Some might say that communism will lift them out of this pit.

Father Lee knocked back the last of his coffee and patted his friend on the head.

—Maybe their conditions are as you say. But that would not excuse them for voting for the communists. We can understand and sympathise too much, and lose our certainty about what is right.

He was all the same slightly concerned about the young man's comments. Surely there could not be conditions which made the mortal sin of communism justifiable? He asked Carlo how to reach these slums and was told he must not go there. Persisting in his enquiries, he reached the area by following the movement of people's eyes as they urged him to turn back. A drunken gypsy sitting with his feet in an open sewer hailed him as he approached his destination.

In the Holy City such a place did exist. With open sewers where shapeless masses of faeces flowed by as squadrons of flies massed for attack. Stained washing was hanging out of windows in a doomed effort to stay dry without picking up smuts from the air. Some men lay in doorways with bottles on every side of them. Hard-faced women whose breasts looked pulled by gravity towards the centre of the earth leaned out of empty window frames with cigarettes stuck brazenly in their mouths.

And the children. They were everywhere. As plentiful as the flies but not as well fed. In this part of the city the people heeded their Pope's strictures on birth control, and even on this hottest of days their children's coughs were a staccato testament to the provenance of the pools of bloody sputum that momentarily lay along the crumbling paths before being vaporised by the sun.

Brief sorrow was replaced by righteous indignation as the powerful heat of the day spread from his face to the rest of his body. Poverty should not exempt parents from the duty of decency. What sort of families allowed their children to romp and play without proper clothing? The youngest were rolling around without a stitch on them, and most of the other's clothing was in tatters. The day was so hot.

And there was a memory or a fragment which came back to him at that moment. For some reason he thought of the cry of a single curlew and the soft bog under his feet and the smell of wet cattle.

The cry of a single curlew.

It was plain for all to see that the olive-skinned girl, beautiful under that dirt, was not wearing any underwear as she leaped forwards and backwards over a frayed skipping rope which seemed on the verge of breaking in two. There was nothing underneath her slight dress.

Unable to turn away, he tried to think of the catacombs and of the faithful holding out against the direst of persecutions. Virgins had their flesh torn by hooks and hot coals thrust against their breasts, and still refused to forsake their virtue. The thought of the coals only increased his heat. The catacombs moved up from the earth and became the sewers.

Knowing was the look the skipping girl directed towards Father Lee. He was sure of this. She must know. In a place like this. He clamped what shreds of personal dignity remained around himself like armour. He liked her. He would have said she was a good girl. Though she must know. They all did. Fortunately he had a bag of sweets with him. Her eyes opened wide when he handed her the whole bag. There was an alleyway.

The heat. And then the chill.

Why the screams? He was not going to kill her. It was just a harmless bit of affection.

Paulo Montale of the *carabinieri* had been searching for two brothers who had committed a robbery earlier that day. He hated these streets and the way they crawled with prostitutes, drunks and, worst of all, communists eager to incite a mob to fury against a policeman just doing his job. The scream intercepted him before he reached the house he was looking for. It was a different one from the other childish screeches rending the air. Montale broke into a run and scattered some kids playing football with a bunch of rags lashed together with twine.

In an alleyway a burly man was holding his right hand over the mouth of a child, whose flimsy dress had been ripped to bits while his left hand tried to hide the evidence of his excitement. The child's legs kicked feebly.

—God bless you, my son, said the man, and Montale

realised just what else was so upsetting about the tableau a split second before he hit Father Lee for the first time.

The priest at the Irish College listened intently to the story from the inspector, before ringing the man at the Vatican who was expert in dealing with such matters. Then the inspector called Montale in and told him not to bother making a report if he wanted to keep his job.

—But Inspector, what this man did to the child. He cannot be allowed to do it again.

—He will not be in Rome after tomorrow. He has an urgent appointment in Ireland. I urge you to forget this.

—But what about the child? Her mother knows as well, and some of the neighbours saw what happened. They followed me.

—The child's father is in prison and her mother is a prostitute. No one in authority would believe her word or that of her neighbours. There is a small gift from the Church in this envelope.

The priest from the Irish College visited Father Lee in his cell.

—You are to return to Ireland tomorrow morning. Your new parish has been told that you were a credit to the Church in Rome. Which, barring one mishap, is true. They have been told nothing of this. Do not worry about it.

His new parish was poor and backward, but it was better than the exile from the Church he had expected. While there, he was responsible for the building of a new community centre. Everyone said he had a natural genius for fund-raising. The compliment pleased him, despite its secular nature.

It was mainly boys in Crosshall. Altar boys. He worked out what families they came from, noting the parents whose tongues tied up in his presence from deference, nervousness and lack of education. Their children were the ones he concentrated on, beginning with accidental touches and moving on to hand-holding and the presentation of sweets and trinkets. The correlation between home circumstances and the size of bribe needed to secure a boy's silence pleased and interested him. Bullying and the promise of damnation would have been as effective, but Father Lee did not want to be a bully unless it was unavoidable.

On Ash Wednesday, Father Lee was in the sacristy with one of the altar boys half an hour after Second Mass had ended when Father O'Halloran, his curate, arrived unexpectedly. Father Lee tried not to worry, and told himself O'Halloran could not have guessed what had been going on before he knocked on the door.

The following day the bishop's secretary, Father Flannery and Father O'Halloran were waiting when he arrived in the sacristy to prepare for early-morning Mass. O'Halloran left when Flannery began to talk.

His first instinct was to deny all. He accused O'Halloran of being a drunk and a womaniser who had bribed the altar boys to come up with these stories. Father Flannery said he knew what had happened in Rome. Father Lee fell to his knees and begged not to be reported to the guards. A short dry laugh issued from Father Flannery.

—Can I stay on in the Church somehow? As a deacon, or even a sacristan?

—Don't be daft. You're a priest, and the Church needs priests. We're sending you to a place in the Midlands called Rathbawn. Don't say anything to young O'Halloran; we told him you were leaving the priesthood. And try and stop this caper if you can at all.

In his early days in Rathbawn, he concentrated on his fund-raising so successfully that his status as a community figure would have had him on the guest list for the opening night of the Majestic Ballroom, even had he not been the parish priest.

McKEON

Measles, German measles, mumps, chickenpox, scarlet fever and whooping cough descended on Seamus McKeon the year he turned eight, pinning him to his bed for months with spots, sneezes and sweats. From his bedroom he heard trains go by including, though he did not know it, those carrying packages to Carnamodda where they would be received by a Henry Caslin not yet promoted to Deputy Stationmaster and ignorant of the existence of Mary Flynn.

On the Friday before he was finally due back to National School, his father brought him for a walk, McKeon's bed-accustomed legs wobbling all the way to the biggest building in Rathbawn, the *Herald* where his father worked as a printer like his father and his father's father before him. Entering the printworks door, down a lane at the back of a building, McKeon was ambushed by noise. The click and rattle and steamy push and clatter of printing. Linotype machines, the new big printing press, the little machines which ran off raffle tickets. The big press was throwing out a horde of *Herald*s to collators who herded them into batches of ten.

His father brought him round the works and introduced him to men who shook hands solemnly, even when their palms were so coated with sweat as to make them slip immediately from McKeon's grasp. They wiped their hands with rags and shook again, properly, before scattering suddenly like western saloon customers hearing a gun. McKeon and his father were left alone to face a man in a sternly tailored black suit.

—Come on, the lot of ye, we're not paying ye to stand around.

—There's a print run on. There's not a lot for the lads to be doing.

—Someone could be sweeping the floor or clearing away loose paper. There's always work to be done, McKeon. And who said you could land your gossan in here? I suppose he is your gossan, unless you've started giving guided tours to the place.

—Mister Tully, he is my son and I wanted him to see where I work. It's a sort of a treat for him. He nearly died, you know.

Those words did not fully register with McKeon at the time.

—The proprietor, his father whispered as Tully stood aside and gave silent permission for the man and boy to travel farther into the *Herald*.

A little office where two bespectacled women calculated wage packets on their fingers led to a huge black door on which McKeon Senior knocked.

—Come in.

His father edged in the door like a man waiting to hear a light bulb crash to the ground. The air in the office seemed so heavy McKeon doubted they would make it to the desk where a little man with his hair tucked behind his ear was decorating a piece of copy paper with a red biro.

—Joseph, how are you doing. Is this the young lad?

The man who had called McKeon's father by his first name emerged from behind his desk and pointed at the photos of the executed leaders of the Easter Rising on the wall.

—I'm Michael O'Donoghue, the editor. We write the stories that your daddy prints. We know all the news. Do you know who those men on the wall are?

McKeon nodded his head enthusiastically. Like most young lads, his favourite parts of history had war in them.

—They're the heroes of this country. When you grow up, young buck, I hope you have a chance to fight for Ireland like those men.

O'Donoghue's spiel was interrupted by a knock on a smaller door which led into a room where the clicking of typewriter keys had counterpointed his jagged ragtime breathing. A younger man entered with a sheaf of paper in his hand.

—Mister O'Donoghue, the County Council stuff is here. How are you doing, Joe?

The change in the voice shocked McKeon. It had been heavy with respect, and then suddenly light with nothing at all. His father made his excuses and left, speaking to his son in the hall as he handed him money for sweets.

—You seen the job I do, and it's the job every man in our family done these past hundred years. I don't want you to do it because you'll get no respect for it. You seen Mister O'Donoghue today, he gets respect and so does young Keenan. They know everything that's going on and they can talk to anyone, even the priests and the politicians. I'm telling you now, a reporter is the thing to be.

He became a reporter to please his father, and when he went to work he walked in the front door while his father walked in the back. The deal was clear between reporters and printers. Reporters did not cross printers, or twenty-seven spectacular mistakes would appear in the short piece they had written on the bishop's Easter message. But the reporters were top dogs on half the money.

McKeon worked on his shorthand till he was allowed to cover a County Council meeting on his own, where, despite the fact that he was a gawky and spotty eighteen-year-old, county councillors had sought him out at the end of the meeting as though he was the man who knew how the Cuban Missile Crisis would end. Men he had seen keeping huge crowds quiet bought him drinks till he could hold no more. He fell across his father when he opened the front door and waited for the bollocking, but there was only a proud smile.

—I know the crack, Seamus, you have to hang around the pubs making contacts, meeting the big people. It's an important part of your job.

In thick notebooks, McKeon inscribed the names of mourners at funerals and the officiating priests at ordinations, the prices of cattle at local marts and the thoughts of the Chairman of the County Board on the iniquitous nature of soccer. He was there when the old President came to Rathbawn for a final spin on the hustings, which left half the pensioners in the town crying with joy and the other half murmuring bitter sentences about dead laughing boys and bastard sons of Spanish Jews.

A bony arm extended from Fintan Beirne's trench coat, scrawling shorthand as the living legend maundered on in the Market Square, the gist of his speech being that he was still alive, and wasn't that a great thing which people should think of when they were voting? When Beirne showed up at the *Herald* in the afternoon, McKeon was the only one in the newsroom. Everyone else had gone to get a last look at the dying chief on his favourite battlefield.

The trench coat, slouch hat and dark glasses made Beirne look like he'd stepped out of a Sean Keating flying-column portrait. The smell of drink off his breath would have killed a roomful of Pioneers.

—How's it going, young McKeon? I see things haven't changed in this neck of the woods as regards timekeeping. Can I type up something here? I have to ring in some stuff for the evening editions, and I want to get it down on paper.

McKeon didn't type anything for the next half an hour. His typing would have sounded awkward and wrong beside the smooth symphony Beirne tapped out, his hands seeming to float above the keys as they produced a flow of clacks which sounded like the musical manifestation of news. The way he breathed and the momentary suck of the teeth before the rattling out of the sentence completed the picture of the real reporter. One from Rathbawn, who had worked in this newsroom before ascending to the heights of national newspaper journalism.

—How are you enjoying your time in the *Herald*, young McKeon? I suppose you're coping well with O'Donoghue. You'd be learning a lot from him, I suppose.

—Ah, yeah, he's been at it a lot longer than me.

—He's not worth a shite. He could have been, but he hung around this place when he should have gone to Dublin. I'm hearing very good reports about you. You're supposed to be a bright lad. Go to Dublin.

—It's easy for you to say. I have a steady job here.

—I'm not saying jack it in for nothing. But there's always jobs advertised. Wait two more years and by then, if you're as good as I'm told, you'll be able to do anything you're asked to do. Then go. I know by the head of you that you want to be famous.

McKeon bided his time. There were occasional consolations, the invite to the opening night of the Majestic, for example.

THE SIXTIES

The Majestic Ballroom had glitter balls hanging from the ceiling, a stage the size of a small village and a neatly painted mineral bar with comfortable chairs, and Henry knew it was doomed. The ballroom days would soon be over. The figures didn't show this, but Henry smelt it on the wind, and he was a believer in hunches. He only opened the Majestic because people in the county town had been good to him, and he wanted to give them something in return.

Jimmy got his drinking done before the Majestic, but the terror that the world would run out of drink while he needed a healer was still in his eyes. He worked the hall like a dervish, knowing that no one there really liked his company. He wasn't there to be liked, he was there to swing things for people.

— Young McKeon, are you enjoying yourself? There's a quare gang of young people out tonight.

— It's not a bad night at all, Councillor, pity there isn't an oul bar in the joint.

— Ah, now, you should be able to go one night without drink.

*

The Caslin brothers appeared, moving like jaguars in mohair suits. Henry asked for introductions. He got them. Story of his life.

—We've always got good publicity from the papers. I think the local paper is very important. If I didn't get the *Herald* every week, I wouldn't know what was going on.

McKeon told himself it wasn't the man he disliked, but the idea of someone who wanted to own everything and win everything. Mister Big Shot in his expensive suit. Father Gerry Lee joined them. McKeon knew him from his trips to the *Herald* office to talk about fund-raising schemes. Harmless.

The *Herald* photographer shuffled over and broached the idea of a shot of the four of them together, Father Lee, Mister Caslin, Councillor Mimnagh and young McKeon. McKeon told him O'Donoghue would never use a picture with a reporter in it. McDonagh wanted the quartet.

Snap.

The photo was taken. The one McKeon came back to look for. Taken when none of the people in it knew any of the important things about each other. It was just a snap of four men standing in a ballroom in the middle of the sixties but, years later, the sight of Henry Caslin, Father Gerry Lee, Jimmy Mimnagh and Seamus McKeon together could be interpreted very differently. That was why McKeon would search for it.

When the group broke up, Henry noticed how people shook Jimmy's hand with respect on their faces and wheedling in their eyes. He saw that Jimmy was a man who mattered. This was an important discovery. At the same time, Jimmy regarded the shape of Henry's head, the way he talked, the way he moved, noticing the way people shook hands with the man. They shook hands with Jimmy because they thought it was a good idea; they shook hands with Henry because they thought he was a good man. You could only like him.

And Jimmy had fallen in love with him. He knew that love was doomed, but that he could make something different out of it, turn it into friendship and dependency and mutual interest and mutual joy. He would take his own ambition and put it at the service of this man.

A week later Father Lee was moved on again. He felt mistreated. It had been just one small incident and he had done a good job in Rathbawn, raising unprecedented amounts of money for the parish. They moved him anyway, giving him a choice between quitting the priesthood or going to America. They said they couldn't protect him any more. It sounded like a threat, so he packed his bags and took a taxi to Shannon Airport, reading in the morning paper that Edward O'Hanlon had been appointed bishop of a diocese in the Midlands. He would be the youngest bishop in the country. The papers called him the rising star of the hierachy. Proper order.

Those papers were full of big advertisements for the ballrooms, but it was the smaller ads Henry noticed. The ones for the singing lounges which had started up in Dublin, keeping people in the pubs and out of the ballrooms. He was seeing the future again, and this time he did not want to be part of it.

It came as a shock to discover that Eugene did not agree with him. Henry tried to explain, but hunches do not translate well into words. Eugene said the ballrooms would never be killed off. There was more money than ever in the country, and talk of joining the Common Market, which would leave the place swimming in grant money. In his efforts to convince, Henry went one step too far.

—What do you mean, Henry? What do you mean by that?

—I'm only saying that we've made money out of the ballrooms because of my ideas.

—Are you saying it's all up to you how well we've done?

—I'm not. But it was me that got the idea for the first one, and all the other things like the bingo. You never thought of anything on your own.

—I never thought of anything? I built these ballrooms and I got the tradesmen in and I sat down with architects and got them designed. I've as much to do with them as you have.

It should have been left at that, but both of them wanted the last word, and in the end people had to come between them. The Majestic office was thick and dark with grudge when they left. The takings stayed uncounted overnight on the table. Their wives advised them to apologise, but neither brother wanted to be the first to lift the phone. They began to suspect there had always been problems between them, Henry thinking of Eugene's lack of interest in school and his post-ballroom carousing. Eugene dwelling on Henry's superior air and glee at being proved correct. The dread feeling that the other might be right drove them to an unspoken stand-off. Work was divided up so that they did not have to meet.

The fact that Henry made the next move did not necessarily mean he was to blame for worsening the rift. Eugene wanted things to stay as they were. Henry wanted them to change. He had to make the next move, and did by calling Anton Dupre.

Dupre was an Englishman who owned supermarkets and an exotic series of rooms in a Dublin street near the canal. He called them a discotheque. Jimmy Mimnagh called him the Wandering Jew, though Dupre was the most secular man you could meet. Henry met him in the discotheque and came away more convinced than ever about the fate of the ballrooms. He thought about getting into the discotheque business himself, but scotched the idea in the taxi. The entertainment business was beginning to bore him.

The ballrooms were a hundred per cent joint-owned by Henry and Eugene Caslin but Henry didn't think he was pulling a fast one, although he knew his brother would not like the deal.

The week after should have been one of the happiest of Henry's life. Mary gave birth to their first daughter. She would be christened Dolores. Then the solicitor's letter arrived at The Hacienda. Eugene's invitation to the christening remained unsent.

Involving the law was a betrayal. Eugene knew how much Henry hated the legal profession for their effect on business, denying the bar licences which might have secured the future of the ballrooms and coming up with their niggly little arguments about planning permission and fire regulations and objections from residents. And Henry could not see how Eugene was in the right. If they jointly owned a hundred per cent, surely he was entitled to sell half to whoever he liked. He had even been scrupulous in offering Dupre a mixture of the most and least profitable ballrooms.

The solicitor Henry hired told him Eugene was in the right. They owned a hundred per cent between them. Neither owned anything independent of the other. Henry settled out of court because he knew he could not win. He felt defeated, despite the fact that Eugene had paid good money for shares which would soon be next to useless. He informed his brother that he would never speak to him again, and kept his word.

Freed from the ballroom business, he became involved with the Rathbawn Leisure Complex, which had been Jimmy Mimnagh's idea. The credit was taken by Christy Dockery. Dockery did things like that because he had been the Party deputy in the town for the past thirty years. Everything in Rathbawn was connected to him. When he got bored he started new ventures to increase his control. He and Jimmy set up a committee of eight men to buy shares in and run the complex. Dockery nodded complacent agreement when Jimmy suggested as a member Henry Caslin, now managing a clothing factory for a Dutch company.

Within three years Rathbawn had a swimming pool, basketball courts, a new soccer pitch, a new Gaelic pitch and handball alleys, which in the eighties would become squash courts. Word round town was that Caslin had been the man mainly responsible. Jimmy told Dockery this, adding

—There's nothing I can tell you about politics, Christy, but it might be as well to show the horns now and again in case there's any mistake about who's running the show at the complex. You're the most powerful man in this town. Don't let anyone forget that.

The sight of the complex gave Henry a tight feeling in the muscles of his arms and legs, which made him feel like jumping to fetch a high ball. He even enjoyed the monthly meetings until the night Christy Dockery stood up when people were reaching for the coats hung on the backs of their chairs.

—Mister Chairman, I'd like to make a bit of a statement. I've sent the text to the *Herald*. I'm becoming concerned about how the complex is being run. We're getting a bad name around the town.

Henry sat bolt upright. Jimmy marvelled at his sharpness. He knew what this was all about. Dockery continued in a voice sharpened by expressing sympathy for Hitler in the forties, welcoming emigration as a safety valve in the fifties and describing contraception as murder in the sixties.

—As a full-time public representative, I'm used to certain standards in the realms of administration. The problem with this committee is that some people spend far too much time doing things like running factories to be on it. There's no room for passengers in this town.

If Henry had not just fallen out with Eugene, he might have let it go.

—I'm the only man here who runs a factory, so I presume you're talking about me, Mister Dockery.

The m in Mister had a grind to it like a scythe being sharpened.

Dockery prepared to unleash one of his favourite phrases. It had a mathematical simplicity. You made a speech that did everything except actually name the person it was aimed at. You let them identify themselves as the target. Then you whipped out

—If the cap fits, wear it.

But he didn't get the chance, because Caslin didn't pause for a second.

—You know and every man in this room knows, that I spend more time working for the good of this complex than anyone else. I'll tell you something else, you can ask the staff out there who spends the most time here, and you can ask the business people in town who's got the most money out of them.

For an awful moment, Dockery expected the complex staff and the business people to walk through the door.

—I'll ask you to exempt me from that last comment about people not doing their work. You do that or I'll resign, and tell the people in town why.

—I'll exempt nothing. If the cap fits, wear it.

A few snickers from Dockery's arch-cronies, but nothing from anyone else.

—Well, I'm left with no option but to resign.

Then something incredible happened. All the other members asked Caslin to stay on. Even the ones from the Party went crying after Caslin like kids after Mammy.

—All right then, I'll stay on. But seeing as Mister Dockery

Mister like a curse. Like rhyming slang for blister. A cold sibilant hiss like the last gasp of steam from a kettle with the element burned out

—Seeing as he wanted to talk about the committee and work, I'll talk about it too. I happened to look at the attendance records of this committee the other day. The man who's missed the most meetings is the Chairman. He's also the only member who hasn't helped out at the complex since it opened.

—Fucking take that back.

—I can't take it back. What you said was an opinion, it might be right and it might be wrong. What I said is a fact, and it's right.

—You're leaving me with no alternative. I resign as Chairman, and I think it's a sorry day for this committee when the choice of the people is overridden like this. This is like the days of Hitler's Germany.

—No one's asking you to go, said the committee secretary.

—No one's asking you to stay either, said Henry, as Dockery trudged towards the door with two cohorts behind him.

Stopping in the corridor to catch his breath, Dockery

heard Caslin inform the committee that, as Vice-Chairman, he would take over for the rest of the meeting.

—It's hardly the first time I had to do it, said Caslin, and everyone laughed.

Dockery toyed with the idea of going back and punching Caslin in the gob, but he calmed himself. He was, after all, the most popular politician in the country and had been for thirty years. Losing a row to some hobo whose oul fella was a drunk with a kiss-me-arse shop wouldn't change anything. Still, he felt bad about being on the outside with Caslin inside, after planning for the opposite to happen. He felt worse when he realised that Jimmy Mimnagh had not walked out after him.

Jimmy stayed talking with Henry after the meeting and went back to The Hacienda with him, reassuring his new friend when he worried that Dockery might be a bad man to cross.

—What you have and want, Christy Dockery cannot take away.

Henry realised that Jimmy was telling him that the opposite did not apply. They could take away what Dockery wanted. He did not worry about a possible reprisal because he was not a man who worried. In fact, only one thing made him nervous. Protestants.

Protestants were different, and all that guff about Wolfe Tone, Henry Joy McCracken and General Monroe being united in the common name of Irishman still did not make them the same. Henry knew a good few Protestants. Or rather, he knew of them. In every town, they owned draperies and sometimes grocery shops. For the few of them in it, they had a lot of shops. Some still owned big farms of land. The ones that were left.

Your Protestant daddy was taking no chances any more. He left his farm to children who'd marry another Protestant, their neighbours not being considered good enough. They'd comb the countryside until some sketch from two hundred miles away married the big-shot Protestant son or daughter. That was the way of them. They kept to themselves.

His mother's sister had spent thirty years in England working as a maid for posh families. People asked to hear her story when she came back first. The story of lords and ladies and the sort of English person you didn't have any more in Ireland. They stopped asking when they heard a different story to the one they wanted.

—They were all very kind. They had a real touch of class about them. They were real Protestant people.

The thought of his aunt taking the Saxon shilling and being grateful for it. Kick me again, why don't you. He preferred Jimmy's version of England where there was a boot in the balls, a sly word or a knife in the guts waiting around every corner for Paddy.

Worst of all were the rich Prods, who looked down at you when you went into their shops and took your money as if they didn't like handling it. But even the Protestant small farmers occupied a place apart. They made such a big deal out of attending their little Church of Ireland chapel, coming out at the end with their arms full of flowers from the altar and standing around for ages outside as if to remind everyone they belonged here.

The boot, of course, was on the other foot when their gang was in charge. There was no chance of the Catholic being let go about his business in the six counties. The land of the B Specials and Beaverbrook and a Protestant parliament for a Protestant people.

Nothing made Henry or Jimmy madder than the thought of the Northern Protestants and their own little state, an offcut of a country which was too small to exist but was maintained by the Brits as a geographical insult.

Their prime minister came to Dublin for the first time.

The Taoiseach went to Belfast. Henry knew he was supposed to feel glad but he didn't. He could tell by the look of the Protestant boss man that he thought he was doing people down here a favour. There was talk on Radio Telefís Éireann that things might soon change. The Northern Catholics were compared to the civil rights marchers in America. Henry was sure they would be delighted to hear themselves put in the same boat as a bunch of foreign niggers.

When Henry crossed the border for the first time in his new Morris Oxford, he tried to think calming thoughts which he could shove like planks over the memories of Malvern Street, the B Specials and the Reverend Ian Paisley. All he could come up with was the memory of his National School history book, which included an account of the Siege of Derry. He remembered admiring the courage of the people inside the city and hoping they would hold out. They did, and then he found out he shouldn't have been hoping that at all.

He held on to that memory and tried to use it as a basis for understanding. You had to have empathy. This deal would be important for the factory.

But what if there were people you could never empathise with? Would that be a failure? Would it be your failure or theirs?

The linen mill was just outside a town twice the size of Rathbawn. Noting the stark military aspect of the place, Henry wondered if the Prods meant their towns to look like petrified rain. The red postboxes and phone boxes added to his unease. The roads were very good. He found himself thinking that the roads seemed a lot better on this side of the border. They probably did massive work on roads near the border out of spite.

Rodney Fullerton ostentatiously looked at his watch, though Henry was two minutes early. He offered to drive

Henry to lunch. Henry reciprocated. They considered getting a taxi, but could not agree who would pay. Both of them drove their cars to the restaurant.

Fullerton. No doubting a name like that. The pop of the wine cork made Henry think about battles of the recent past and the ballads which commemorated them.

—And the leader was a Limerick man, Sean South of Garryowen.

—Are you hummin' an oul tune to yourself there, Mister Caslin?

—Not at all. You can call me Henry, Mister Fullerton.

—You'll have an oul drop of wine, Henry.

—I don't drink.

Fullerton raised his eyebrows theatrically. His smile was less sarcastic than it might have been and less friendly than it could have. Henry removed a folder from his briefcase. Fullerton finished the bottle of wine while Henry made do with one glass of water. He hadn't known whether Prods drank. Did some of them not regard it as a papish sin or a Paddy disease?

Back in the office, Fullerton went big on the red-faced effusiveness. Henry relaxed sufficiently to forget where he was for a few seconds. His host stressed how much they had in common. Businessmen had more in common than any other group. They were an international class. One day there would be no nations. Only businesses. He read out the contract, stressing the address of his firm. The road, the town, the county.

—I'm afraid you have the name of the county wrong, Rodney.

—No, I don't. County Londonderry.

—There's no such place as County Londonderry. It's County Derry. Londonderry is only a makey-up British name.

—I hope you're not trying to insult me, Mister Caslin.

This factory is in Londonderry. It's also in the United Kingdom.

—No one calls it Londonderry.

—No one I know calls it anything else.

There was silence for a few seconds. Starlings chattered outside the window. When they stopped, the quiet was unbearable.

—Can you just change it on my copy of the contract. To Derry.

—No. That's not the way we do business up here. The county is called Londonderry.

—I'm being reasonable. What about the Siege of Derry? It's the Siege of Derry ye won.

—I don't care about reasonable. I said no. Listen, why don't we look in the atlas and whatever name is there goes on the contract?

Fullerton battered his fist down on the red letters. Londonderry.

—See now, Henry. The *Sunday Times* atlas, the greatest atlas in the world and it says Londonderry. You couldn't get better proof than that.

—It proves nothing. It's a British atlas.

—Ah, now, let's face it. Who in the world would pay any heed on an Irish atlas? If there was such a thing.

He didn't seem to be joking. How much did these names matter anyway? Henry signed the contract and the conversation returned to the territory of business and money as Fullerton walked unsteadily with him to the car.

—I'm glad we exchanged addresses, Henry. I might give you a shout sometime. We can take advantage of the fine fishing ye've got down there.

—I'm afraid there's no fine fishing near Rathbawn.

—I thought the South was all fine fishing.

—No, that's a sort of cliché. It's like the idea we have down there that everyone up here is a B Special.

Henry started the engine. Fullerton leaned in the window.

—Everyone here might not be. But I am and I'm proud of it.

He wasn't joking this time either.

—Nice doing business with you.

Back on his own side of the border, Henry reflected on the superior way Fullerton had acted. He didn't mind it that much. All the same, the man should be careful. Some people might take that kind of behaviour very badly indeed.

In America Father Lee found himself undone by money. The root of all evil. The Yanks and their obsession with the dollar caused his downfall. The neighbouring diocese had been hit with a massive court case. One of their priests had been interfering with youngsters and they did nothing when they found out. The cover-up cost them a million dollars after a lawsuit. Father Lee recognised the priest. They had once masturbated side by side in a small private cinema which specialised in footage of Asian youngsters brought home by GIs returning from the Vietnam War.

Extensive enquiries were carried out in other dioceses, mindful of their parlous situations. Father Lee hoped against hope. He'd been well enough behaved in Schuylersburg Falls. Just some light feeling and fondling of the altar boys, and one incident with a small girl who'd got a bit panicky and suffered an awful asthma attack.

He was brought to the airport in the early hours of the morning and told that when he arrived in Shannon, he would be met and told where to go and what to do from now on.

—Will I lose the right to say Mass?

—No, of course not. But you're not going to be allowed to work in a parish. Not for a while, anyway. We can't have this behaviour. If the American media heard, they'd rub our noses in it.

—Ireland is different, thank God.

The monastery was in drumlin country where slanty black rain disimproved gloomy scenery, the birds screamed rather than sang and the cows sounded like they couldn't be bothered getting the moos out of their throats. The abbot and the monks knew Father Lee's record. They would not associate with Father Lee, but did not feel they could tell other people what to do. Father Lee was a free human being with his own mind, and anyone who desired his company was welcome to it. It was not up to the monks to keep children away from him.

He had developed the ability to make friends with children and extract trust from their parents, who would let him bring the kids on little trips to the seaside. On day trips he would stop the car on the way to the beach and tickle the puzzled children, repeating the game on the way back but this time inserting his fingers into their openings. On weekends he brought boys to tourist resorts where he would book them into the same guest-house room as himself. The boys would be forced to masturbate Father Lee on the Friday night and would be raped on the Saturday until he got tired.

The kids were selected from the poor housing estate which backed on to the monastery grounds. The people there still had respect for the clergy, a respect they bore around on their crushed backs like snails carrying large and cumbersome shells. They were convinced that their suffering would always be there, and the Church assured them this was so. Their children were ideal victims.

An emboldened Father Lee began calling to the houses of his children with sweets and gifts for their parents. Some children became agitated by these visits, and a couple even

pair of them while they made their minds up. They shouted after him. He flashed his NUJ card out of his back pocket and kept moving.

At night, the noise of the day's comings and goings seemed to hang suspended in the building. The light from the courtroom he was headed for flung a streaky skulking shadow down the corridor. He looked down at it as he walked on, the steel tips on his shoes making his footsteps theatrically loud. The guards at the door shook their heads when he tried to get past them. It was ten twenty-eight.

—Boys there's a court on and I have to report on it. It's my job.

—The court is on in the morning. Were you not told that?

—It's on now. I know it is. That's why I'm here.

—It's a special court. You can't come in.

—Have you law on that? I'm entitled to come in unless the judge has made an order for the case to be held in camera. Come on. There'll be an unholy row if ye don't let me in. Ye'll end up on television.

—Listen, Seamie boy, I'll just check with the judge about it. But I can't go in until another guard turns up. It'll be just ten minutes.

McKeon heard the rasping cough which Judge Monteith employed to announce the beginning of proceedings.

—I'm going in now. If you want to stop me, you'll have to arrest me. There'll be some stir about that, and it's you that'll get blamed.

When he walked into the court, the two sets of solicitors looked at him, the guards looked at him and Judge Monteith regarded him as though he was shit which had turned up on the ends of the judicial wig. The Minister for Justice, Edward O'Higgins, stared at him while the guards gave their evidence.

It must have been some party. The Minister had fallen

out with his driver and made off in the Merc himself. Within a mile he had mounted the footpath, destroyed six litter bins, hit a man who was currently in traction in the Mater Hospital and turned the car over. The superintendent explained apologetically that they had no other option but to book him for drink-driving before glancing in McKeon's direction and shaking his head. The judge did the same before pronouncing the sentence once and fast. That didn't work. McKeon's local-paper shorthand got the details perfect.

—Disqualified from driving for a year and fined fifty pounds.

O'Higgins had to be helped out of the witness box.

McKeon spent the next morning in a room at the station fielding questions from management and the legal department. All the questions merged into one big one. Are you sure? If he had even hinted he wasn't, that would have been that. They were giving him a way out. He stuck to his guns. Truth prevailed, helped by the fact that O'Higgins had described the station as an anti-national nest of homosexuals and Protestants and was campaigning against an increase in the licence fee.

The case made McKeon with the young guns. He had hammered another nail in the coffin of a corrupt Establishment. A young woman from Belfast who talked about the female orgasm in a loud voice during coffee breaks asked him back to her place that night. He hadn't the confidence, but appreciated the offer.

In Toner's a couple of weeks later McKeon saw the pock-marked man talking to Fintan Beirne. They smiled bashfully when they noticed him. McKeon knew who the man was now. He was familiar with too many paranoids not to have heard of the Special Branch. He wondered if it mattered that he'd got the right story for the wrong reasons before deciding that investigative journalism was like sadomasochism. If someone's using you for their ends and you're also getting a lot out of it, everyone is happy.

Anyway, someone who'd wanted to ban the Midnight Court couldn't complain about being screwed by a court at half past ten.

The rural TDs who had been McKeon's friends in his first months in Dublin shied away from him in the Dáil restaurant after the O'Higgins story. Christy Dockery spoke to him to explain that he couldn't speak to him anymore.

—I know you're only a young fella trying to get on, but there was a lot of our people think you did a wrong thing.

—The law should be the same for everyone, Christy.

—Ah, I suppose, but O'Higgins is an alcoholic, he'll be dead soon enough without you speeding him on his way. I hadn't you down as the sort of gossan that'd be harsh.

The loss of Christy and his mates didn't bother McKeon. The older reporters would always get on better with them than the younger ones could. The youngsters would have to make their names by not getting on with them.

Henry Caslin was also looking into the future. He had seen it once before in the shape of an old parish hall. This time it was a field which a local development association was trying to sell. No one wanted it except Henry, who saw it as the perfect empty canvas for the art of making money, a placid clean face on to which Henry could apply the cosmetics of his dreams.

The future was baby food. Henry wanted a line of little blue cans stretching out to infinity and filled with both sweet and savoury mush. A little bit of his home county in every young Irish stomach. Baby food had been chosen because hardly anyone else was making it. The rule of sex, politics and business. Three of the four cardinal points of Henry's life, the fourth being his family, which now included two daughters and a son. Their baby faces came to his mind when he and Mick Dowd from the meat factory planned the new business. Dowd knew about canning; the other investor was a Dub garage man named Foster who had just sold Henry his first Merc.

But it wasn't Dowd or Foster that Henry sought out when he saw the perfect field for the factory. He drove home to Mary, and then they called round to Jimmy. The three of them stood on the side of the road with rain falling on their faces and their arms around each other. When Henry pointed at the field, Mary and Jimmy could already see the workforce hurrying to their jobs, the beautifully cambered roads leading up to the plant and the big sign which read BB Baby Foods. They heard the crisp rustle of company notepaper competing with the sound of curlews, notepaper with Henry's name at the top. He kept pointing and talking, and they saw a fleet of lorries carrying the precious cans all over Europe. The scutch grass disappeared under the weight of their dreams.

The next week the North caught fire.

The blaze was kindled by two simple and seemingly harmless words which lacked the heroic tang of rising or war. Civil rights. All they were looking for in the North were fair elections, decent housing and some sort of reasonable life for Catholics. How could you argue with that?

The Prods showed how. With batons and tear gas which television stations brought over the border into living rooms where men cursed, women wept and children bit their nails in frustration as they watched splendidly isolated RUC men batoning the defenceless to one side of the screen and then back again.

Derry and Londonderry. Now Henry saw what there could be in a name. Himself and Jimmy watched the baton charges on telelvision, and the sight of blood trickling down the heads of demonstrators gave them an itchy feeling in their scalps. Henry wanted to punch and bite and kick and be on the streets of Derry with a baton in his hand to show those arrogant, those well-fed, those planted Protestant bastards what a fair fight was like. Jimmy shook with temper beside him. Henry spoke first.

—The fucking bastards. The fucking cunts.

Normally he never cursed.

—It's not, it's not fucking right, Jimmy.

His heart seemed to be jumping sideways and trying to drill its way towards the fresh air. His saliva tasted bitter and he felt helpless.

—We can't just stand idly by. They're our people up there, and we're letting them be attacked by savages. Something has to be done.

Jimmy continued to listen.

—We should get guns to them so they can defend themselves. The Irish Army should go in and sort out the Protestants. Anyone who can use a gun should go up there.

Jimmy nodded agreement. The beating continued on the screen. Happy RUC men flattened the remaining protesters. The stones fired in retaliation looked like joke gestures made by children against adults.

—If the Catholics had guns, those RUC fuckers wouldn't be so smart. It's a war, Jimmy.

—It's a war, Henry. We should be up there.

McKeon lobbied hard to get to Belfast or Derry. They were the places to be. But too many senior people wanted to go, so he had to hang around Dublin and talk to left-wing students who squatted houses in Georgian Dublin. They told him they were going to bring down the system. He felt like telling them they were a hundred miles too far south. History was going on over their heads. Their world seemed unreal in this time of blood.

His interviews with the students were never used. The screen time was taken up by the spreading riots, the first civilian casualties as armoured cars shot up Catholic flats. He watched his television and waited for the first RUC men to get killed, feeling a certain amount of relish at the thought. Most people did in those days.

For the first time since Rome, Father Lee felt connected to a greater community. He watched the marchers being beaten and thought of his own childhood in a village where the tricolour could not be flown, remembering his father's fear of the policemen who swaggered up the lane for no other reason but to make sure that fear continued. He prayed for the safety of his people and told everyone where he came from, letting his anger show. People said it was good to see at least one priest speaking out. He organised socials to raise money for the Citizens' Defence Committees in the North.

Jimmy put out feelers. It wasn't hard done. Every county within a hundred miles of the border was swarming with men from the North looking for assistance. First they talked about medical supplies and the humanitarian aspect. When their listeners nodded they talked about self-defence. Finally they spoke of guns, and the best ever chance for a thirty-two-county Republic.

The pictures continued to be the same on television. Armoured cars and tanks and guns against stones and bin lids. Nothing seemed to have changed. Jimmy thought of the great paintings of the flying columns who had put the Black and Tans to flight. The riots were like knife strokes which slashed and distorted the pictures. The country's foundation myths were being retrospectively mocked. Jimmy parked his Austin Cambridge outside a monastery near the border and met three men in the sacristy of a small chapel.

—Just give us the money. You provide the money, and

our Defence Committee will decide how it's spent. We're the people on the ground.

The people on the ground. There was no better way to describe the Northern Catholics.

The man with the beard began by talking about blankets. Jimmy nodded. The man moved on to guns and bombs, words which did not yet automatically conjure up a picture of punctured flesh, splintering bones and limbs cartwheeling gracelessly through the air. Different words upset Jimmy, words which showed that the man with the beard had no respect.

The man called Jimmy's country the Free State, which made it sound a mere province with no power other than to issue its own stamps and paint postboxes a conservative colour. Jimmy winced every time he heard the f-word, and each use reversed the cache of arms away from the Irish coast and back towards the Central European warehouse where they currently lay.

—Statelet.

That was what the man with the beard called the North. The word sounded childish and loaded with spite. A war in a statelet would be fought round corners. This man was not asking for help. He was presuming on it. He didn't say he wanted a United Ireland, either. He wanted a free one. He told Jimmy neither part of the country was free. The words were a backhanded slap across the face.

—Your security forces.

Security forces was a phrase Jimmy liked. It named the baton-charging, the CS gas and the men rampaging through Catholic housing estates where women and children shuddered behind damp, paper-thin walls. You changed that. It implicated the guards. The guards were not security forces, but your man was saying they were. The word your decided it for Jimmy. He said he would go back to Henry and see what he said, now that Jimmy had been fully apprised of the situation. There would be no money. Henry needed to be protected from this insane spiral. There was no way out of it. It was like honeydew, like the Venus flytrap.

—You realise there will be no problem with the guards or customs or anything. This has government go-ahead. It has the nod at the highest level.

Jimmy nodded.

—What you're really saying is that there's no way Henry Caslin will provide money to buy arms. That's what you're saying, isn't it?

He nodded again. They walked out of the sacristy. The man with the beard stood on the gravel and talked to his two companions. Heads were shaken. Words had created the difficulties. Gestures confirmed them.

—Fucking cowardly wee Free State cunt.

Letting on not to hear, Jimmy hoisted himself painfully into the Cambridge and drove away, looking in the rearview mirror at Charlie Burns, Myles Duff of the Special Branch and Father Gerry Lee who had arranged the meeting. He needed a drink. The rioting was still on television in the local pub. It seemed different to Jimmy now, and he wanted it to be a long way away. He began the process of filing it in a corner of his mind with other memories which could only be recalled inadvertently. Thousands of people all over the country were doing the same, feeling as though their next-door neighbour's house had gone on fire. Sure they wanted their neighbour to be safe, but first they wanted to make sure the blaze did not spread any further.

One other thing. Duff had reminded him of a management mole planted on a building site. He didn't know how Burns had not copped this. Anyone that gullible didn't deserve money.

*

Father Lee apologised to Burns for Jimmy's behaviour.

—The only thing the Free Staters want from the North is contraceptives.

What happened in Belfast turned Dublin into a city of whispers. Long black cars tailed customers home from pubs where patriotic ballads were sung. Passport-sized photos were affixed to little files. Reports were copied. Doors started closing on the men from the North.

The pock-marked Myles Duff began to phone McKeon at home. When they met he walked with a bounce and swagger which announced the arrival of his moment in history. He spoke from behind his hands.

—There's a load of money gone missing from the Defence Committee funds. Check it out.

—The Irish Army were going to train a bunch of young lads from the North. But they changed their mind. Have a look at it.

Without ever going there, McKeon had become involved in the North. He was becoming well known. He never revealed his sources. He met Duff at the zoo one day. The place was full of children throwing food to the animals and parents who saw nothing wrong with the idea of a zoo. Simpler times.

—It's going to be the biggest story of your life. I'm doing you a favour.

The monkeys picked fleas from their chests and offered them to each other.

—Three Ministers. All up to their bollocks in gun-running. They won't even deny it. Take these documents, it's all in it. Think about it, Seamus, three government Ministers bringing guns into their own country for the use of subversive elements. There's a conspiracy to destroy this state. Either you're against it or you're with it.

On the way home McKeon bought three bottles of wine in an off-licence because he couldn't face the documents sober. That night every crack and warp in the wood of the flat startled him. The three Ministers, including the one they called the Tough Guy, had gone behind the Taoiseach's back and brought guns into the country for distribution to the IRA. The Special Branch had infiltrated the operation and intercepted the guns. There would be prosecutions, but everything would have been hushed up if the documents had not found their way to a certain eager young television reporter.

The Ministers resigned when the story broke. The government shook. Duff came into his kingdom. Everyone forgot about the North as the Ministers went on trial for gun-running. They got off because everyone wanted them to, and did a little dance of joy outside the Four Courts for a couple of seconds. People forgot them then. Timing had been their enemy. They had got on the wrong side of the cusp between the time when everyone felt something should be done and the time everyone knew nothing could be done. They had lost, Duff had won and McKeon had become famous.

One of the Ministers killed himself two years later. McKeon was asked if he was happy now. He told himself it had nothing to do with him. He was a reporter, someone who said what happened. It did not matter why it happened. He was not a camera but a photocopier.

The Party tore itself apart at its annual conference. The three Ministers were denounced from the platform and stalked away with abuse clinging to their backs. In another country they might have had placards hung round their necks and been paraded through the streets. Here, headlines were attached to their names and their disgrace proclaimed by newspaper vendors.

Jimmy knew things would never be the same again for the Party. This was good. Destruction was the best friend of the future. Christy Dockery backed the gun-runners and made a speech in Rathbawn about the heroism of the armed struggle. He suggested the guards got out of the way and let the IRA at it. The next day a restaurant was blown up in Belfast, glass flying through the air to sever the arteries of resting shoppers. People began to realise that words meant and cost something.

The sixties were over.

THE SEVENTIES

Henry had been right about the ballrooms: Eugene went bankrupt as people stopped caring about showbands. Unfortunately it was beginning to look like he had been wrong about baby food.

It had seemed so easy when they started off. All you did was put some mush into a can and then sell it. The first problem was that babies didn't like the food. The second was that canning baby food was different from canning meat. Cans of BB Baby Food tended to blow up in hot weather and shower shoppers in Banana Dessert, Lamb Hotpot or Turkey Goulash. The punters did not forgive BB.

Dowd introduced the little Englishman to Henry. Bloody Sunday was not long gone, and Henry wasn't sure if he could be bothered talking to someone from a country where shooting thirteen unarmed civilians dead was seen as acceptable behaviour.

—Michael here tells me you own this big baby-food factory. Says it's costing you a mint. My name's Trevor Bright. I worked in baby food in England.

Henry had a picture of the little man sitting at a desk while up to his neck in a morass of Braised Liver.

—I know all about the business. I've got the contacts

and everything. I can give you a dig-out, mate. And I'm fucking whizz at market research and product development as well. You interested?

Market research and product development were new words to Henry. They sounded peculiarly English. Bright continued talking while Dowd made faces behind his back. Henry kept listening and invited Bright round to The Hacienda.

The man was right about himself. He was a fucking whizz. Henry thought he might be a genius. Bright had handed him a list of two hundred contacts and the best places to stay in every town in England. By the time Henry got back from his tour, Bright had invented four new flavours of baby food which would be contained in a new kind of tin covered in a new wrapper bearing the company's new logo.

The roof was leaking in the rented cottage Bright shared with his wife, Dowd's sister, so Henry gave him cash towards a new house. He got the money back in profits within a month. The cans had stopped exploding and babies began to reach for them on the supermarket shelves, screaming until their mothers plopped the beloved cans of BB into the trolley.

Bright was in Rathbawn because he loved Linda Dowd and because one of their daughters had jumped off a fifth-floor Elephant and Castle balcony after a bad trip. Linda spent six months in the Maudsley Hospital afterwards, and promised she would return to her real life if moved back home to Ireland. Her husband gave up everything for love and hid his pain by creating a new product, while his wife lost her mind in different surroundings.

Eventually she would kill herself. Bright knew this, but he still needed money to make her remaining misery as comfortable as possible and to send his daughters away to school so they could be spared the sight of their mother.

He asked Henry to make him a director of the company. Henry told him he would be looked after, so Bright went home happy and drank warm champagne with his daughters. When he brought a glass up to his wife she lacerated her tongue by chewing the rim off.

Henry found Bright a strange sketch. He was always coming up with a baffling new phrase. Workers' democracy and profit sharing were the latest gems, and Henry was not going to countenance them. He would yield to Bright's superior nous in the field of baby food and marketing, but the man's lack of knowledge about the workings of Irish life stuck out like a lovebite on a nun's neck.

If you gave the BB workers any say in how the place was run they would walk all over you. They'd want to make things easier for themselves until they ended up not doing a tap. Henry was in charge because he had put in the work and the money over the years. The day they had enough cash to start their own factories they could have all the say they wanted.

And profit sharing. Stop the lights. Why give something to anyone when you don't have to? Henry decided not to sign over the shares which would have made Bright a director. He did not inform Bright of this. The Englishman would be better off not getting involved in the running of the company in case he got like Eugene and thought he knew it all. That way everything would just end in tears.

While Henry was busy telling himself how little he owed Trevor Bright, he still found time not to notice what Jimmy was doing for him. Jimmy had brought him into the Party, but it was still a surprise to his protégé when the news was broken that the local elections were two months away. And Henry got an even bigger shock when he was selected as a candidate for the county town, despite the fact that Christy Dockery tried to rule the motion out of order on three separate occasions at the convention. Still, he was pretty sure of getting elected until Mary told him he might not be.

—Why not? Jimmy says I will, and I think I will. People like me in this town.

—Yourself and Jimmy aren't women.

The gnomic nature of his wife's response meant that Henry didn't get much sleep that night. When he thought about it for a bit, he could see no reason why a single person in the town would vote for him. By the time he hit the Land of Nod he had decided to give up on the idea of politics. After all, it was Jimmy's idea. A vote was documentary proof whether people liked you or not, and life was hard enough without taking risks like that. Mary woke him at eight in the morning.

—Do you want me to tell you why you might not get elected?

—Ah, it's OK, I won't run, love I'm not that interested.

—You will run, and you'll win as well. You'll top the poll if you listen to me. But do you know what you can do for me? Get dressed and look in the mirror.

He thought he looked a bit tired but not too bad. The suit looked grand. The hair was tidy enough.

—Tell me what's wrong with you.

—Nothing, Mary love. Well, I'm a bit shattered and I know I'm not the finest-looking man in the county.

—You are the finest-looking man in the county, to me anyway. But look at your clothes. What do you look like?

—I look like meself, Henry Caslin.

—You do. But you look like Henry Caslin the ballroom owner. That's what that suit makes you look like.

He looked in the mirror again. He was proud of these suits. They were something of a trademark with the wide lapels, long collars and big buttons – a sartorial expression of what he stood for. Confidence, risk-taking and the willingness to do the unexpected. Ditto the flowery shirts. He was hurt.

—Well, that's who I am. These are the clothes I wear. I thought you liked them.

—I do like them. And I'll vote for you because I love you. But not everyone in this town loves you, not everyone even knows you. They won't like that suit when you go out to the Dublin Road looking for the posh vote. They'll think you're a cowboy.

He gazed into the mirror a third time. Maybe she had a point.

—What will I do?

—It's what we'll do. We'll go shopping.

By the time Mary steered him into Davitt's barber's, Henry was resigned to adopting a new image.

When he took his suit and his haircut out on the Dublin Road the next day, Henry was invited in for tea five times. Three women with barrister husbands asked him which university he had attended. He was tired but happy when he returned from his first ever day of canvassing.

—Mary, is there any chance of a drop of tea?

—There is of course, love, we're in here.

Mary was sitting in the kitchen with five women, the only one he knew being the lady who cleaned the house and had two sons in prison.

—Sit down, love. I was telling Anna here how you were running for the Council, and she said to make sure to call round to her house and look for a vote.

—And your wife said there was no need to wait for you to call, that you'd have a chat with me here, me and the sisters. It wasn't my idea, Mister Caslin, I'd have been happy enough if you'd come to the house.

Henry could see how uneasy the women were even before they started stroking the furniture and ornaments as though they were animals, fascinating to the touch, which might be startled if woken suddenly. Every time political words failed him, Mary filled the silence with the offer of digestive biscuits.

—We'll have every woman from The Butts in the house wanting to have tea with me. You must be going mad, Mary.

—There'll be no more of them, they're nervous of houses this big. But those women are related to everyone in the place.

—You know, Mary, maybe it's you that should be running.

—Ah, love, I couldn't be bothered.

Everyone knew after a week of the campaign that Henry would be elected, but that was not enough for Jimmy. Merely becoming a county councillor would actually diminish Henry by making him part of quotidian local politics. He was bigger than that. What he needed to do was poll an astounding number of votes.

Personation was dismissed as inefficient and risky, but kept in mind as a fall-back option. Jimmy flourished the voting cards of the recently deceased like a prestidigitating magician.

—I have it. I know how we'll get you this massive vote.

—Speak up. It's not the dead people again, is it?

—No. There's a gang of people in this town who never vote. Hundreds of them who have never been asked their opinion of anything.

—Who?

—The gyps.

There were plenty of tinkers housed in Rathbawn all right, and caravans dotted on the outskirts of the town. There were nearly enough of them to elect a candidate of their own.

The problem was that you couldn't talk to the tinkers or depend on them. They lived in their own world, and hardly acknowledged the presence of the settled people. They couldn't read, they couldn't write and Henry wasn't sure if they were all there. A gyp's life seemed to consist of begging and drinking and fighting and beating his wife if he was a man, or of having twenty children if she was a woman. He wasn't even sure they were entitled to vote. It seemed a waste if they were. Still and all.

—It's a great idea, Jimmy.

—It is. I'll draw a plan tonight. We'll call it Operation Gyp.

—We will. Only not out loud.

Most of the tinkers lived in The Butts, an estate where the locals were too disheartened to keep them out. Jimmy suggested a visit there the next day to meet the tinker big guns.

The next morning, as he prepared for his visit, Henry was surprised at how much thinking about the tinkers annoyed his head. They were like Protestants, wanting to be different even though they had no right to. The Protestants counted change behind the counters of shops, and the tinkers huddled by the side of the road beside piles of scrap metal. Both gangs said they were happy the way they were. Outside normal life.

You couldn't ignore the tinkers. There they were with their big inbred heads and their jabbering chat, a paw stuck out on every street on every town in the county looking for bobs to spend on drink. They put their children out begging in all weathers. They would take the eye out of your head with a belt if you turned your back, but if it came to a fair fight they'd whinge and run off, apologising as they went

—Ah, come on boss, nothing was meant, nothing was meant.

The thought of having to ask them for something made

Henry sick to the pit of his stomach. He brought a few bags of old clothes and some loaves of stale bread with him in an attempt to maintain the appearance of superiority.

On the way to The Butts Jimmy told Henry that the tinkers wanted bathrooms in their houses. They both got a fit of giggles. A few hundred years of slashing in the fields and now they wanted inside toilets. Jimmy said they probably wanted to sell the fixtures for scrap.

The Butts did not seem completely Irish to Henry. The streets were too narrow, the houses too close together and soccer was played instead of Gaelic. No one said hello to him or Jimmy, but holed curtains the length of the street twitched back one by one like Busby Berkeley dancers. Rain beat against the wooden boards which subbed for glass in the window frames of certain houses.

—The knackers are well at home in this place, said Jimmy cheerfully.

A Sacred Heart lamp winked at Henry in the hall of the first house they visited. The woman of the house wasn't bad-looking, but she had the cut of a gyp about her. In the kitchen her husband and three other men sat at a table.

For the first hour the tinker spokesmen acted like they'd cut their tongues out and sold them to their relations for drink money. They talked back, every sentence prefaced with qualification, shot through with apology and finished with uncertainty. Henry still picked up the gist. They wanted their houses to be repaired as often as everyone else's, people from the same families to be moved into houses near each other, front gardens to look out at and kerbs that prevented water flowing under their doors, turning kitchens into swamps every time the clouds burst.

What Henry wanted to do by the time they finished talking was run the gang of them with a shotgun. What he did was set Jimmy to work registering the whole crew.

On the day of the election, Henry and Jimmy spent time

cursing every tinker that had ever walked. By half two they had not seen a single one. A sole member of the Ward family arrived at a quarter to three, and seemed unconcerned by Jimmy's invective.

—No panic, lad, no panic at all, it's just a bit early in the day is all.

Operation Gyp's final phase commenced at half past three. Henry's rivals looked on with betrayed expressions as every tinker from The Butts made their way to Rathbawn's National Schools to vote, saluting Caslin and his supporters as they arrived. Caravans arrived too, full of men and women registered by Jimmy on the basis that they were camped inside constituency boundaries. No one else realised that these caravans would clear to the four corners of the province once democratic duty had been done.

The older men and women did not even know who they were supposed to vote for. Jimmy bustled into the polling booths along with them, handing them fags as he explained where to put the tick, sometimes just making it himself and rushing outside to help the next bunch of voters.

Christy Dockery accosted Henry as the last of the caravans rattled into the distance.

—There's something wrong with someone who needs the gyps to elect him.

—They're citizens of this town like anyone else. Anyways, I didn't need them to elect me. I needed them to make shite out of your pals in this election. When there's a general election, it'll be your turn.

The final tinker to vote paused on his way out of the gate and planted a hand on Henry's shoulder.

—Good luck now, Mister Caslin. The travelling people are all up for you, we know you'll do right for us.

The look in the man's eyes told Henry that his new followers would remember the promises he had made. He wondered idly if it had been an entirely good idea to make them aware of their power. And then he was struck by a blessed thought. The tinker's vote counted for exactly as much as the County Surgeon whom Mary had charmed with cheese and wine at a party for the staff of the County Hospital. They had one vote each. That was democracy, and Dockery wasn't wide to that.

Democracy was the best business. It was even better than baby food because everyone was a potential customer. They were all there to be won. People who would be grateful for a hello and an acknowledgement, people who needed promises and people who needed their self-importance stroked. The next day Henry was elected on the first count with three times as many votes as his nearest rival.

McKeon, noticing the result, wondered if he had under-estimated Henry Caslin, before telling himself that he was moving in a world which the baby-food king would only ever aspire to. In Mulligan's of Poolbeg Street he drank with poets, journalists and artists known by tourists for their access to wellsprings of wisdom, truth and political success.

At the bar they talked about the world to come. Mc-Keon and some poets who'd published one book of verse in ten years as well as Sarah Bergin, his newsroom buddy and expert on the female orgasm, Sian Guiney who was bringing the new faith of public relations to Ireland, Pete Hopkins, a promising film-maker for whom lack of money prevented him from shooting any footage whatsoever.

Pete's wife Moira, who worked on a women's magazine where the female orgasm would only have been discussed if you could knit it, hung around the outside of the circle, always managing to be the one who missed the final stool and ended up staring at an important back as the conversation heated up.

Those who owned the important backs lived in the country's first apartment buildings, which they ventured home to from the country's first ever discotheque and had sex which they regarded with seriousness. Sex was not a matter of hedonism and pleasure, it was a liberating act which struck at the repression inherent in Irish society.

McKeon's women were girls to him, and together they drank champagne and ate dinners in the first restaurants with foreign names. Waiters and maîtres d' smiled conspiratorially at him from behind the backs of his latest companions.

Fintan Beirne arrived very drunk in Mulligan's on the Friday after McKeon had slept with Sarah Bergin for both the first and second last time. McKeon had not seen much of Beirne recently, and when he hailed him heard muttered curses from his new friends before they all fell silent.

—Mister McKeon, how the fuck are you doing?

—Fintan, it's good to see you. I haven't spotted you in ages.

—I'm still on television, don't be so fucking smart.

—I meant in the real world.

—Television is the real world, don't slag it off. You're pulling a good living out of it, in your fucking apartment with your fancy women and all those clothes and so on.

The way Beirne caught McKeon by the shoulder was either affectionate or threatening. The surroundings stayed silent.

—Anything wild going on, Fintan?

—You'd know, how the fuck would I know, I'm not supposed to know about anything any more.

—For Jesus, sake, said Sian.

—Cheer up, Fintan. Come on, things are going great for you.

The words got suddenly stuck on their way out of

Beirne's mouth, and he just stood there with his jaw dropping before he knocked over a pint, propelling Carling Black Label all over McKeon's new suit.

—You're doing so well but never, never forget who gave you the start and never forget your friends. Never let things get on top of you.

He turned to Sarah Bergin.

—And you mind your own business . . . cunt.

The silence did not depart until a couple of minutes after Beirne had.

—I'm surprised at you, you're the only person in Dublin who talks to that sad alcoholic bastard, said Sian as if that was the last word that could be said on the subject.

After the pub, they hit for a theatrical hotel where all-night drinking was possible and could be justified by reference to the creative temperament. When McKeon woke up, everyone else had left. He staggered out the door and made his way to the steps of the Gate, where he sat down and began to drift off again under a poster for a play which explored the alienation of modern man in a seemingly futile world. Someone tapped him on the shoulder.

—Seamus, are you all right?

—Are you OK?

Pete and Moira Hopkins. Neither had ever previously instigated a conversation with McKeon.

—We saw you inside. Moira was worried about you.

Books rose to the roof in the rooms of their cold-water flat in Hatch Street. Moira made McKeon rasher sandwiches and tea while Pete explained how he would make the definitive film about Modern Ireland if only someone would give him the money. Moira said she was sure they would. Pete said it was a privilege to have McKeon in the house.

—It's a flat really, but we'll have a house soon.

—After you get your film made.

The first paper sellers of the day were walking to their stands when McKeon left the flat and saw Pete and Moira kissing at the front door, unaware of him looking back.

It was a frustrating time for McKeon. He was a reporter without much to do because real news could not be reported in 1976. The Republican heroes of a few years back were being arrested now. Their families would get phone calls a week later to say they'd fallen downstairs or beaten their heads off walls in custody. If the families went looking for them, they did their stint inside as well. Everyone knew what was going on, but no one said a word. McKeon suggested a programme on the allegations. His bosses told him to take the week off and go to the racing in Cheltenham. He'd enjoy it there.

On the plane over, McKeon sat beside a man from a Dublin newspaper who was writing a feature about corruption in horse racing. The men in the seat ahead of them bet on how long it would take the jet to get airborne, what brand of orange juice would be with their breakfast and what province the stewardess was from. They finished by betting on which of the two flies crawling up their window would make the top first. McKeon and his flight companion took rooms across from each other in the Queen's Hotel and promised to keep in touch if anything that looked like real news came up.

All McKeon had lined up was an interview with the gambler they called The Kid. The Kid had cleaned out the Tote in Galway the year before with big-money bets on no-hope horses. He had been a semi-finalist in the World Poker Championships, and would eventually become a financial speculator rumoured to be behind the economic collapse of at least two small Central American countries. One day he would walk away from Cheltenham promising truthfully that he would never bet, drink or smoke again.

But that was a long way ahead of him, and when McKeon met him in the bar of the Queen's he felt he was talking to a man who could never lose.

—I do enjoy seeing you on television, McKeon, said The Kid when a fairly harmless interview ended. I don't know a lot about news, but you're supposed to be good at what you do. That's all any of us can be.

—Have you any big bets planned this time?

—I have something I'd like to tell you about. I want to tell you because someday you'll be able to make a great programme about it. Someday when my money is made and it won't matter who knows it. Promise you'll make that programme, and I'll cut you in for a little bit.

McKeon raised his eyebrows at the word 'little'.

—A little of this is a lot.

The horse's name was Barrow Lad. The Kid won more money on him than anyone had ever won before on a British horse race. He won it because of a lack of knowledge.

Nobody knew that The Kid was the real owner of the horse. Nobody had the foggiest notion that he'd previously raced under another name as a useful novice hurdler before supposedly being destroyed after a training accident. And nobody had a clue that the jockey had been pulling him back so hard all year that the only way to make Barrow Lad go slower would have been to fit a reverse gear.

The bookies did know that the horse was 50–1 for the opening hurdle race of the day but they couldn't anticipate that, the minute they opened, The Kid's men would pour into betting offices in every decent-sized town in England and Ireland and load money on to Barrow Lad. By the time they realised what was going on, it was too late. The horse started at 10–1 and The Kid had a massive on-course bet just for the style of it.

McKeon had five hundred on Barrow Lad, and when

his fellow journalist called to his room the morning of the race to check rumours that something crooked was going on, professed ignorance. When the race was over McKeon watched The Kid leaving the course surrounded by a bunch of heavies who protected him from a potential lynch mob of bookies and officials.

—Mister Cassidy, isn't there something very irregular about the betting on this race? There's talk of an enquiry.

—No one will prove anything. Anyway, I've got my money, we all have including your mate from RTE. We're having a party tonight and you're welcome to come.

It was five in the morning when the piano arrived in the hotel: The Kid, suddenly fancying a sing-song, had sent some of his gang out to wake up the owner of a musical-instrument shop and buy his best model. He bought a hundred more bottles of champagne when it arrived.

McKeon was as drunk as he'd ever been, but what happened brought him back to sobriety. It began with the hands being clamped over his eyes, hands that were clammy and smelt of sick. It was Pete Hopkins. His face looked and smelt like a pile of wet coats in an airing cupboard.

—Pete, how are you? What are you doing in Cheltenham? How's Moira?

—Moira's fucking great, y'know, Moira's great. She had a kid there a few weeks ago. We called him James after somebody.

—I'm delighted for you.

—I'm very happy, said Peter Hopkins, but the words did not seem to fit him.

—So what are you doing here?

—Got some work doing a promotional film for Bord Nag Capall. The glories of the fucking Irish horse. Fuck the fucking Irish horse.

—Don't knock him, you're drinking his champagne.

Hopkins flung the glass out of his hand. It shattered off

the fireplace but so many glasses, fixtures and promises were being broken at this stage that nobody passed a remark.

—And don't give me that television-station shit. I fucking hate ye and all, and the country and the Irish horse.

—Peter, stop it man. Go home or something, this isn't like you.

—I'm sorry. But they've ruined me. I'm a ruined man. They all did it, especially your people.

Six years for the poor bastard. Six years starving and scraping and thinking it was worth it because when young he had read about Van Gogh and Keats, and about Hemingway who in Paris had been very poor but very happy. He looked at Moira supporting him and felt bad about it because the impulses about who should be cradling whom had still not changed, and maybe never would.

Then his luck changed. The television station commissioned him to make the film he had always wanted to. They gave him enough money to make it properly. He brought Moira out to dinner the night of the good news and brought her out again the next night. He told his friends that the poverty is over and that the really talented artist does not starve in a garret, but is recognised when the time is right. His mind replaced *A Movable Feast* with *The Great Gatsby*.

—*Faith of our Fathers*, directed and written by Peter Hopkins.

He made the film. In Cheltenham he describes it line by line to McKeon, whispering the technical directions in his friend's ear. Beginning with a jumble of images. Suffering children, famine dead, the poor in the Dublin lockout.

—That comes up you see, Seamus, and I use James Connolly's quote that the Church in Ireland has always been unfailingly on the side of the oppressor. We fade then into a shot of a bishop coming out of his palace and stepping into a sports car.

He hums part of the soundtrack. Hymns and Irish traditional songs whose performance was supposed to guarantee their singers a place in Heaven.

—They're used very ironically, though, Seamus. I've got them with extracts from stories by McGahern and O'Faoláin about the stupidity of the Church, and interviews with people brutalised by the Christian Brothers.

Shots of orphanages and Magdalen Laundries intercut with voices Pete had salvaged from the void. Voices saying things which McKeon had never heard before. Voices which meant the station would hang on to the documentary and make sure it would not be shown. All of Pete Hopkins's work had been for nothing because he could not ignore these voices. He tries to explain why to McKeon.

—Do you know what I found, Seamus? Do you know what I fucking found? I met all these people, these kids, people who were once kids and still are because they were never able to look after themselves again, but yet they were never kids because do you know what was going on?

But McKeon does not comprehend.

—Look, Pete, I'm sorry the station didn't use the film. They'll release it in a couple of years when the sex thing is more open.

—They'll never let it go. I thought when I started that I was making a film about how they repressed us because they hated sex. But they didn't hate sex. They screwed little boys and girls every chance they got, they loved that kind of sex.

—Fuck it, stop it Pete, I'm as liberal as anyone else and I'm no apologist for the Church, but there's no need for that kind of chat.

—These people I interviewed who'd been in the orphanages and the Industrial Schools. They'd never told anyone before. It was the same story with all of them. The Church was preaching against sex, and it was full of men who liked screwing little boys and girls.

—You're fucking fantasising, Peter.

A man wearing a deerstalker and a sportsjacket jumped in and thumped Pete in the face. Pete's nose began to spurt blood.

—We'll have none of that filthy fucking perverted chat in this room. I have a cousin a priest. I'll kick you around Cheltenham, so I will.

McKeon held the man off and got Peter to the door. A mixture of blood and foam on Pete's lips meant that everytime he spoke little red bubbles formed and then burst.

—The station have ruined me. They've killed me because the truth is too much for them to take. I understand. It's too much for me to take as well. But they shouldn't have done this to me.

His eyes looked like the word suicide, and made McKeon realise that he'd been wrong when he looked at him and Moira together. He thought he was seeing a love they both had, but it was just Moira who possessed it. His love was tied up with his film, and there was nothing she could do to change that. There was something awful about the thought of a woman looking at the man she loved and realising she couldn't bring him back from despair because he didn't care enough about her to come back. He would live inside his head instead of her arms. It was his choice. McKeon dreamed about Moira that night and forgot her the next day.

He was too busy and too successful to worry about anyone except himself. A couple of months later he won a national broadcasting award for a half-hour report on a trip by a bunch of Dublin feminists to Belfast to buy condoms. Mindful of the impending awards, McKeon had made the expedition sound terribly serious, and edited out the arrival at Connolly Station where people started blowing up the yokes and letting the air escape, so johnnies flew over the taxi rank like tiny transparent seagulls.

The report ended with McKeon holding up a packet of condoms which he had bought from a vending machine in a Belfast pub. His expression and his grip suggested they might explode at any second. He felt this closing image was what clinched the top prize.

At the same time as the train gang were flittering condoms around Connolly, people in Rathbawn couldn't get hold of rubbers for love nor money. This led to an inordinate dependence on the withdrawal method, a contraceptive equivalent to British policy in Northern Ireland. It relied a lot on chance, it was embarked upon because there didn't seem to be any alternative and eventually it led to disaster.

Orla Leavy was eighteen and without much sense, so she believed Larry Lynn when he told her that what they were doing was completely safe. It was not. She waited for her overdue period to arrive, and after a few weeks jumping off walls in the hope of inducing a miscarriage was faced with the fact that people were going to find out she wasn't a virgin.

At BB Baby Foods she worked a machine which stuck labels on cans. She quite liked the job and had never missed a day. Now when she worked she thought of how carefully husbanded wages might enable her to buy a second-hand pram and some nice baby clothes for the kid which she planned to name after its father, despite the fact that Larry had skipped town on hearing of her predicament.

She was one of those people who don't look like anyone in particular, and even her friends would have found it difficult to pick her out on a crowded street. Her hair, her eyes, her height, everything about her suggested a cunning master criminal contriving to bamboozle the cops by assuming an appearance with no distinguishing features. Henry had never noticed her in BB before the morning he saw the bulge of her stomach and, a split second later, the ringless nature of her fingers. He made enquiries, was told the story and asked that Orla be given two weeks' notice and four weeks' pay. There were no complaints.

The girl herself would not have made any fuss, had Trevor Bright not come across her cleaning out her company locker as big grey tears dropped down her swollen face. When he found out what had happened, he told her to sit in the canteen while he found Henry. The girl sneaked out of the canteen and ran for home the minute his back was turned, thus missing Bright's interception of Henry at the very machine she had formerly worked.

—Where's the girl who normally works this machine, Henry?

—Don't worry about it, Trevor. How are we doing this week? Any news on the Sainsbury's front?

—Where's the girl who normally works this machine, Henry?

—Is it any of your business, Trevor?

—As a shareholder, it is actually.

—I sacked her. I gave her her cards, I put her down the road. It's not the first time we did that to someone.

—You sacked her because she was pregnant. She was a good worker Henry, you weren't fair.

Englishmen, as far as Henry could see, were convinced there was some set of rules which governed everything in life. They used the word fair two hundred times a day. Fair to Henry was a place full of animals and three-card tricksters.

—Look, I had no choice. I don't want that sort of example being set in this factory. That sort of crack has no place in BB.

—Fucking listen to yourself, mate. You're not a priest, you know. You're a businessman. As long as she does her job it doesn't matter what else she does.

—I'll speak to you about this later . . . mate. Anyways, that's not the only reason I sacked her. I had complaints about the standard of her work as well.

It was one of those times when Henry didn't know what to think so he talked to Mary, who told him exactly what he had been thinking all along.

The factory was full of married men. An unmarried mother in the place would cause scandal. It might encourage other young ones in BB to think they could carry on the same way. A woman with a young child shouldn't be out working anyways. When it came down to it, Henry just didn't like the idea of someone like that working for his company and taking home his wages. Did he not have the right to choose who worked for him?

Making his first and only cup of coffee of the day, Bright was surprised by a determined-looking Henry.

—I'm warning you now, Trevor, yesterday's carry-on isn't good enough. I won't put up with it again.

—You what?

—Listen, what you did was unforgivable. You attacked me in front of the workers. How are they supposed to have respect for me and this company if they see you shouting at me, how?

—Now hang on. This is about the poor girl you sacked.

—She should have been glad enough to have a job to hold on to. We employ people who wouldn't get work any place else in this town. They don't have the education or training for anything else, only working machines, and we treat them well. They're happy here, so don't you go stirring them up.

—You're twisting things, Henry. The crux of the matter is—

—I don't want to hear another word about it, it's finished. Come on and forget about it, good man.

Henry had a little laugh to himself at how daft Bright was.

—You're twisting things.

Bright and his English rules again. Of course Henry was twisting things, that was what you did to win arguments.

A string of youngsters visited Bright's office over the next week and told him they'd complained about Orla because she was lazy and asked that she be sacked. When a couple of them said they hadn't even noticed that she was pregnant, and one enthusiastic young lad said he was sure Mister Caslin hadn't either, Bright realised he was out of his depth and tried to forget about Orla Leavy.

Henry did not want to forget. Bright had acted as though he was an important man in BB, as important as Henry himself even. He wasn't. The man's English contacts belonged to BB now, and Bright himself had trained a local lad to do his job in case he ever fell sick. Henry typed meeting agendas and mailed them himself. He couldn't get them off his hands quick enough.

Everyone at the meeting knew that something strange was going to happen, but they were still surprised when Henry moved his motion.

—I propose that Trevor Bright be replaced as Marketing and Development Manager.

Henry picked a spot on the far wall and kept staring at it so that he did not have to see Bright's face. His peripheral vision caught the expressions of Jimmy and of Mick Dowd. They looked terrified by what they could see in Bright.

—Henry, mate, come on, what's going on here?

—Order. As Chairman, I have to insist that you follow proper procedure. A motion has been proposed and we're going to vote on it. There's no time for speeches; people have to make up their own minds.

Only Bright wouldn't shut up. The threads of his thought were flimsy, but he began to knit them into something attractive. The room fell quiet and heads began to nod as he listed everything he'd done for BB. When Henry moved to hammer his hand on the top of the table and cut Bright off, a mutter from the floor dissuaded him. Bright was recovering his confidence as his hands drew graphs and pie charts in the smoky air.

—And, furthermore, as a twenty-five per cent shareholder in this company.

Henry couldn't resist it any longer.

—I'm sorry, but you're not a shareholder.

Bright was convinced that Henry had lost it now.

—I am, Henry, remember, we agreed it. I've held twenty-five per cent of the shares for the past year.

—I'm very sorry, Trevor, but I don't remember any such agreement. If twenty-five per cent of the shares had been transferred to you then we'd have had a meeting like this to agree the transaction. There was never any such meeting.

For a few seconds Bright stuttered and gabbled incoherently before letting go a blizzard of abuse. An impressed Henry counted seventeen swear words he knew, four he suspected he'd heard before and eight he was sure were site-specific to whatever part of London Bright came from. The fact that the abuse was delivered in a Cockney accent was bad enough but when the words 'thick Paddy bastard' and 'spud-picking cunt' were heard, that put the tin hat on it as far as the board members were concerned.

—We don't go for that sort of language here, Mister Bright. Remember where you are, not where you come from, said a smiling Henry.

Bright walked out so he could hate in the open air. Henry decided to sack Mick Dowd as well, because the feeling of sacking someone had made him feel good.

The solicitor's letters piled through the Caslin and BB

letterboxes for a few months afterwards and then suddenly stopped.

They carved her name and a sad little message on Linda Dowd's tombstone. Her husband forgot about BB Baby Foods and returned to London with two daughters whose eyes looked like empty shop units with the lights turned off. He never was a fucking whizz again. For the next couple of years any BB triumph was greeted by Henry shouting on the factory floor

—Didn't I tell you we didn't need Trevor Bright, didn't I?

He shouted this with added fervour when BB clinched the deal to supply Sainsbury's. Hundreds of thousands of English kiddies shovelled a little bit of Rathbawn into themselves every day as they built up the healthy bones which would spend most of the eighties lounging on a couch at home watching daytime TV in between trips to the jobcentre. BB became such a legend with Sainsbury's that one of the top brass decided to call into the factory on his way back from a fishing holiday in Connemara. Knowing how relaxed the Irish were, he didn't bother to call Henry until he was in the town itself. Henry put the phone down and panicked for a second before rounding up Jimmy and some of his election team to act as a reception committee.

—It was a lovely little plant, although the first thing I noticed was this ruddy great black flag flying in front of it, the Sainsbury's man explained to his curious colleagues on his return to home base.

The tour itself was a massive success, and added to Henry's reputation as a charming Irishman with an ever-present twinkle in his eye.

—This is the main factory area. Most of these people have been with us since we started, and they're always willing to go that extra mile to do the best for the company.

—Smashing. Super. Oh, just one thing, what was that big flag out the front for?

—I'll tell you what, you'll be very interested in this particular kind of canning machine we have over here. I'll just give you a good look at it now. How was the angling abroad in Connemara?

—Very good, thank you, Henry. The people were lovely of course, very hospitable. What does that flag out the front stand for?

—We're very hospitable in Rathbawn as well. We'd be known for being hospitable. All over Ireland if you mention Rathbawn, the word you'll get back in return is hospitality.

—I'm sure you know that you're regarded as one of our most valuable suppliers, Henry. And this factory is an absolute credit to you; I don't think I've ever seen a more contented workforce anywhere. Oh yes, there's just one thing I'd like to know, out of idle curiosity.

—We won't let you go without having a little dropeen to drink. Jimmy, bring Mister Flint into my office and pour him a glass of brandy. And remember that a bird never flew on one wing.

The glow Henry felt after the visit was even greater than that felt by Flint, after Jimmy poured seven glasses of brandy for him. Yet he was troubled by the realisation that the same kind of praise from an Irishman wouldn't have meant as much to him. Why was it that you could only believe you'd done well when someone said it to you in the same accent that a hundred years ago had been ordering your great-grandfather out of his pitiful hovel? Why was it that every time you did well you had one eye on the Brits to see how they'd react? It was as if they were an old girlfriend who had said you'd amount to nothing, forcing you to devote your life to proving her wrong. He decided that these questions didn't matter a tinker's curse as long as Sainsbury's kept coming up with the money. No one minds being patted on the head by a right hand if the left is handing you a fifty-pound note.

—So, Richard, what was the big black flag actually for? Flint would be asked when he concluded the tale of his visit to BB.

—Do you know, Caslin never quite got round to explaining.

As Flint drove away from the factory, Henry breathed a sigh of relief before a tear came to his eye as he looked at the black flag and thought of the brave sacrifice made by Larry Lynn, killed by machine-gun fire the week before as he tried to ambush a British Army patrol near the border.

The cry of the curlew repeated in Father Lee's head as he entered confinement in the monastery. It alternated with the memory of the abbot's voice.

—Confinement will do you good. It will give you a chance to meditate, to contemplate, to think. It will help you overcome your urges.

The word urges was emitted in a voicelike spasm of the throat. The abbot was unable to name the acts of Father Lee.

—You must contemplate and think on the face of God.

A pattern had become ingrained in Father Lee's life like a piece of dirt trodden irremovably into a soiled carpet. As life would eventually be found out by death, Father Lee would be found out by faceless accusers. A child would speak. A query at the gate of the Church would be rudely and emphatically dismissed. The man who had dismissed it would take action against Father Lee.

He had wondered aloud if the abbot would be able to confine him to his room. It was a free country, after all. The abbot repeated his argument about the helpful nature of solitude.

—You cannot force me to undergo confinement. I am

not even a member of your order. I come under the authority of the diocese, and I know my rights under canon law.

—I'm sorry to have to tell you this, but the confinement may be necessary for reasons of personal safety. Two of your accusers have threatened to exact retribution. They mentioned a military body which I think we are both familiar with.

—That body would not act in such a manner.

—These are strange times.

He saw no one. The room became a place where time stood still. And because it stood still and did not flow naturally, it began to pile up and fill the corners of the room. Like dust it moulded itself to the shapes of the corners first, before beginning to colonise the rest of the room. Great heaps of time rose from floor to ceiling and began to thicken, until Father Lee could hardly see his hand in front of his face. He came to feel that the room was filled with a solid ice block of time within which his head and body were encased. That time hung there and made him scream until, exhausted, he did begin to contemplate. But it was not God he found, it was himself and the memories of his sins.

A lump of hair the size of his fist came away when he tried to pull those memories out of his brain. He emptied his sleeping pills into a glass of water. Drinking, he told himself that the agony was over.

He woke in a hospital run by nuns, who saved his life once more when he broke the bedside lamp and slashed his wrists with the jagged fragments. As he recovered, he realised that the abbot would not risk confining him to the room again. Instead Father Lee was informed that it was thought advisable for him to travel to England, where arrangements had been made which would enable him to forget the traumas of the past few months. The thought of frontal lobotomy caused him to shiver fearfully, but the abbot put his reprieved mind at rest.

—Father Lee, I am sure what you did was not harmful. This is not by any means the first such case I have had to deal with. We merely need to take prompt action because often the level of public complaint is, I feel, wildly out of proportion to the small amount of damage there has been to all, to the children, if indeed you can call them children, society being so saturated with media-generated sexual images that they grow up so much faster these days.

At Heathrow Airport a man in a corduroy suit held up a cardboard placard with Father Lee's name written on it.

—I'm glad to see you, Father Lee, he said, my name is Doctor Brian King. Welcome to London.

This room was not much bigger than the one in the monastery, and though it was not locked, Father Lee saw men patrolling the grounds when he looked out of the window. He did not care. Where would he go? The television on a stand opposite his bed showed the details of a trial from his own country. A gang of men had been charged with murdering Catholics. They had beaten them, tortured them and slit their bodies open with butcher's knives. At times Father Lee felt amazed at the absolute evil present in the world, and wondered at the fuss over his own minor wrongdoings.

—You are what is known as a child abuser, Doctor King told him.

Father Lee shook his head and said that he was not. Doctor King read details of statements made by children in Ireland and America, going through them painstakingly as though he was a patient teacher guiding a pupil through some labyrinthine mathematical process. Finally Father Lee agreed that child abuser seemed to be the correct term. Doctor King said that he could make him stop committing these kinds of acts.

—It won't be easy. But I can. If you want to stop. Do you want to stop?

—I do.

The words came out before he could think. Doctor King clapped him on the back. That night Father Lee stayed awake, seeing in the dark of the room the blackness of his heart, his mind and his future. He wanted to tell Doctor King that it was the past which hurt most, and which could not be wiped out.

Ten of the other eleven men sat, like Father Lee, cradling themselves as though wishing to disappear into their chairs. Their hands shook as they held their cups of tea. Eventually they gave up the effort and left the cups on the ground without even noticing the pain of their scalded knuckles.

The odd man out's eyes were set so far back in his head it took some time before you noticed that one was green and the other brown on the top and a ripe rose-hip colour on the bottom. His hair was shaved to the quick, and his chin not shaved at all. He sat with his legs apart and was the one who spoke when Doctor King asked who would like to get the proceedings under way, rasping out an east London accent so strong as to appear inauthentic.

—My name is Andy and I am a child abuser. I am here because I am sorry for what I have done, and because I know I have ruined people's lives. I want to change and not to do wrong to children any more.

As Andy spoke, his fellows gradually shifted position in their chairs, uncurling out of themselves like time-lapse-photographed plants flowering. Doctor King joined in the applause when he stopped speaking. Father Lee saw Andy wink, and knew he must be blinking back a tear.

The group members beat each other for the next six hours with the blunt instrument of confession as their hatred of themselves expanded and filled the room, touching everyone except Doctor King, who cajoled and coaxed and encouraged and did not once judge as generations of children were verbally re-desecrated by middle-aged men who now knew they were not alone and fervently wished they were.

When the circle had become almost cosy, Doctor King introduced new people. Younger men and women. The group was not to talk but to listen. A young woman stood in the middle of the circle and told what had happened to her. How she had been abused by men like them, and how it had led to dark nights of suicide attempts, prostitution, eating disorders and the loss of her own children. How she could never forget and would never forgive. Others had come through like wartime survivors, but it did not lessen the pain they expressed.

Father Lee's sleep was not easy that night. Maybe someday he would be able to forgive himself for what he had done, and come to terms with what he was. But he could not find the children he had despoiled and make them come to terms with him. He could forgive himself. They could rebuild their lives. But there was no joint solution to the offence. There could be no peace between them.

Andy's voice jolted him awake in the games room the next morning.

— You're a priest, ain't you, Gerry.

Father Lee looked for Doctor King, and heard him joking in the corridor with the orderlies. A long way down the corridor.

— A few priests did me when I was a kid.

The creeping, surging desire for dangerous knowledge welled up inside Father Lee.

— When I was six, my father and mother used to hire me out to people. They'd have parties in the house and all the other local paedophiles would come over. I'd be the star attraction. A couple of them were priests. I'm always able to tell a priest. By the look and by the smell.

He put his nose to Father Lee's collar and sniffed, before ejecting a laugh which caused his false teeth to rattle and almost slide from his mouth. Father Lee felt himself approaching the familiar stage where nausea and interest melded. He began to listen to Andy's stories.

The childhood with parents whom he reckoned had bred him for sport, bringing him to special parties and weekends away until he fled the house at ten and lived rough, charging for what had been given away free in the past. He had turned to drugs, drink and armed robbery in search of the sensation which would convince him that he was a bad enough person to have deserved his life. Above everything else he was a liar. He was the king of liars.

—All you need to do, my son, or should that be my Father, is tell one big truth and one big lie. You tell the complete truth about everything you've done and then you say you're sorry. And they believe that lie, because they've heard the truth before it. They think if you know you've done something wrong then you want to stop. It comes from your Church, mate. Confession and the absolution of sins. Except I know that nothing is really wrong.

His philosophy had taken him through Alcoholics Anonymous, drug rehab, the probation services and now it would convince the purveyors of child-abuse therapy.

The dozen were brought to a minibus when summer started, and were driven up the motorway. The driver turned off at a junction where a brightly coloured sign indicated that they were approaching an amusement park. As they left the bus, Doctor King explained that they were at the park in order to get used to being around children without feeling their old sexual urges.

They had been warned to stay close to their helpers, but

Father Lee soon gave his the slip. He did not have any intention of going near a child; he was just bored. Part of him felt outraged by the trip. The minibus and the fairground had made him feel like a member of some small-town youth club. Maybe this was fair treatment for Doctor King's other patients, but Father Lee was an educated man who had held positions of trust and responsibility in the community. A man respected by politicians, solicitors and doctors could not submit to the indignity of being squired around a playground. He was still considering his humiliation when he saw Andy racing towards him. Andy grabbed him by the hand and they ran towards a rusty white-panelled van which waited for them at one of the exits.

The van driver told Father Lee that he was a mate of Andy's. They were all going to east London for a bit of fun. In the back of the van he heard Andy talking to a drunken twelve-year-old with the face of someone making the worst of a bad lot.

Father Lee left the Hackney house the next day. The minicab took him past hundreds of streets and lanes that looked the same. Past Asian families in cheap clothes who carried string shopping bags, past huge Victorian buildings converted into pubs with broken and barred windows, past youths in football jerseys chatting to pregnant teenagers and handing them cigarettes. He did not look back, because he did not care what happened to the boy after he left. He had shut his eyes to the possibility of ever being anyone else but Father Gerry Lee, Child Abuser.

On a tube-station phone he told the abbot that he had checked out of the course because it seemed anti-Catholic. The abbot listened without much apparent interest and said he was washing his hands of the whole case. The next phone call was to Bishop Edward O'Hanlon, who sounded no different than he had been in the seminary. Bishop O'Hanlon asked where he'd been lately.

—It's a bit shameful, to be honest, Edward. I just had a little problem with the drink and I've been drying out abroad in England. I think I'm grand now. But it was difficult, you know.

—Ah, Gerry, it's a terrible curse. You know yourself, we all have to watch it. It can be a lonely life in the parish. You're over it, you say.

—I am, Edward. I was wondering if . . .

—You don't have to ask me anything. Aren't we friends? Listen, there's a parish in Belfast that could do with a new parish priest. Would you be interested? They have a problem getting good-quality people up there because of the, you know, situation. I think you'd be ideal for it, seeing as you know the political ins and outs so well. By the way, I'd better tell you this first since you're my oldest buddy. They're going to make me a cardinal.

Henry Caslin wanted to move up in the world as well. That was why he was running in his first general election. He shouldn't have been because Christy Dockery was the sitting TD for the Party, and nobody but nobody challenged a sitting TD until Jimmy decided it was time for Henry to make a little bit of history. Henry hammered Dockery at the convention, and took to the highways and byways of the county. The Party was set fair to take power from the coalition. It was a good time to be a new candidate.

Jimmy planned the campaign with TJ, the man from the good land in the south of the county, and Mel, the mountainy man from the north of the county. They looked at maps and drew up lists of everyone who lived on them, writing down the names of the local football teams, where the people worked, the names of their children, anything they had ever done. They made out suitable greetings for every voter in the county so that these voters would know Henry cared enough about them to remember the football medals they'd won or the fact that they were well known for their home baking or had a brother who had done fierce well in America. Henry practised the perfect smile for the susceptible, the mournful look for the grieving and the naïve glance for the uncertain.

Sometimes on the road he realised how little he knew about his own county. Like the day mountainy Mel brought him to the town where a young girl had bled to death giving birth in a grotto. A dozen houses were set apart from the rest of the place on a road dotted with caravans.

—The tinkers, is it?

—No. Different than, but no better.

By the time they reached the first house, people were in the doorways of all the others. The man there didn't speak when Henry said hello to him. He relaxed when Mel leaned across Henry and grunted something. The man seemed to relax. Henry pushed past him and walked into the hall. It was dark, but he could make out the shadow of a woman. He put his hand out to her and drew it back when he saw she was breastfeeding. The man of the house tapped him on the shoulder.

—Do you want to see the house?

The man fiddled with a length of brown cable which hung across the hall and the place lit up. It was all holes.

—Rats. The fuckers.

Probably only a small percentage of the holes were visible to Henry, as most of his vision was taken up with small children who looked roughly the same age. He looked at the woman. She nodded.

—All mine. All twenty-one of them. Six of them have to

sleep out in the caravan. We're all on top of each other here.

The smell of piss slunk around the house. Goats were tethered in the back garden and a skinny dog lay beside a smoking turf fire in the kitchen. The tips of Mel's shoes slid uneasily around the bare floor. The woman spoke over the sound of them.

—What are you doing here? We're only a bit behind on the rent.

—I'm Henry Caslin.

—Who?

—I'm running for the Dáil. I want your vote so I can represent the people of this area.

—Our vote wouldn't be much good to you.

—All right then, said Mel, and Henry heard the tips move towards the door.

—Will you make us a cup of tea, missus, asked Henry.

The tips stopped dead as the woman instructed a child of indeterminate age and gender to boil the kettle. Henry did not regard the tea too closely when it arrived. A glance told him it was floating under a film of grease and contained some suspicious black particles. He did not particularly want to know exactly where the grease came from and what the particles were. He took a sup. One of the children tapped its mother's arm.

—Mammy, that's the dog's cup.

—Don't worry love, we'll give it back to him when the man's finished.

On the way out Henry passed through a cordon of bearded men, and women who held children they hardly looked old enough to have given birth to. Questions slid quickly into his path.

—Will you get the houses fixed?

—I will.

—Can you do something about the rats?

—I can.

—You wouldn't have a few bob on you? I'm in the pure horrors from drink.

—I would.

—Why did we never see one of ye before?

Henry couldn't answer that question, but Mel did when they'd driven a bit out the road.

—Nobody wants to think of them being there.

—Who are they?

—That town had one of the biggest workhouses in the country eighty years ago. We closed it when we won independence. But some of the people had nowhere to go and they didn't know what to do with themselves, so a few houses got knocked up cheap for them. They're there since, interbreeding and intermarrying.

—Why does no one do anything for them?

—Because they spoil the effect.

They were to finish the day in Drumbaldry, the journey to which began with a turn off the main road and then another, with the sequence continuing until Henry had counted a dozen turns, each off a small road until he felt like he was at the heart of a Celtic spiral. The car climbed and made Henry think of westerns he had read as a youngster which told of mesas, gulches and canyons, where the cowboys would try to hide from hordes of Apaches only to find the pesky redskin varmints had got there first. It felt as though Mel was leading him into some trap. Finally Mel stopped and told Henry to get out and look at the view from the mountains. He had taken one step out the door when his chauffeur caught him by the arm.

—Steady there, now. We don't want a premature by-election.

Under the dark of the night was an even deeper black. Mel dropped a pebble. Henry reckoned it must have caught on the way down, and had turned to walk away when he heard it hit the bottom.

—Did we miss the turn for Drumbaldry?

—Ah, no, Henry. Drumbaldry bes a bit remote. It's another couple of turns up the mountain.

The turns continued to take them inward. Even Mel seemed unsure of his way, and was relieved to find the wooden sign.

—The Mountainside Inn, two and a bit miles.

A bit in Drumbaldry turned out to be what was called a fair bit in the rest of the county, and a trek anywhere people weren't used to walking long distances. There was no outside light at the Mountainside Inn, and the curtains were drawn. They picked the pub out from the shining eyes of the sheep dogs sitting outside the door.

A young man wearing a battered stovepipe hat was pointing a shotgun at the barman when they walked into the pub. Henry got ready to dash out the door, but Mel pushed him forward and advised him to wait a minute.

—Put the gun down, Timmy.

—I will not. I'll shoot you dead, Michael James.

—You will not.

The shout from the crowd drew a few derisory laughs, and the men at the bar turned back to their drinks. The landlord was equally unconcerned.

—Will you do something with that gun, and not be acting the bollocks.

The man in the hat pointed the gun at the ceiling and pulled the trigger, bringing a cascade of ancient plaster down on the drinkers at the bar and shattering a couple of glasses. The landlord reached over and took the gun off him.

—You can get out now, Timmy, you'll not be served again tonight.

—I'm not barred, am I, Michael James?

—You are not, Timmy, you're not that big of a deal.

The pub laugh stuck in the collective throat when Mel stepped forward and stood on a sheep which was warming itself by the fire. The squeal of people's livelihood in pain grabbed attention in a way the waving gun had not.

—Hello, Mel, it's seldom you come, said Michael James.

—Michael James, I have a man with me that'll be running in the oul election. I'd say he might want to say a few words to the lads.

A quick leap brought Mel to the spot recently vacated by Timmy. Within a couple of seconds he had a drink in front of him and looked like a natural member of the company. He looked away when Henry tried to catch his eye. The candidate was on his own.

—My name is Henry Caslin and I'm standing for the Party, and if I'm elected I'll do me best for the people of Drumbaldry.

—You'll not come next nor near Drumbaldry till the next election, and you'll be fucking right, said a man who'd taken his false teeth out of his mouth and was trying to cut the edge off a lump of plug tobacco with them.

—In all fairness, you're an awful bollocks to come up here. Sure we have no time for ye at all.

He reeled off the spiels he'd dragged round the county but it was like playing handball with a half-solid ball. The harder he threw the rhetoric, the faster it came flying back, freighted with an additional cargo of insults and bodily noises, some of which he had never heard before. His explanation of how the Party had always made people proud to be Irish was met with a chorus of laughter.

—Would you ever get on out of here, y'oul bollocks.

Not one of them had looked Henry in the eye since he'd entered. They'd stayed hunched at the bar with one shoulder drawn up as if they were cold or waiting for a skelp, their voices low and indistinct like radio interference.

A sheepdog nuzzled Henry's leg as he left the Mountainside Inn. Then it bit him. He looked over the dark precipice beside the car and felt himself fall as the push connected with his back.

—You were gone only for me, said Mel who could have changed the course of history had his hands been less broad than his sense of humour.

Henry was surprised at Mel's good spirits.

—Mister Caslin, you're a great bit of stuff. They had fierce time for you.

—They did nothing only insult me.

—If they didn't like you they wouldn't have bothered. They thought you were a mighty man. I'd know it from their eyes. Amn't I one of them?

—Will we get many votes here?

—We'll get them all. The Party has every vote out of this patch these last fifty years. They don't want anything except the TD to land up to the Mountainside the time of an election so they can give him stick. You'll see them again in another four years.

They continued up the mountain, Henry's ears filling up as the headlights picked out tired-looking sheep who looked like they couldn't go any farther. Potholes and craters assailed the car, which finally ran aground in a deep fissure traversing the road.

—We'll leave it here and get it out on the way back, said Mel.

Half a mile on he parted a canopy of bushes and revealed a small byroad.

—Drumbaldry Lane, Henry.

A house lit up like the apparition at Knock laying wait for them at the end of the lane. Henry had never seen such a clean house. White from top to bottom with a gate that shone, neatly trimmed hedges and sheep who looked like they'd been in a bath running around outside. A stone path ran up to a front door which Mel gently pushed in. A small wizened man sat in a kitchen lit up by a rush lamp.

—You're welcome, Mel, is it that time again? The four years do fairly fly.

The strange, halting nature of the old man's voice made him sound like he was trying to speak a new language or use a new body part. Henry thought the man might be recovering from a stroke before he realised he just wasn't used to talking.

—This is Tom Harte, Henry.

—Tom Harte. Mel, I don't believe it.

The greatest guerrilla of them all. Swooping down with his small band of mountainy men, ambushing Black and Tan patrols, burning the RIC barracks in the county town and cutting off a Free State contingent sent to find him before picking them off one by one. Everyone thought he was dead until the fiftieth anniversary of the Easter Rising was marked by the appearance of his autobiography, *Fighting for Irish Freedom*, a story of derring-do and narrow escapes written in the style of Zane Grey, which claimed pride of place on every dresser in the county.

Mel told Henry not to mention the book.

—He doesn't even know it was written. The lad that did it thought Tom was dead, so there'd be no harm pretending he'd found this manuscript and publishing it.

Tom asked his visitors if they'd excuse him while he made tea in the scullery.

—Or do you want anything stronger, Mister Caslin?

—I don't drink, Tom.

—Good man, Mister Caslin, I'll vote for you then.

—He got barred out of the Mountainside forty years ago and never took a drop since. It's twenty-five mile to the next nearest pub.

Altitude seemed to have loosened Mel's vocal cords,

and he whispered Tom's real story as they waited for the clank of cups to announce his return. Tom and his cousins had set up their flying column out of boredom, and sank into complete torpor when the fighting was over, pretending for a while that news of ceasefires hadn't reached them and killing a few uniformed representatives of the new state, which pardoned them because of Tom's legend and also the impregnability of his mountain lair.

In the forties an Irish-American film director had wanted to make a film based on Tom's life. He brought John Wayne up the mountain to meet the legend and Tom challenged Wayne to a shooting match, picking tin cans off a fence with a shotgun, winning easily before telling the director that the star could not be allowed to play the part.

—Sure he couldn't. He cannot do the things I can. It wouldn't be right.

Arriving unannounced behind them, Tom handed a cup to Henry.

—I heard you telling that John Wayne story, Mel.

—You're still some man for one man, Tom. You have ears like a bat.

—Only that wasn't the end of the crack. I told him I'd give him a second chance to show he could do what I did. I gave him two border collies and sent him over the side of the mountain to bring a dozen sheep back to the house. Myself and yon director sat out in the rain waiting for him. It was the next day when Wayne lands back, and never mind the sheep – he had even the dogs lost. His clothes were soaking to his skin and out the far side of him. He tried to be brave and he says to me, 'Mister Harte, I'll play you in that film.' I says to him, 'The hell you will.'

On the way down the mountain, Mel turned off the engine and let the car freewheel so he could practise his steering.

—I thought you'd like to meet him. So you could see the kind of man that set this country free. Their likes won't be here again.

—They surely won't.

Henry continued his campaign and found more parts of the county whose remoteness was as much temporal as geographical. He bought the *Herald* works and printed full-colour posters of himself which decorated every lamp-post, handball alley, billboard, telegraph pole and football-field wall in the county. Up in Drumbaldry the legend was cut into the side of the mountain

—Vote Number One Caslin.

McKeon anchored part of the election broadcast on national television, and did an unintentional on-air double take when Caslin's result came in. The man had got the fifth highest vote in the country.

In Rathbawn, Henry stood on the back of a truck beside the monument to the town's War of Independence martyrs and told the crowd what was going to happen with the Party back in power. People would make money, the EEC would give money to the farmers and the government would give it back to everyone else. Afterwards he shook hands along The Crescent, oblivious to the presence of disgruntled supporters of the deposed Christy Dockery, who made their move at the entrance to the town's first ever shopping arcade. Mel got hold of three of them. The fourth might have endangered Henry's new suit but for the materialisation of a young garda on the scene. Henry asked the name of his rescuer.

—Garda Paul Clarke.

—You'll go a long way, Garda Clarke.

The man was forgotten until Henry was a few months into his new job as TD. Busily quashing summonses, he noticed Garda Clarke's name coming up a few times. He got on the phone to the man's superior, who agreed to lose a summons against Heaney's pub for after-hours drinking. Heaney was a first cousin of Mel's, and also a thick fucker who wouldn't close his pub while there was any possibility of a customer even thinking of a jar. One of the duties of a local Party TD was to get him out of trouble when he was nabbed by the cops.

The summonses caper Henry enjoyed immensely. The local guards sent him a selecton of legal documents and he got out the red biro. The parameters were understood. Nothing serious could be taken out, and if Henry took the piss by squaring too many summonses he would pay for it the week after. Or rather, his supporters would. Henry regarded the system as the essence of democracy. People came to his clinics and detailed the offences they were due to be charged with: drink-driving, drunk and disorderly, found on in a pub, driving without insurance, reckless driving, minor assaults, failure to pay court-ordered money to the banks in time, and he took the lash of the law off their shoulders if he could. He was an elected representative, and he gave people a direct contact with the legal system. What could be more proper? A self-righteous shimmy of the shoulders drew the red biro through the summons against Heaney and his customers.

The next summons against Heaney arrived two weeks later and got the same treatment. Garda Clarke was once again involved. A week later came another summons. The red biro again. When the same thing happened a week after that, Henry realised that this battle could not be won by calligraphy alone. Garda Clarke had to be made to realise that he couldn't undermine the public's faith in the democratic system. Henry phoned Jimmy and told him they were going out to Heaney's for the night.

A dozen people were in Heaney's when Henry and

Jimmy arrived. At closing time Henry ordered a Coke for himself and a triple brandy for Jimmy. John Heaney got on the phone, and by half one most people from the surrounding villages were in the pub, drinking away with the door wide open. The several singsongs which were going on stopped when everyone heard the sound of a squad car approaching. It was ten minutes later before they heard the trudge of garda shoes outside. So many cars had been parked near Heaney's that Garda Clarke had been forced to leave the squad a mile away. The pub fell quiet as he walked in and saw Henry Caslin TD and Councillor Jimmy Mimnagh sitting at a table in the middle of the floor. Henry broke the silence.

— Well, Garda Clarke, what'll it be, a pint or a transfer?

The humiliation felt by Garda Clarke could be seen running just under his skin like ripples of damp under wallpaper. There seemed to be just two choices. A sulky exit with laughs and jeers sticking to the back of his uniform and taking an awful long time to wash off. Or a taking of names which left Henry no alternative but to ring the Minister of Justice and arrange a transfer to some particularly unpleasant crime hot spot. Instead, Garda Clarke smiled, pulled over a chair and sat between Henry and Jimmy.

— A pint then if you're buying, Mister Caslin.

Now Henry was sure the youngster would go a long way. He gave John Heaney a ring to let him know that from now on he was on his own, and let Garda Clarke know he had done this. Garda Clarke did not thank Henry, but he did begin to talk to him when they met. Football would have remained the sole subject of their conversations had it not been for Councillor Dickie Carberry.

Carberry had been one of Dockery's henchmen in the Party, and even Dockery was aware of the man's status as a pure-bred bollocks. He was reputed to be OK if he wasn't drinking, but as no one had ever seen him sober this was difficult to prove. Carberry sneaked whiskey into the Council Chamber, tried to assault anyone physically who disagreed with him and usually ended up voting the opposite way to which he had intended, if he was still awake when the vote was taken. He had been left the council seat by his father, and would have lost it but for the timely action in 1969 of a mob of Protestants who attacked a bunch of civil rights marchers as they crossed a bridge which no one south of the border had previously heard of.

His joining Sinn Fein at this opportune time meant that Carberry's outbursts, drinking and paranoia were suddenly seen as protests by a principled man against a democratic system in which he had no faith, rather than as sociopathic aberrations. He began to talk about armed struggles, winning back in the North in the morning and putting bullets in the Brits, even going to Drumbaldry in an effort to get Tom Harte to pass on the Republican torch. He and his entourage were beaten up outside the Mountainside Inn by men who mistook them for sheep rustlers. The mistake was not altogether incomprehensible, given that Carberry's new right-hand men were a stonecutter with forty-seven convictions, a young lad born in Manchester who'd just got out of jail for putting his teenage wife through a plate-glass window and a chip-van owner who'd turned to republicanism when his effort to firebomb the social welfare office for cutting his dole failed. Henry saw them around the town selling *An Phoblacht*, and remembered a speech he'd once made about the IRA in the North being comprised of the most respected men in the community.

Still, he felt guilty that forty years of dreaming about the heroic recapture of the fourth green field he had ended up watching the battle unfold on *Scene Around Six*.

Carberry might not be perfect, but at least he had the guts to stand up for the Republican cause. Jimmy disagreed, telling Henry that Carberry was a disgrace to any movement.

—He's even a fucking disgrace to alcoholics.

But Henry knew who was in the right. Then Carberry told him how the cops were harassing him and his followers. They had been stopped selling *An Phoblacht* because they didn't have a permit; the houses of two old ladies had been ransacked by gardai just because their sons were Republicans and the young lad from Manchester had been clapped in Portlaoise Prison.

—He's a political prisoner, said Carberry to Henry.

—He's a political prisoner, said Henry in the Council Chamber.

On the front page of the *Herald* appeared a photo of the young lad surrounded by a black border. Garda Clarke did not want to talk football the next time he met Henry in the Imperial.

—Barry Brogan isn't a political prisoner, Henry. We caught him trying to rob the takings from the cinema.

—What about ye ransacking the houses of those two oul ladies in Balinascran?

—It was a pity we had to do it, but we recovered four rifles, two hundred rounds of ammunition and a rocket launcher.

—And what about not letting them sell their newspaper? Isn't that against freedom of speech?

—They could get a permit if they applied for it. But they won't because they don't recognise the state. They don't think this state exists any more than the one in the North, and they'll bring their war down here if they have to. It's not like the War of Independence, Henry.

When Henry continued to protest about the arrests of

Carberry's cohorts, Garda Clarke tried to blank him. On a wet Wednesday when eight people had been killed in the North, Henry made a final effort to strike up a chat. Garda Clarke gave a two-word answer, walked across the street and took down the number of Henry's double-parked Merc.

Armed men robbed a bank in the next county the day after, and headed for the border. Garda Clarke received a call seeking assistance and found the getaway car abandoned at a quarry near Rathbawn. The robbers were long gone. He radioed the station and was told to remain beside the car as it might yield some valuable forensic evidence. He had a laugh about how everyone talked in cop-show jargon these days, and walked up to the car. A booby trap blew him into a million pieces when he opened the front door.

The birds ate flesh from the trees around the quarry for months afterwards. The local undertaker buried an empty coffin, and what was salvageable of Garda Clarke was swept into plastic bags and burned. The IRA claimed responsibility for the killing.

It was agreed to cancel that night's County Council meeting. Instead people would just talk for a few minutes about what had happened. Everyone had spoken when an hour was up except Carberry, whose slowness to rise and shuffling during the minute's silence was put down to the usual DTs.

—I think Dickie Carberry should round off proceedings, said Jimmy, who had just returned from meeting the family of Garda Clarke's teenage fiancée.

—I have nothing to say, replied Carberry, and inspected his nails.

—I think you should tell us what you think of what happened today, said Jimmy, you know, like if you think it was wrong. Unless you're scared.

The scared sounded like it was spelt with seven a's. It was a taunt travelling forty years down the line from the National School yard.

—I'm not scared. I'm a member of the Republican movement, and I didn't come in here to be blackguarded.

—But you'll condemn Garda Clarke's death, said Henry as if he was just beginning to understand the point of an obscure Hitchcock sub-plot.

—I can't condemn it. Garda Clarke was involved in the pursuit of an IRA active service unit, and as such was aiding and abetting the enemies of the Irish Republic.

—But it was wrong.

—It's easy for us to say it was wrong. Garda Clarke as an Irishman should not have been where he was at the time. The Garda have a record of harassing members of the Republican movement, and I'm afraid to say this killing was an act of war. He got what he deserved.

Henry crossed the floor to Carberry and caught him by the collar.

—You're scum, Dickie Carberry, and you'll be awful sorry for this.

—Oh, typical, using violence against me, and you'd be the very one going on to me about being a supporter of violence.

Something changed right in front of Henry's eyes as the four Clarkes, all army men, carried their brother's coffin to the cathedral. Something everyone had believed in was ebbing away. It was a painful growing-up for a town which wanted to curl up and go asleep, so it could wake up in a country where everything had stayed simple and old myths did not kill neighbour's children.

Missus Clarke showed him photos of her son Irish-dancing as a child, at Irish College in the Connemara Gaeltacht and playing for the county hurling team. She told him the boys had been brought up to be proud of the country, that Paul had seethed when he saw British troops march into Belfast and that the word Londonderry still annoyed him, before realising that the word still did not apply to her son any more.

—He was a Republican, Mister Caslin, but when he got into the guards he couldn't believe what he was up against. He said you wouldn't believe the sort of characters that are involved in the IRA.

—He didn't mind me sort of defending those Sinn Fein lads in the Council, did he?

—He didn't mind. He said you didn't know what you were talking about.

Henry never forgot Garda Clarke. Every day he spent in the Dáil, he looked across at his secretary and remembered the day he had picked her up from the airport as she returned home for the funeral of her fiancé, accepting his offer of a job for life once she stopped crying. They sat together silently in a small office, he watching her sorrow decrease slightly and she noticing his vast impatience increase massively.

His impatience was unusual. In the weeks after the 1977 election, the people were as happy as Larry. They had voted for the Party because they wanted to get back to those uncomplicated days before modern life began. The Party leader, the new Taoiseach, was the visual and mental embodiment of those hopes. He smoked a pipe, took tea with the clergy and wore sensible knitwear, which showed he would never get excited about anything. Had the TDs under his control been as relaxed as him, there might have been a happy end to his dreams of a country where nothing much happened.

Most of them were.

But all of them weren't. Henry Caslin certainly wasn't.

Neither was Mickey Kelly. He'd been a cop and become convinced that only politicians were above the law. It was where he wanted to be. The showband days were over, so this was the best way to meet impressionable young women. Noel McCarrick was the opposite. His business had burned down two years ago and he hadn't claimed insurance. He wanted no blot against his good name, and he didn't want to sit waiting on the backbenches. Gerry Gilligan, the Canny Dub, had tramped every yard of every street in the toughest constituency in the country. He had worked so many hours in his constituency office that he ended up marrying his secretary because he didn't know how to talk about anything else except politics. They were driven by different kinds of dedication, but they wanted something to happen and someone to point them in the direction of power. They could not live in a country run by the Man With The Pipe whose old rival, the Tough Guy, noted the impatience of the four neophyte deputies, sent them messages and requested meetings. In his diary Henry noted an appointment at Leopardstown Racecourse.

When Henry and Mary arrived in the Owners' and Trainers' bar, the Tough Guy presented them with an expensive pair of binoculars each. Henry had picked three winners by the time the horses for the last race reached the parade ring, and the Tough Guy suggested that the wives take a walk down there.

—Mary pet, could you go down there and keep this man's wife company. Put a few quid on Latin Flyer.

—You're betting on Latin Flyer? My horse is going in this, Imperial Realm.

—But Latin Flyer is going to win.

The Tough Guy's snort made him sound like a horse himself. He drew up his shoulders and leaned across the table. Henry couldn't believe how big the man had got. He looked all of five feet and six inches now.

—Did you bet on my two other horses, Caslin?

—I didn't. And they both lost and both of my horses

won. You can call me Henry. I'd prefer you to call me Henry.

He knew how sensitive the Tough Guy was about his horses. They reminded him that he was rich in the same way that his expensive paintings and private island did. The ability of his horses seemed a matter of indifference to the Tough Guy. Their loyalty was all he demanded. Once he had been thrown while galloping one of them. He shot the horse in the head, putting three more bullets into it even though it was already dead. He told the story himself. It impressed Mickey Kelly and struck Henry as a waste of time, effort and money.

—Just fucking listen to me now Henry. No, I'll call you Caslin because that's what I want to call you. I want to be leader of this fucking Party, and I should be fucking leader already, of the Party and the country. The fucker who's in charge is fucking useless. I want his arse kicked to fuck out of the job and I want some tough fuckers to run a campaign for me. I heard you and your buddies might be the fuckers who could do it.

The Tough Guy had spent years on the margins, exiled by the disgrace of the arms scandal, a story which Henry recalled had been broken by Seamus McKeon. He wondered did the Tough Guy think saying fuck all the time made him scary? The man should go up to Drumbaldry and see where fuck got him.

—So, Caslin, you fucker you, are you fucking prepared to be on my team? I know you're a man who wants to go fucking places. Listen, we're both men with money, we can talk to each other on the fucking level here. I might be tougher than you, but I don't have much more money than you. Not that much.

Ah, thought Henry, but I made my money from hard work, and no one knows how you made yours. He told the Tough Guy he would dedicate himself to the task of getting rid of the Man With The Pipe. The Tough Guy smiled. Latin Flyer came in at fourteen to one. Imperial Realm came in fifth, and flinched as if imagining what a bullet in the fetlocks felt like. Mary arrived back bearing the prize for the best-dressed lady and Henry walked away with her. The Tough Guy called him back as racegoers drunkenly bottlenecked at the door of the bar. He suddenly pulled Henry's head close to his and whispered, the breath coming out in a sharp, painful jet

—And listen to me, you Midland fucker. If you double-cross me on this, or ever fucking double-cross me, I'll cut your throat and throw you over a fucking cliff. Just so you know.

Henry's dissembling grin was born out of eight hundred ancestral forelock-touching years.

In the car park, Mickey Kelly was searching for his car. A drunk woman trailed after him with the hem of her long white dress dragging through stones and gravel. He was a man who loved womanising and tolerated women. The week before he had crashed into a river while driving the lead singer of Mamacita and the Amigos home after a night of illegal poker games which had put three grand into the pockets of his Italian suit. They had waded through the water after sodden twenties which raced away from them like panicked paper fish and Mamacita, real name Concepta, told him he'd surely have to leave his wife after having this much fun with her. He was not going to.

—You won, Mary, said Kelly. This one didn't win, of course. All week buying clothes and all morning getting ready so we missed the first race. But she couldn't beat you Mary. A bit of a disgrace, that and the age of her.

The wild, pained look in Moira Hopkins's eyes made Mary took away, in the process taking in the way her dress was buttoned completely incorrectly. Her husband had killed himself just before she met Kelly. Six months ago.

—Jesus, Henry, he's some fucking man though. We're all hardy enough but he really is the Tough Guy.

Henry's mind said

—He's not so tough.

Henry's mouth said

—He's the toughest, all right. And he's picked the right men.

The right men began to meet in a late-night eating house on the edge of the city's nightclub strip. Jim's Place opened only in response to a knock on its louvered door. It was owned by a Cavan widow who told herself she ran a high-class establishment, refused admission to drunks and sat in the darkness watching streetwalkers and shift workers eat chicken curry. When the four men in suits began to arrive regularly and soberly at three in the morning, she reckoned her long search for a better kind of customer might be nearing an end.

Jim's Place was Henry's idea because the restaurant had no drinks licence, and he knew that subterfuge did not mix well with alcohol. The Gang of Four met every night for four weeks, and only saw the Tough Guy on television. If their mission was discovered their commander would deny all knowledge. They met and planned and waited for the outside world to provide them with ammunition, which finally arrived in the shape of a document waved excitedly in the air by Kelly.

He had squared a rape charge for a man with a brother high up in the Army. The man swore he would do anything to repay the favour once he and his family had finished driving the woman out of town. Kelly mentioned that anything discreditable to the government which his brother could turn up would be welcome.

—You mean discreditable to the opposition, said the man, smirking at Kelly's mistake.

—No, I mean discreditable to the government. And don't ever fucking even think of laughing at me again, or I won't be around to help you the next time you have too much to drink after watching porno movies in McCann's.

They stayed in Jim's Place till eight in the morning, as the future of the Man With The Pipe changed in concert with the light outside the windows. Perusing with great pleasure the document marked 'Confidential'. A small map showed a piece of land near the border where the IRA had brought down a couple of British Army helicopters. The Brits flew over this area to avoid making a massive detour necessitated by the illogicality of the border. Their only other option was to fly over a small piece of countryside in the Republic. The Irish government had just given them permission to do this.

—What do you think? asked Kelly.

—I think it's a gross derogation of our national sovereignty, and a disgrace that it's been hidden from the Irish people. It threatens our neutrality and could lead to British troops being based on this side of the border, said Henry.

—Do you really? asked McCarrick.

—Does he fuck, said Gilligan, and the four of them burst into happy laughter.

When Henry sprang the Air Corridor question on his leader the next day, the Man With The Pipe was caught sufficiently unawares to mumble that as it was only a tiny bit of Irish air involved, surely it wasn't that important. Henry said this showed just how far into the British pocket he'd sunk. Party deputies who remembered that the constitution claimed sovereignty over the whole island never mind the bit this side of the border, booed their leader. Opposition deputies who'd given up the idea of ever winning a vote again wondered what was going on.

The Gang of Four had given themselves two years. They achieved their task in just three months because they were joined by a fifth ally, the most powerful member of the group. Reality. The Party had promised to send him the way of the snakes, but he returned. He told the people that the economic crisis would not end just because the Party said it would. The country would not be re-united and the crew over the border would continue killing each other no matter who was in charge down here. He whispered that people who'd done thirty years across the water and returned to build their houses and raise their children at home would soon be driving their new cars to airports and ferry ports to send their kids back to England.

Reality could be ignored as long as he remained an abstract genie made of smoke and shadows. But once he took on human shape his power could not be denied and there would be no forgiveness for the man responsible for his transformation. The Man With The Pipe was forced to become the banshee singing the song of economic death outside the national house.

He took the pipe from his mouth and turned up on the telly at a time when people were expecting an American cop show, an English soap opera or another news bulletin, where film of real blood and real bullet holes in sledge-hammered doors underlined another grim truth. They settled back in their chairs and said

—Ah, look, it's the Man With The Pipe. Good old Man With The Pipe. He's going to make us all feel better.

But this time he did not. Instead, he told them they would all have to tighten their belts because the country was going broke, and if they weren't careful men from banks they'd never heard of and had certainly never borrowed from would come in and run the place. He was sorry, but the Party seemed to have made a bit of a balls out of things.

It was time for the Tough Guy to leave his tent. He and his backers made speeches telling people that the Man

With The Pipe was being too gloomy, and that there was no need for this belt-tightening at all. What was needed was new leadership.

On the morning of the leadership election, the soon-to-be-ex-Taoiseach confidently told Seamus McKeon on television that he had the full backing of his Cabinet. He was right. All fifteen of them backed him. There were seventy backbenchers, and each one had been told by Henry that when the Tough Guy became leader they would leapfrog over the people sitting in front of them. They all believed him, although they knew that four of the fifteen jobs were already spoken for.

The Man With The Pipe had one final shot remaining in his locker before he took the whiskey and the revolver out of it.

—I want there to be a public vote in this election. Party rules have no provision for a secret ballot.

He was right. Nobody had ever challenged a Party leader before. He had put in the roll-call rule the week before, when his opponents' eyes had been off the ball. It would need a vote to change it, and he knew the backbenchers weren't that keen to defy a leader in public.

—Can we not have a secret ballot to decide whether we have a secret ballot or not, said Henry.

—I've covered that, said the Man With The Pipe, looking enthusiastically at his would-be betrayers beginning to quail and wonder how Caslin would get out of this.

—There's nothing to say we can't have a secret ballot on whether to decide to have a secret ballot on whether we have a secret ballot.

The Taoiseach's pipe fell out of his face. He lost his position after four votes, and the Tough Guy walked out into the street, holding his bejewelled hands in the air while Henry sneaked away to collect Dolores and Dearbhla from *Star Wars* and Henry Junior from the zoo.

His just reward was prefaced by a call from O'Sullivan, the Tough Guy's press secretary, a man who spent his life in a constant flinch.

—The Tough Guy wants to see you, Henry. He says get your ass in here pronto.

Get your ass in here pronto. O'Sullivan repeated the Tough Guy's hard-boiled utterances in the unconvincing and ingratiating manner of a priest telling dirty jokes. It was he who ushered Henry into the Taoiseach's office, where the Tough Guy was spinning a large metal globe with his finger like a secret service boss in a spy movie. Henry almost expected him to stop it suddenly and say

—Caslin, we're sending you . . . here, before pointing to some Pacific island where the forces of evil were up to no good.

The thought made Henry smile, which provoked the Tough Guy into assembling his face by stages into the usual snarl. Henry felt like asking him if he realised that the person he was trying to convince of his toughness was himself. He did not, because it would have been a waste of time. The Tough Guy was obscured from his own sight by a veneer of play-acting which had hardened into a solid wall of self-parody.

—Sit down to fuck, Caslin, and stop smirking like some inane fucking turf-cutter's jackass.

The command only made Henry smile all the more, and he put his hand to his face to mask an encroaching laugh which he stifled in a pretend cough.

—I'll get straight to fucking business, because you know I'm a man who doesn't beat around the bastarding bush. I've got a fucker of a job for you. Minister for Justice. Do you want it?

The imperious nod of the head with which the Tough Guy dismissed Henry did not really work, and as Henry left he saw the new leader ease out of his chair and position himself once more by the globe. Mickey Kelly was re-knotting his tie in the corridor. He had the rumpled look of sheets left at the bottom of a laundry basket and eventually forgotten. Kelly clocked the combination of amusement, curiosity and very mild censure in Henry's expression.

—Castlebar International Song Contest. Hungarian young one who came third. Seemingly they don't have strip poker in Budapest.

His secretary Martina placed the call to Mary in The Hacienda. He knew that Jimmy would be waiting beside her at the phone. The news would not be real until he spoke to them. It was their ministry too.

—Mary. They've made me a Minister. We've got Justice.

—It's great news, Henry.

—It's great to have you to tell it to. I love you, Mary.

—I love you too, Minister.

—Stop.

Mary loved it when he used the word stop in that way. He didn't use it the way it was written down. The correct English way they taught you in school, and that made the word sound forbidding. An order to halt with a faintly Teutonic tone. In Henry's mouth the word turned to

—Shtop.

The h introduced and deliberately lengthened. The s like a kettle enjoying a brief moment of steamy significance. This way the word was not an admonition, but an expression of pleasure which sounded Irish and coquettish. The sound of the cute hoor winking and blessing a harmless effrontery with a smile. The laugh of a child who wants the tickling stopped but enjoyed it while it went on. Mary could have listened for ever to Henry saying that word. Once he started, she would never want him to stop.

When the phone call finished, Jimmy gracefully extended his arm to Mary and led her in a paso doble through the house, followed by two giggling daughters and a sullen son who watched as the duo leaped into the swimming pool in the back garden.

From their office window, Henry and Martina watched the elongations and dilations of gardai shadows pacing under street lamps, and looking ruefully at their public representatives celebrating the Tough Guy's ministerial largesse by falling out the door of Buswell's Hotel bar. Normally Henry would have been there but this night he wanted to talk.

—Do you think I'll be a good Minister for Justice?

—I do, Henry.

—Do you think, you know, Garda Clarke would regard me a suitable Minister for Justice?

—I told you often enough, Henry. He thought well of you. And he was a good guard. He never concerned himself with who was Minister. He didn't think it was his business.

—Do you think much about him?

—A fair bit. Often good thoughts. I do think he's keeping his eye on me.

—It wouldn't be any of my business, but have you seen anyone since, like, are you seeing anyone at the moment?

—I'm not. I don't think I'm fully over Paul yet, nor won't be for a while. The girls do be on to me to go out and try and meet someone else. I couldn't be bothered to be honest with you.

—You're only twenty-two, Martina. You should be out enjoying yourself. It's three years . . .

—I enjoy meself at work. I have a good oul life. I'm not looking for a man, Henry.

—I know, and I know I go on a fair bit about this, but when I think about what me and Mary have, the whole love crack, I think you deserve the same. Whoever gets you will be a lucky man.

—He'd need to be luckier than Paul.

The driver of Henry's ministerial Merc had red hair and shelves of flesh under his eyes that looked like they wanted to slide down his face and escape. He told Henry he'd met his wife in a Caslin ballroom. They shook hands and luxuriated in the freemasonry of happily married men, like nuclear physicists wondering why others found such easy equations so difficult.

—By the way, my brother-in-law is up for drink-driving in Cork.

—I'll keep an eye out for it.

The petitions of the convicted to the Minister for Justice implored him to use his prerogative to reduce or cancel the sentences and fines imposed, by the judiciary. It was like old times for Henry on his first day in the office as he searched for drunk drivers, tax evaders and temporally challenged publicans. When he reached the magic fifty of his constituents, plus the late request from Cork, he sighed, rested his cramped right hand and swore that after this special day of celebration the ministerial pardon would be restricted to cases of obvious injustice or absolute political necessity.

—Martina, would Garda Clarke have minded me, you know, exercising my right as Minister for Justice in regard to those petitions?

—No, Henry. He would have expected it.

Her elevation to the post of ministerial secretary enabled Martina to move into a house of her own and put brick walls between herself and well-meaning invitations to Barry's Hotel, the Ierne, the TV Club and sundry other venues where a man's first line was to ask if you were a nurse, and his last a dismayed admission of failure before you even got to make up your mind. Henry worried she might never meet Mister Right now.

Worry about Martina aside, being a Minister was mighty crack. After Cabinet meetings, he and Kelly and McCarrick would hop into their Mercs and race down to an Italian restaurant whose merit was denoted by exorbitant prices. Last there footed the bill. The skill and flagrant disregard of the rules of the road displayed by his driver meant that Henry's wallet remained relatively unscathed.

People were encouraged to ring the Ministers at the Dodo. The ceremonious promenade of a white-phone-bearing head waiter to their table seemed intrinsically connected with power. Henry's calls were mainly from Mary, Kelly's from his justly suspicious wife and from Moira Hopkins, whose pleas and complaints burst from the receiver into the ears of his fellow Ministers and other nearby diners. After hanging up and informing the manager to tell any further callers that he had left, Kelly would mime the cutting of his throat or the placing of a bullet in his head.

Kelly should have been told that his life would be vastly improved by the severing of ties with misfortunate Moira, but Henry was scared the man would storm off and leave him in the company of McCarrick, whose realisation of the vast and frightening responsibilities of the Minister for Finance had turned him into an obsessive, speaking of nothing but public-sector borrowing requirements, deficit budgeting, monetarism, the gold standard, the European monetary system, capital gains taxes, stagflation and Keynesian pump-priming. Only when the papal visit loomed did he talk of anything unconnected with economics.

What amazed Henry most about the papal visit was the revival of interest in objects of devotion from the past.

There was Dick Brogan and The Firemen with Welcome John Paul, Mamacita and the Amigos with Papa You're

Welcome A Hundred Thousand Times, Katie and the Treasure Seekers with Walk With The Pope and the Bushman Showband with We're Totally Yours Oh Holy Father. He was surprised Tom Nolan had not got in on the act yet. The showband stars had returned from the dead, and any doubter just had to put his fingers into the centre of their records to make certain.

The day the Pope landed and kissed the tarmac at Dublin Airport was a day off for McKeon. For this big occasion, the station had rounded up men from the old guard of the fifties and sixties who could achieve the right note of pinched reverence as they annotated the footsteps of His Holiness. It was disguise day for station and country, reminding McKeon of the film where an old beggar lady's friends pretend she's rich to impress her posh daughter who's come to town. Ireland was pretending to be pious and back in the nineteen-fifties, because no one wanted to spoil the Pope's illusions.

The idlers from the station, some university lecturers, writers and artists met in a house off a Georgian square with beer-garden umbrellas shielding them from the sun, and a biblical plague of wasps which would have worried anyone superstitious. But none of them were superstitious. And, although McKeon glanced occasionally at the blank television screen in the corner of the dining-room, he told himself that this was a reflex action rather than a wish to see what was going on. In the garden, he lay back in a deckchair with a panama hat pulled down over his eyes and thought of Moira Hopkins wheeling her young son James towards the Phoenix Park. The thought made him smile. Two young women whom he had once interviewed at a protest against the strip-searching of Republican women prisoners arrived at his chair. One made an announcement.

—We've had a hard morning, spray-painting graffiti

against the visit. A couple of times we thought we'd get lifted by the pigs.

—Why did you do that? Could you not let people who want to see the Pope just enjoy the day?

The other woman's face loomed through the canopy of wasps.

—That is just such a fucking male thing to say. This visit will set women in Ireland back a hundred years. It's all right for you, your rights aren't threatened by the oh so Holy Roman Catholic Church.

McKeon took another draw on the joint in his hand.

—Oh, OK then. What sort of stuff did you write?

—The usual. No Pope here. Not the Church, not the State, women will decide their fate. Keep your rosaries off our ovaries.

—Sure the Pope probably doesn't know what ovaries are, said McKeon.

This statement seemed to satisfy the two women, and they drifted off towards the barbecue as McKeon hit the house.

Tiptoeing into the living-room, he was just about to plunge towards the control panel of the television when he realised that he had been beaten to the punch by a young woman who wore an expression of complete guilt as their eyes met.

—I'm just . . . watching it, she said.

He handed her a spliff and sat on the couch. The volume was turned down so low they couldn't hear the Pope. The camera panned across the Phoenix Park, which looked like Woodstock. Same numbers, same joy. McKeon realised that he was in the wrong place, and that in years to come he would be asked where he had been on the day of the papal visit and he would say in a garden near St Stephen's Green, having the same conversations as many times before.

—We can't stay watching this, said the woman.

—I know.

—It's a bit awful that we can't.

—I know. Are we all supposed to pair off and go to bed together?

—I suppose. I better warn you that I might want to talk about some very strange stuff when we're there.

—It's OK. I'm pretty broad-minded.

She was too. She even joined in the enumeration of the memories which had drawn them to the television set. Pride in a few First Communion dresses and suits. Holy wells and late-night processions. The feel of a plaster holy statue and the sensation when you kissed its chipped toes. The foreboding atmosphere on confirmation morning, heightened by the smell of incense. Days in the rain selling prize-draw tickets to help black babies. Returned missionaries rumoured to have learned magic from their savage charges. The unmitigated peace felt in the moments after First Confession. Long Easter Masses with a chorus standing in for the mob who wanted Jesus crucified. Being dragged groggy from bed to say late-night rosaries with elderly relations. The movement of small white arms scooping Knock holy water from fonts.

They fell asleep to the sound of Leaving On A Jetplane, coming from the garden, the day having turned out some way special after all.

In the VIP section at the next day's Youth Mass, Henry bumped into Tom Nolan as a choir of young people sang before the Pope's sermon.

—Wait till you hear this song, Henry, just wait till you hear it.

Henry checked his leaflet.

—Is it Sing My Soul, Tom?

—Is it f . . . sorry God, no it's not. I think they might spontaneously break into a song that's not on the sheet.

The Pope told the young people of Ireland that he loved them, and the crowd went apeshit as the choir broke into song again. Soon everyone was singing along with them, Tom Nolan with special gusto.

—He's got the whole world in his hands,
He's got the whole world in his hands,
He's got the whole world in his hands,
He's got the whole world in his hands.

Henry looked quizzically at Tom.

—I slipped the choir fifty pound each to sing that. It's a religious song, you know.

—He's got you and me brother, in his hands,
He's got you and me brother, in his hands,
He's got you and me brother, in his hands,
He's got the whole world in his hands.

—Why did you do that?

—I'm bringing it out tomorrow as my new single. It'll be hard kept off the top of the charts now, no matter what Dick Brogan or Mamacita or The Bushmen do.

—Tom, you're a miracle worker.

The next morning Jimmy walked around the village where, a hundred years previously, Our Lady was said to have appeared against a church gable now surrounded by glass and sheltered indoors in the shadow of a huge Roman-style basilica. Cripples and the ill came to touch the crumbling plaster which was reputed to have miraculous powers. Jimmy looked through the glass at the palsied, the spinally damaged and the cancerously thin being helped towards the sacred spot. His reflection was suddenly thrown back at him. A man with a twisted back limping slowly across the tarmac. Another cripple. He took his place in the line. The only unaccompanied supplicant.

After an hour his turn came. Walking towards the wall, he tried to feel some source of energy which told him that once the world of eternal life had slipped through and touched this village. There was nothing. He thought of New Testament stories which stressed the absolute importance and power of faith.

—Lord, I am not worthy to receive you but only say the word and my soul shall be healed.

The Roman centurion whose son was cured because he believed. But Jimmy knew that he would never be healed because in the moment before he touched the wall, he realised that he did not have that kind of faith.

Jimmy listened keenly in the basilica to the Pope telling people to remember the faith of those poor farmers of a hundred years ago, and to resist what was mistakenly termed progress. The twentieth century, said the Holy Father, was a catalogue of depredation. Jimmy thought he was referring to the Nazis and the communists and other killers, but they did not come up at all.

Instead, the Pope talked about abortion and contraception and homosexuality, which had been created and promoted by the permissive society and the mass media. These evils must be resisted. The crowd clapped and whooped and hollered, and Jimmy felt shattered because he believed the Pope was wrong.

When he had met Guy, he had not even seen a television set, had rarely gone to the pictures or listened to the radio. The media did not make him do what he did. He had decided for himself. And the sound of people cheering the Pope's wrongful statement showed Jimmy for a second what it must be like to go outside the sanctuary of the Church. He could see how people who had disobeyed or did not fit in with the Church's teaching would regard Her as a force for meanness and spite and perhaps even evil.

Father Lee led the pensioners from his Belfast parish in song as their spluttering minibus was passed by sleeker models from wealthier parts of the statelet. Only his renowned genius for fund-raising had enabled the trip to be undertaken. His parishioners were poor, but Father Lee had made sure they would make the trip because this would be the best day of their lives. They clapped rheumatically along with a sing-song.

—Sean South Of Garryowen.

—Roddy McCorley.

—A Nation Once Again.

That one they especially liked. So Father Lee had launched straight into it as the minibus moved away from the checkpoint, his voice strong from years of sermons and parish announcements rising over the crying of the old women and the confused mutterings of the old men, whose humiliation seemed an even more awful emotion than the terror felt by the women. He sang because he would not let the greatest day of these people's lives be spoiled by the men in uniforms who had sprinted alongside the minibus and waved their guns at the driver. They pushed Father Lee aside and forced the old people off the bus. They made theatrical attempts to search their belongings, and left them standing in the cold for an hour until Father Lee told his people to get back on the bus and tried to lead them there. A young man barred his way with a gun.

—These people have to get back on the bus.

—I'm sorry, Pat, but you ain't going nowhere until I've had my orders.

Father Lee wanted to take the gun off the young man and shoot him in the head. Instead he demanded to see his commanding officer, basing this request on his viewing of *The Colditz Story* on television where this was the response of the British to unreasonable behaviour by their German jailers. They were all for fair play, the British. On television. Father Lee repeated his demand. A couple of the old women urged him not to make the soldier mad in case he got hurt. It occurred to Father Lee that death here could be some sort of atonement.

The officer in charge arrived and asked Father Lee where he was going.

—To see the Pope across the border.

—I didn't know the Pope was Irish, Vicar.

A vein throbbed in Father Lee's head. A dozen soldiers watched him intently.

—He is visiting Ireland. I am bringing these people to see him.

—That depends. I have the authority to hold you here all day, and then you wouldn't see the Pope, would you?

They were held for another hour. Then Father Lee sang his heart out and told jokes and played card tricks, until by the time he escorted his parishioners off the minibus they were looking forward to the Pope rather than backwards to the British Army.

Perhaps it was because he had seen the Pope in Rome when life seemed more hopeful, but the day was a disappointment for Father Lee. Worst of all was the sermon. The Pope preaching that violence in the North was not justifiable in any circumstances, and then doing the routine of getting down on his knees and begging the men of violence to lay down their arms. Father Lee felt like charging up to the altar and explaining what had happened at the checkpoint, and how a million worse things happened every day to the Pope's flock in the part of the island he hadn't bothered to visit and how these days added up to tens of thousands.

A man in purple robes appeared beside the Pope. Cardinal Edward O'Hanlon. Radiant with piety. The sight of his old friend filled Father Lee with despair, the thought of the road he had taken himself rendering the ceremony and all surrounding it as meaningless to him as the most incomprehensible of creeds.

It was easy for the Pope to pontificate because he did not have to live in Belfast. Belfast forced you to make your position clear. The sermons of Father Lee let his parishioners know how he felt about the robotic presence on their streets with its electronic speech, armoured body and whirling metallic accomplices in the sky. He was pleasantly unsurprised when a man with an orange beard and a lisp who had asked him to store guns in the old days on the other side of the border turned up at the parochial house and explained that several volunteers would like to receive Communion and confession on a regular basis but could not as they were in hiding.

—There won't be any difficulty about that.

—They're very sensitive about confession, Father. Some of them are reluctant to go in church because they're afraid the British have bugged the boxes.

—There's nothing they won't tarnish, is there?

He began to hear confessions and distribute Communion to men whose identikits would occasionally turn up on the news alongside footage of bullet-riddled cars, burned-out hotels and photos of unmistakably Protestant heads whose appearance was always followed by the details of children left behind. It annoyed Father Lee that no one ever mentioned how many children a dead Catholic had left behind. He began to visit prisoners and twice hid wounded men overnight in the parish house. His contact assured him that the British would not raid a priest's house.

—The propaganda risks are far too great.

Some of his parishioners had sons locked up in Long Kesh. They began to arrive at his house to try to explain what they had seen there, something beyond the usual beatings and filth, something they were unable properly to describe. Anyone who had seen what was happening in the H-blocks was being driven mad. He would have to see it for himself, they said, because there was no imagining it.

Father Lee knew what the Blanket Protest was. The prisoners had refused to wear prison clothing and chosen to spend their days in the cell wrapped in their regulation blankets. He saw that this was unpleasant, but not how women who had lived through a dozen years of bombings, shootings and the fear of both would regard it as an unspeakable nightmare. The words the Dirty Protest he first heard on the bus to Long Kesh. He did not know what they meant, and in fact they meant nothing. The words had nothing to do with what he would see, because they belonged in an ordinary world of language and explanation.

As usual, the warders went through the rigmarole of blaming him for every Republican action of the past week, asking him if he was happy that a hotel full of wedding guests had been decimated by a bomb whose ingredients included sugar and petrol. The sugar made the petrol stick to the bodies of the revellers. The petrol caught the flames of the explosion and turned the Protestants into human torches, like the Christians burned by the Romans.

Father Lee wanted to say

—I feel the same way about them as you do about the dead from Bloody Sunday, McGurk's Bar and the Romper Rooms. They are not my people. Let their own mourn them.

But he stayed silent until the search was concluded by warders who seemed unusually scared, and acted like men doing maintenance work on a nuclear device. As if in close proximity to something which could destroy their world if its power were unleashed. They shook their heads as they unlocked the final door and allowed Father Lee to precede them.

The strange hollowness in the prisoners voices could not

solely be accounted for by the acoustics of the wing. They shouted phrases in Irish, a language they had obviously learned in jail as the absence of accent made it sound like a West Belfast dialect. Half a dozen voices took up a chant

—I'll wear no convict's uniform

Nor meekly serve my time

So England can call Ireland's fight

Eight hundred years of crime.

The warder with Father Lee slowed his step as if wishing to delay their arrival at the first cell. Here was held the grandson of Maisie Donnelly, the woman who sewed Father Lee's vestments. Suddenly a smell became apparent, an odour far worse than the normal prison tang of slop pots, bodies washed in meagre rations of water and decaying, inedible food.

—Here you are, Father, your people. Except they're not people, they're fucking animals, shouted the warder as he walked back down the corridor to the echo of bars rattling in contempt and the four-line poem being repeated in a strong monotone.

The eyes were what moved Father Lee to tears. Because they were Maisie Donnelly's eyes, and this connected to the world outside the prison. He would have called that the real world, but for the fact that there seemed to be an awful reality about the prison which was broken down to the bare essentials. Everything normally beneath the surface was here smeared across the eye of the observer.

A world composed of shit.

Maisie Donnelly's eyes shone in her grandson's sockets the way the sky does when unsettled by the weather. With the clarity which presages disaster. Two thin, bearded men wrapped in blankets approached the bars of their cage.

—How's about you, Father.

Their long, matted black hair was like desiccated seaweed. When they began to speak to Father Lee, the singing and shouting stopped suddenly and was replaced by an urgent chatter of voices, which sounded like starlings on Belfast telephone wires singing a pleading song

—Father. Father. Father. Father.

These young men had grown up watching television, playing football and going to school. They had appeared to be anchored to a world which, though ringed by Saracen personnel carriers, FN rifles and Molotov cocktails, seemed still part of God's inventory.

At the moment of realisation, Father Lee wished that he could have been a good enough man to feel the appropriate outrage against the circumstances which had removed them from the world.

The shit lay caked against the walls. In the corners the covering was more of a thin veneer, which showed what the walls must have looked like in the first few weeks after the prisoners had decided to stay in their cells and slop out there, daubing the excrement on their surroundings. Father Lee thought of hands that had once held hurleys, hammers and other hands picking up the shit and painstakingly distributing it on the walls within which their owners had to sleep each night and eat each day. The prisoners were living inside medieval canvases of the horrors of Hell.

You could see that the protest had been taking place for some time, by the caking of the shit on some sections of the wall where it bulged outwards and threatened to slide on to the floor. The tiny white pinheads of maggots moved casually around these areas. Father Lee felt intense urges to scratch himself as he moved from cell to cell, receiving more and more details like an ancient bard hearing the narrative of a disastrous battle from the ghosts of the vanquished.

Watching the television at home that night, Father Lee wished for an explosion to wipe out copious numbers of an enemy who had reduced the ancestral line of Plunkett, Pearse and Tone to dozens of empty-eyed young men living in their own shit. When it did not come he rang Cardinal O'Hanlon and blurted out what he had witnessed in Long Kesh.

The cardinal's voice was pained. But there are different kinds of pain. There is the pain of mortal agony. And there is the pain of finding that a splinter has entered the bottom of your foot and will be awkward to remove.

—It's difficult, Gerry.

—It's difficult to understand how men could be kept in conditions like that in a so-called civilised country. The Church must condemn the authorities.

—You said that the men smeared the faeces on the wall themselves.

—But that's not the point, Edward. You know they shouldn't be left like that. They're not asking for much, just the rights to wear their own clothes and to associate freely, which they had in the past anyway.

—Mmmm. Francis Donnelly is a parishioner of yours isn't he?

—He is.

—Do you know why he's in jail?

—He joined the IRA. Most of the young lads in the area did. The Donnellys were burned out of their house by a Protestant mob. That young fella was beaten up by the UDR when he was fifteen. What do—

—He put a bomb under an RUC man's car. The man was taking his five- and four-year-old daughters to school. The three of them were blown to smithereens. Gerry, they won't have the opportunity to protest about anything.

Dresden. Hiroshima. Saigon. Father Lee wanted to list examples of the inevitable brutality of a just war, but he kept quiet and listened to the cardinal explain why he could not tie the Church to the Republican movement.

—I'm sure you remember when the Pope got down on his knees, Gerry.

—Yes, I do, Edward, and now he wants the Northern Catholics in the same position, thought Father Lee, but he appealed to the cardinal on the grounds of pity and charity. Asking him to visit so he could see for himself, and agreeing that he would have to be very careful and avoid making a political statement.

At the gates of the prison the cardinal spoke with his usual imprecision, but this did not matter because no one heard his message or passed any heed on the carefully neutral moral he had extracted from the stories of the men with the shining eyes. Instead they watched the distress in his eyes and the sweat on his forehead and could tell he had seen horror.

The men on the Dirty Protest were visited by television crews, religious leaders, politicians and hosts of other intermediaries, who stood outside the prison walls in the sunshine, talking about helpful discussions and matters of grave concern. The shit continued to pile up and change colours.

Father Lee's contact arrived one night with a case of whiskey and a request for a favour. The local unit were holding a tout whose informing had been responsible for the death of three volunteers in an SAS ambush and the arrest of ten more, two of whom were currently on the Dirty Protest. Unfortunately there was no option but to kill the tout, and in the long run save the lives of young volunteers by making prospective grasses think again. All week the man had begged to make a final confession to a priest and the unit, not being vindictive men, felt it would be unreasonable to deny this request.

—The only problem being, Father, there aren't many priests we can trust. We need someone with an understanding of the realities of the situation.

The light in the informer's room was of such low wattage that Father Lee was reminded of a photographic darkroom, but he could still see how badly the man's face was marked. He had to be asked to repeat his sins several times, as a lack of teeth rendered his speech almost incomprehensible. A wasp buzzed around the light in the room, and outside in the hall a young man with dyed blond hair softly sang a Bruce Springsteen song. A girl in a tracksuit top asked him to sing Elvis Costello instead.

Father Lee gave the man a light penance. Three Hail Marys and three Our Fathers. Normally he was stricter, but these were exceptional circumstances. Outside the door the banter continued. Blondie were mentioned. The Clash were dismissed. The penitent dropped to his knees and grabbed Father Lee by the waist.

—Father. Father. Help me. Help me, please. You have to. They're going to kill me tonight. They'll listen to you if you tell them not to kill me. They'll listen to a priest. Father, you can get me out of this.

The man's hands were clasped over his head, the broken fingers protruding at strange, anti-geometric angles. Father Lee said nothing. The man's voice grew shriller until it blended in with the buzzing of the confused wasp.

—Father, I didn't want to get me confession heard at all. I don't care about that. If you bring me out the door with you, they'll let me go. You have to help me, Father. You're holy, you're a priest.

This continued for several minutes until the man's voice began to grow faint, as his eyes found Father Lee's and saw they were empty of consolation. Father Lee stepped over him and walked to the door.

—You asked for confession. I have forgiven your sins and you are now in a state of grace. May God be with you.

The boy with the gun had switched to a Van Morrison song when Father Lee walked past him. He touched his forelock to the priest, strolled into the room and closed the door behind him.

That night, Father Lee explained to himself why intervention on behalf of the tout was impossible. He had not been brought to the house to make an appeal for clemency. The IRA would not have heeded him. Matters of military discipline were none of his business. It would not have been honest to try to rescue the man when he had been invited there to hear a confession. He felt angry with the tout for putting him in an awkward position. The man had shown bad faith in making a confession solely because he thought the priest might rescue him. Father Lee let his contact know he was not keen on performing many more such sacraments.

There were just two more. Both touts were resigned to their fate and made fine confessions. Father admired the foresight and faith of these women. The first man's concerns had been inverted. Father Lee had been there to help him attain eternal life, but the man was just worried about his mortal existence, unable to see that the priest was giving life just as surely as the blond gunman appeared to be taking it away.

He had no sympathy for touts. No one who had seen the men in Long Kesh could have.

Prisoners usually welcomed Father Lee. They knew which side he was on, and that they would receive news from home without the sour addition of moral lectures or urgings to renounce the path of violence. Occasionally he would have to suffer a hostile reception from a recent convert to Marxism, and sit patiently through a half-hour rote denunciation of priests as lackeys of the ruling class, running dogs of venture capitalism and dealers in the opium of the people before returning to tell the boy's mother there was nothing to worry about. He admired the dogmatism of the

Marxists. It showed a passionate desire for belief which made them good long-term bets to return to the fold.

The young man in Crumlin Road, serving eight years for taking a lift in a car which had a pistol stowed under the back seat, turned his back on Father Lee when the priest arrived. He rocked backwards and forwards, a list of well-wishers and news from his home street passing by without altering one iota the steady autistic movement of the thin back and hunched shoulders. A warder motioned to wind the visit up. Thinking of the anticipation with which the boy's mother would be awaiting his visit, Father Lee tried a final gambit.

— Think of your mother, like a good lad. Give me some message. I'm seeing her this evening.

The rocking slowed slightly. This emboldened Father Lee.

— Think of your little brothers and sisters. How can I tell them their brother has nothing to say to them?

The look in the man's eyes was of a wild dog at the exact moment when it loses its nerve and decides to attack.

— You fucking bastard, Lee, I know what you are. If you go fucking near my brothers and sisters, I'll fucking kill you stone dead. Don't think I won't.

A shaking Father Lee sat in his car with his head against the dashboard, his mind running methodically through the decades till he matched the mad eyes with those of a Belfast child he had found lost on the beach at Portrush and lured into some secluded sand dunes littered with brown glass beer-bottle shards. The boy had cried an unusual amount, he remembered.

His mind also ran through the stern punishments visited by his Army on the perverts and deviants whom historical chance had rendered casualties of war. He dreamed of his booby-trapped body lying on a border boreen, a placard reading 'Pervert' hanging round his neck and of beatings, kneecappings and the blindfolded journeys in Ford Cortinas from which no one returned. In the morning he rang his contact and arranged a meeting in the cocktail bar of Europe's most bombed hotel.

The cocktail menu bore an air of tacky desperation, some of its concoctions burdened with risqué names. Sloe Comfortable Screw Against The Wall. Sex On The Beach. He noticed the young punters, whose religious affiliation was masked by the desectarianising effect of affluence, focus on these names and then flush when they noticed his priestly eye upon them. They settled for more unambiguous choices. Long Island Iced Tea. Banana Daiquiri. His contact ordered two coffees on arrival, surreptitiously sniggering at the list of drinks.

—What do you think of this place, Father.

—It's . . . different.

—You said this was urgent.

—It is urgent.

Suddenly Father Lee felt so calm that he had to strain for the requisite worried tone.

—I'm getting worried about the help I'm giving to the volunteers.

—I understand. It can be a worrying line of work. Do you want to take a rest?

—No. No. It's not that. I'm worried about what the British will do if they discover me.

—There would be no proof of anything against you. And they'd hardly jail a priest.

—It's not jail I'm scared of. It's just that I hear a lot about MI5 and their tricks. You know, you told me about it once, black propaganda. A priest, I think, would be very vulnerable to any sort of whispering campaign.

He could see how his contact was taken in, and how the man's imagination only stretched to imputations of womanising or embezzlement. That was good. If the truth did reach his ears, he would regard it as proof of the unusually perverted nature of the British rumour machine.

—I would be worried that if they tried to blacken my name it could leave me in a very awkward position. People should know better, but you'll always have the few saying that there's no smoke without fire.

—Don't worry, Father. I'll see that any rumours are dealt with.

Three wee girls were skipping on the footpath as he drove home. There was an expensive packet of sweets on the dashboard. The day was nice and hot.

The newspaper headlines said the government was in disarray and that the Tough Guy might be gone in a couple of months. He was losing most of his support, said the reports. These reports had chapter and verse from confidential Cabinet meetings, exact details of every fuck-up and disagreement. Which was why Mickey Kelly and Henry would be spending the night at the Tough Guy's place.

Kelly found the yacht journey out to the island pretty hard going. Twice he leaned over the side and got sick. One of the crew shouted

—Man overboard.

It was meant as a joke, but Henry saw it as the perfect description of the Tough Guy, who had subjected them to a two-hundred-mile drive down the coast. The Tough Guy had become rich in the sixties and no one knew how. They knew so little that there wasn't even enough there to make rumours. His prize possession was this island, ten miles off the coast on a rough stretch of the Atlantic. Monks had lived there once, to show their fanatical devotion to God. The Tough Guy lived there from time to time to show his equally fanatical devotion to the deity of his self-image. The two other passengers on the boat were bigwig cops. Henry knew them to see. They were as puzzled as he was.

The Tough Guy greeted them when they landed. Henry realised that he had underestimated him. He had merely thought the man was a bollocks, when in fact he was stone mad. The Irish wolfhound sitting at the feet of the tweed-jacketed Taoiseach seemed to sense this sentiment and growled at Henry. Kelly threatened to get sick on it.

Wellingtons and waterproofs were provided for the new arrivals on the island. Henry felt like he should be running ahead of the Tough Guy, beating small wildfowl out of the bushes. It worried him that the Tough Guy probably felt the same way. It rained, but the party continued to tramp round the island, their eyes misting over from the reflection of wet black rocks against a weak sun that didn't know whether it wanted to come out or not. The Tough Guy, Henry, Kelly, the two top cops and the bodyguards.

—I am a man of Ireland, said the Tough Guy, the flora and fauna of this country fill my heart with a joy that only a true patriot can feel.

A wild duck flew off a rock just in front of them. The Tough Guy expertly shot it down and a bodyguard trotted gun-dog-style to fetch the dead bird.

—Pinch me and see if I'm dreaming, Kelly whispered to Henry.

—I'm going to do something with that duck, said the Tough Guy.

In the big house, port and cheese were handed round as a caterwauling mix of pipes and whistle played in the background. The Tough Guy cocked an ear to the din, downed his port in one and licked his chops.

—That tune I find to be the embodiment of the Irish national spirit.

The record sleeve told Henry that the tune came from Bulgaria. The Tough Guy ordered everyone to sit down in the red leather armchairs which had been pulled into a laager in the middle of the floor. He cleared his throat and began to speak in his podium voice.

—Our Party is a great one. It is not just a political party, it is a national movement whose spirit is one that goes back to ancient times. As leader, I consider myself the chieftain of our Celtic tribe.

He unfurled a copy of the day's newspapers, which continued the usual Cabinet leaks but also a story by a female political journalist which said that a senior member of the government would shortly move a motion of no confidence against the Tough Guy. There were quotes from this unnamed minister, who said the Tough Guy was in his final days as boss.

—We in our Party are not mere politicians in the English or European state. We are keepers of the national flame, custodians of the Irish spirit. An attack on the leader of the Party is both treasonous and anti-national.

The cops nodded, and the Tough Guy continued. There were people whose anti-national attitude made them threats to the state. The unnamed Minister was one and the female journalist was another. They wanted to belittle and do down the head of the country and everything the Irish people held sacred. Henry wondered if the cops were going to say anything. Something like, stop, can we go home now, or this is daft. But they just kept looking at the Tough Guy as if he was talking perfect sense. And the longer Henry listened, the more sense it seemed to make.

—We can't let this continue. It must be stamped out. I've called you here today to enlist your help in carrying out an operation which will finally prevent these people from making a mockery of our great country.

Henry and Mickey didn't say a word on the boat back to the mainland. They just thought of how they had agreed to bug Joan Brosnan's phone. A Special Branch man who talked a lot about 'subversives' and 'the fabric of the state' had explained to Henry about wire-taps when he'd been appointed Minister for Justice. It was generally IRA, or anyone the Branch said might be in the IRA who were targeted.

No one had said that Joan Brosnan might be in the IRA but she would be bugged all the same, as would the other people on the list the Tough Guy handed to Henry. Members of the other parties, members of the Party, some more journalists, an actress who might be having an affair with one of the opposition front benchers. Along with the first transcripts, Henry dealt with resignation letters from listeners who had signed up to keep tabs on bombers and gunmen, and now found themselves listening to conversations not very different from the ones they had in their own homes.

For the first couple of weeks Henry didn't listen to the tapes. Then he decided that it would be remiss of him not to check on the work he had authorised. Soon he was listening for a couple of hours every day. It was strange how eavesdropping on people's conversations made you dislike them. Their thoughts given voice and rewound sounded venal and unimportant. If they had been important, they would have been doing the listening. Henry felt like he was playing a game. He and Kelly would swap stories about what they'd heard on the tapes, and then authorise another dozen taps.

Sometimes he asked his driver to bring him past the houses of people who were being bugged, so he could imagine what surroundings they were in when they had the conversations he'd heard. He basked in his superiority. The participants only got to hear a conversation once. The Minister for Justice could hear it as often as he wanted.

Finally Operation Boatman hit the eureka button.

—Joan. Hello.

—Hello. Who is this?

—Noel McCarrick. I thought you might be interested in hearing what went on at today's Cabinet meeting. I think the oul fucker is on the run.

—I think you're doing the right thing. Noel, I warned what he'd be like in government, how he'd humiliate people like you in front of your colleagues.

—I'll move that motion against him soon. I think once people see someone standing up against him, he'll be on the way out.

—By the way, do you think we should be careful about talking like this on the phone? He's capable of anything.

—In fairness now, we're not living in Russia.

—I have a plan, said the Tough Guy in a surprisingly calm voice when he heard the tape.

The next morning the Tough Guy handed Kelly a small tape recorder. Henry watched from down the corridor as Kelly met McCarrick that afternoon. He had hidden the tape recorder in Kelly's desk drawer. The microphone lead was wedged between two telephone books on top of the desk. Kelly and McCarrick walked into the office.

Kelly rang Henry that night. They met in Jim's Place and listened to what had begun like a hundred bantering conversations from the past.

—This is the good bit, said Kelly, and ordered two cappuccinos before turning the volume up.

—Noel, I'm not very happy with the way our man is behaving as leader. I know you're loyal to him, but I wonder, do you have any reservations at all?

And it all came spilling out of the Minister for Finance. Who was backing him. When they were going to move against the Tough Guy. How much they'd like Kelly on board. If he thought Caslin would join them. All lovely informative cut-your-own-throat stuff, but still only the overture.

—I have a few financial worries, Noel. That's the only thing stopping me helping you get rid of your man.

A split second before the next sentence, Henry remembered McCarrick's obsession with economics, and assertions that market forces could solve all the problems.

—How much do you need?

—Oh, well, it's immaterial, but fifteen thousand pounds could see me right.

—Fifteen thousand pounds. It's a shame to see you crippled politically because of that. It's not a huge amount.

—It's enough when you don't have it. I'm in hock to the banks, so I don't see where I'll get the money from. You don't have any ideas?

Kelly's voice had fluttered at that stage. Henry wondered why before he noticed that there had only been a couple of minutes left on the tape. Time in which either Operation Boatman would be completed successfully, or the conversation would join the great mountain of pointlessness due to be shredded at the end of the month.

—Listen, some of the people backing us are very, very keen to get rid of the Tough Guy before he does any more damage. They're people of substance, if you get my drift.

Reel him in, Mickey.

—How do you mean?

—Listen, if you were to support us, we could make that fifteen thousand available to you, maybe even top it up to thirty. No questions asked. Support us, and the money is yours.

—No questions asked, did you say?

—That's what I said. I could have that money for you tomorrow.

The motion of no confidence was moved before the next meeting of the parliamentary party. The media predicted victory for McCarrick and his cohorts. Just before the vote was taken, the Tough Guy placed the little tape recorder on a table in the middle of the room.

—Support us, and the money is yours.

The conversation was replayed half a dozen times. The tape was finally switched off to allow Mickey Kelly to speak. A litany of financial misfortune which had left him open to attempted bribery and constant assaults on his integrity was detailed. He had carried the tape recorder with him to protect his good name, as he could stand the rumours no more. He was sorry he had done this, but . . . And Kelly began to cry. Henry thought this was doing the dog on it a bit. The Tough Guy put a fatherly arm around the Minister's shoulders.

—Mickey, I know it wasn't strictly correct, but I also know you're a man who'll go to any lengths to protect his honour. Like most of us here, your integrity is the most important thing to you.

Murmurs of agreement were almost drowned out by the sound of biros scribbling out No and replacing it with Yes. When McCarrick left the Cabinet offices, his promised Garda escort was not there. Instead there were six of the Tough Guy's constituency workers who knocked him on the ground, kicked him in the balls, jumped on his chest and eventually trapped his arm under a chair until they heard a satisfying breaking sound. Their leader gave an imperial thumbs-up from the balcony above. Henry had been on his way to help McCarrick when Kelly grabbed his arm.

—Don't do it. If he'd won, we wouldn't be Ministers any more. We'd be fucked. That's politics.

A courier arrived as McCarrick nursed his broken arm at home. His faith in human nature was just about to be restored before he noticed a strange smell from the package. Feathers and entrails fell onto the floor as he undid the final knot with his one good hand.

—Get well soon. I thought this might be a suitable gift. A dead duck which I shot myself. *An Taoiseach*.

Henry didn't join in the celebrations. McCarrick's broken arm came between him and full enjoyment. He listened again to the final batch of tapes before joining Mary in an Italian restaurant near the Dáil. He was just leaving the restaurant when Joan Brosnan rushed out of the cloakroom and held his arm. She was frightened and crying and drunk.

—They're there. They're waiting for me out in the dark.

Mary caught Joan by the arm and tried to soothe her.

—Who's out there, Joan, good girl.

—The men. The Tough Guy's men.

—Ah, now, fuck it, said Henry, and prepared to storm out.

He knew what a paranoid she was from listening to her phone calls. She was always worried about being bugged, and even though she was being bugged there was no way she could have known. It was just her suspicious mind. He wanted to lay into her and tell her it was over. Finito. Her side had lost fair and square. You could say what you like about the Tough Guy, but he wasn't some kind of mobster.

Mary saw all these thoughts collecting on Henry's face, and broke the connection between the brain and lip with one look.

—Henry, if Joan is scared, I'm sure she has some reason. Put on your coat, pet, and we'll walk you to your car.

Someone had laid a line of broken bottles across the windscreen of Joan's car. Henry tried to shut out the noise of Joan screaming and Mary's breath coming fast and irregular. He picked the note off the windscreen with some thoughts of throwing it away, in case the Tough Guy had signed it himself. He had not.

—Dear Bitch. You lost. There are plenty more of these for your ugly face. Be careful what you write in future.

Mary insisted on bringing Joan back to the restaurant,

where another half-bottle of brandy was poured into her while Henry called a couple of guards he trusted and told them to keep an eye on her house for the next few days. He had seen the car parked across the road as he picked up the note. Two of the men who had broken McCarrick's arm were in the front. One of them waved.

The Tough Guy called in to Henry's office the next day.

—I hope you see what I'm prepared to do to stay on top. Anyone who wants to beat me has to go all the way with me. I don't think anyone can, do you, Henry?

Henry stared him down. Thinking. Not so tough. Not so tough. Not so tough. Scary. Different thing.

THE EIGHTIES

When McKeon saw Niamh McNiven for the first time, the word which came to mind was geometry. Her arms seemed to hang in identical fashion to her hair. Her legs seemed connected to her arms as if they were the same limbs, all four of them just incidentally separated by her body. Most women's bodies were disconnected. Their breasts would not seem to belong to the same body as their stomach, for example. But Niamh's body looked teased out of one block of marble. From the tips of her toes to her twitching little lines of eyebrow, she was all in proportion.

—I said I thought your speech was very good. I watch you all the time on television. You're my favourite journalist.

He had come to Buswell's to launch a political biography written by a colleague, a book so devoid of interest it seemed to have been treated by a powerful cleaning agent which left no trace of incident. The biographer arrived over and told McKeon he'd stand him dinner in the Dodo. He invited Niamh along as well. McKeon was surprised at the thrill and delight he felt. Later the man would tell him he'd presumed Niamh was with McKeon because of the way she stood in relation to him. It almost looked like she'd practised this stance in the mirror.

In the Dodo, she pulled her chair over beside him and asked lots of questions about himself and his career and how he'd come to be such a success. It wasn't the most original line of conversation, but it felt somehow different. So different that when the biographer gave him a randy thumbs-up as he left the Dodo, he felt intensely irritated. It isn't one of those, he wanted to say. He bought another bottle of wine and questioned Niamh about herself with a fervour he'd recently been unable to capture on prime-time interviews.

She was twenty-six. It seemed far too young, until he remembered that he was only thirty-six himself. He just felt a lot older than his age. She seemed younger than her age. Like someone who needed to be looked after. Her apartment was in a section of Georgian Dublin notable for the youth of its offices and the venerability of its prostitutes.

—I'd invite you in for coffee, but I'm out of coffee.

—I love tea, or anything like that. I'd love a cup now.

—All I have is a bottle of peach schnapps left over from a Christmas party.

—I love peach schnapps. It's my favourite drink. It's a pity you can't get it more places.

She came back with two glasses of peach schnapps and wearing a dressing gown. Because her clothes smelt of smoke and food from the Dodo, she said. He tried to apologise for this, but could only produce an underwater noise, a gurgle, a bubble. Sounds from a language just invented.

—Would you mind if I kissed you.

—Sorry?

—It's OK.

At half five he looked at his watch and realised he was due at work in two and a half hours. When he mentioned this fact, she revealed herself as naked underneath the dressing gown.

For three days they stayed in the flat. Letting the phone ring, the papers be published, the television news report the beginnings, middles and ends of stories, letters pile up on mats, friends, meter-readers and Jehovah's Witnesses knock at doors and go away without an answer. Going through the gamut of sex. Starting with the tender and portentous, moving all the way to the familiar, frenzied and experimental and then back to the tender stage again, before two pairs of exhausted eyes winked at each other and closed in sleep for another half a day. Leaving the apartment, he felt like a forlorn deserter.

He took two weeks' holidays so he could be with Niamh. The first week in bed with talk which was itself sexual in intensity filling the gaps between lovemaking, such as they were. Some part of McKeon's body was always stiff, and Niamh was tireless. She worked out at a gym, she said. To stay in shape.

—Tell me everything, they both repeated as if they could talk through the whole life they had not spent together.

Other boyfriends had meant nothing. It was all right, he said, she did not have to tell him. She said she wanted to. A couple of well-known actors, a conceptual artist who had become famous by painting himself blue all over and living in a dustbin for two days to commemorate the Great Famine, and a footballer with six Irish caps.

On the second week they went to Paris, and McKeon bought presents with manic intensity. Niamh explained that she had no money and could not buy gifts back. He said that did not matter, and stretched himself to the financial limit in an effort to display his love empirically. It was like working out. It had hurt before you knew you were doing enough. He had wanted to show her Paris, and was slightly thrown off his stride when she knew it better than he did. In shops on the Place Vendôme, thronged with elderly grey men and bright young women whose make-up looked theatrical, he bought her expensive jewellery and scent.

Niamh took him to the Musée d'Orsay and tried to explain the wonders of Monet, Manet, Degas and Cézanne. She had gone to art college and spent a summer holiday copying paintings in the Louvre. He much preferred the paintings there, but did not tell her. She led him through Impressionism, cubism, fauvism and pointillism with an insistence more gentle than anyone else's acquiescence. Back in Dublin, she brought him to gallery openings.

An excess of love made McKeon feel like a connoisseur. He even endured the show by Niamh's artist ex, which consisted of a film of two stationary farmers looped three hundred times in the background while the man himself threw porridge oatlets into the audience. It was a protest against the current famine in Kampuchea.

—She's some woman, said the performance artist as he stood beside McKeon in the Project Arts Centre toilets.

McKeon nodded beatifically. The man did up the buttons on his 501s and finished the sentence.

—But there's no keeping her.

In the bath at Ashford Castle, Niamh told McKeon that she wanted to know everything he knew. She soaped his balls to the point of erosion as she talked.

—I'd love to be a journalist, Seamus. There's an ad in the paper today for journalists at RTE. I've applied but I haven't a hope of getting it.

He had never asked her what she wanted to do, because he knew that what was really important to her was loving him. But he didn't see why she couldn't be a journalist. She could do anything. He rang the head of News and asked for a meeting, reminding his old friend that ten years ago he had rescued him from being beaten up by British soldiers.

—Yeah, I can swing it for you, Seamus. There's just one

thing I want to warn you about. The unions are strong in here, so if I get her this job we can't take it off her in the future.

Why would anyone ever want to take anything away from Niamh?

In the Dodo he waited unconcerned for an hour and a half. Secure in the knowledge his Niamh would turn up soon. The waiter arrived with the white phone.

—Seamus. Oh, I'm really sorry. Listen, when I heard that I'd got the RTE job, I had to tell all my friends and they just came round and threw this surprise party for me.

Whoops and cheers and squeaky modern jazz in the background. A few people shouting

—Hello, Seamus.

—Oh, God, it's hectic here. I suppose I can't leave them now. I could be there in another half an hour. Or you could come over. I mean, it's a very young crowd, and you won't know that many but it would be cool if you were here, I could leave them to their own devices and we can spend the night talking to each other.

—Listen, love. It's grand. You stay there. I'll call tomorrow. OK? Love, I'm so proud of you.

He was. Though he'd squared the job, the achievement still seemed hers. Let her have this night of glory. He wasn't a possessive type like Mister Performance Art who had smeared indelible paint on her front door so he could see which of their friends had visited the house, only stopping after a visit from two unamused cops with bright blue hands.

—Seamus, you're the best, baby, mmmmm, mmmmm. I want to love you and fuck you for ever.

Imagine. She'd said that in front of a whole room of people. He was going to marry this woman.

*

Two police cars followed Father Lee and forced him to the side of the road as he drove from the prison towards his parish. An RUC man opened the passenger door, climbed in and said

—I think you know what this is about, Father.

Perhaps delusion was beginning to take hold of him, but Father Lee did not have a clue what this was about. Then it occurred to him that his visits to the prisoners were regarded as untoward, and that this was a blatant attempt at intimidation.

He was taken to a square grey-breeze-block barracks surrounded by barbed wire, where he was given tea and told to wait for the officer in charge. A deep brown rind ran around the inside of the cup. Four of the last half-dozen policemen to use the cup were dead. The other two were learning to cope without the bottom halves of their bodies.

News of Father Lee's arrest caused consternation to descend on the narrow streets of his parish, and ignite the religious feelings which were both central to and strangely unnamed in the conflict. The men he visited said their prayers, received their sacraments and knew the major dividing line between themselves and their jailers, but still called themselves Republicans or nationalists to avoid using the word Catholic. Inside, they knew where the deep root of the war lay.

One side had not said

—A Unionist parliament for a Unionist people.

The other did not say

—Unionist bastards, when their popular parish priest was pulled in for questioning.

Their indignation was tinged with a feeling of release. The internment of a uniformed soldier of the faith had temporarily broken the shackles of euphemism. Women banged bin lids on the pavements in protest, and exhorted

Cardinal O'Hanlon to do the ecclesiastical equivalent. The cardinal began enquiries into the reasons for his old friend's incarceration.

The people of the parish were kept warm by communal outrage, but there were those who knew why Father Lee had been held and hoped he would stay in the police station for ever. They were the ones who shifted uncomfortably in the shop when neighbours worried out loud that the priest might not be getting enough to eat. They were in the cold: no one more so than Kieran Armstrong.

After the arrest, Armstrong began to drink alone and make quick dismissive hand gestures in reply to offers of darts games. He thought about informers. In 1798, in 1848, in 1867 it was informers who sold the pass. McErlean betrayed Roddy McCorley who was hanged on the bridge at Toome, Niblock led troops to the hideout of Henry Joy McCracken who died upon the gallows tree. Armstrong drank to avoid including himself in a mental triumvirate.

As a youngster he had carried bricks for a man whose brother had been executed for planting bombs in Coventry during the Second World War. The man had been betrayed by one of his comrades. The informer was followed all the way to Australia and his throat was cut in the sleeping car of a train rattling towards Perth.

Such were the rules of war. Armstrong knew them, though he had been unable to pass them on to his son Patrick, who had waged his own campaign in the middle of the struggle going on all around him. Houses and cars in the neighbourhood were in constant peril from Patrick. Armstrong could not understand his son. The boy had been bright at school, bright enough to know where these stints of burglary were leading. There was nothing to do but throw him out of the house.

His parents kept their ears open for news of Patrick, who progressed from sleeping rough to living in Turf Lodge with a woman whose two kids had been semi-orphaned by two paramilitary organisations with opposite aims but identical methods. One night, as he watched *Match of the Day*, he heard her answer the door, stand aside as five men entered the sitting-room and say

—Here he is.

In hospital he told his father this was the fifth kneecapping. The IRA had decided it was the final one. They did not want to have to kill him, they said, so they would inflict as much pain as possible in an effort to finally frighten him straight. Patrick had thanked them profusely for their consideration. The doctors said they had never seen knees so badly damaged. The bones had almost been reduced to powder. Kieran asked his son to forgive him. Patrick held his father's hand and told him not to be daft, but Kieran thought of the complicity of understanding and felt more bitter towards himself than towards the masked men.

He pushed his son's wheelchair up and down streets as he returned any money Patrick had stolen and paid for damage he had caused. Some of the neighbours, he knew, had travelled to the Sinn Fein office, asked what could be done about his son and then distanced themselves from the implications of their question. Receiving the money would force them to concentrate on the moral balance sheet.

In dark corners of disco bars he watched his son wheel himself around, talking to women who loved his survivor's glamour and men who regarded him as an unfortunate reminder of what could happen. On the way home one night he asked Patrick the question which had always bothered him.

—You were a bright wee kid. We thought you'd make college. What happened to you? There was never a thief in the family.

The answer made Kieran run away and leave Patrick to wheel himself home. He walked the streets until he felt Patrick might have gone to bed. His son was still up when he got home.

—Whatever about anything else, did I ever tell a lie? Did I ever squeal when I got those beatings? Did I ever try to escape? I'm your son.

Listening to the story a second time, he knew there was not one word of a lie in it. A tale of school trips, First Confessions and Christmas parties. All the ingredients of community life recast as opportunities for Father Gerry Lee. He passed the story on to the RUC. It made him feel like an informer, and he told them he would not testify in court. He had started them in the right direction, and it was up to others now. He had made a slight hole in the wall, and if everyone else did the same then the wall would crumble. Patrick told him the names of others. He saw them on the street, coming home from work, pushing prams, hanging around outside the bookies'. Keeping their secret secret.

Detective Clive Hunter knew that neither Armstrong nor his son would stand up in court and say their parish priest was an abuser. He doubted if anyone would, but he pulled Father Lee in all the same because he thought that, being a man of God, he might welcome the chance to confess all.

Father Lee smiled when Hunter told him this, and made reference to the B Specials, who had been disbanded in the seventies for a brutality too great for even the Brits to bear.

The questioning was the B Specials up to their old tricks, thought Father Lee. Marching him into a police station at gunpoint just because of some harmless fooling around with kids. The B Specials could not bear to see a man standing up for the risen people. With them it was always croppy lie-down. But the croppy would not lie down, and Father Lee would not be dissuaded from visiting prisoners by bullying from the likes of Hunter.

—These are very serious allegations, Father. Do you want to talk to me about this?

Father Lee just laughed at Hunter. The big Protestant head on him.

—Sooner or later, Father, you'll have to answer charges on this.

This didn't seem very likely to Father Lee.

Kieran Armstrong finished his final drink and hit for home. Eight hundred yards from the pub, a car pulled up and four strong Protestant men dragged him into the back seat of a blue Mark Four Cortina. Half an hour later, they dumped his body on a piece of wasteland across which the people of two Belfasts faced each other. Father Lee mourned another Catholic victim, but people soon forgot about Kieran Armstrong. What was about to happen would make all other deaths seem strangely unreal.

The prisoners had continued to live in their own shit and people outside got used to the idea, inserting the name of the prison and the protest into the lexicon of news and politics and rational conversation in pubs and clubs and canteens, while the shit piled up and the maggots grew in size and multiplied. Nothing changed except to get worse, and the prisoners realised that there might be no way back from this battle unless the world could be made to understand its enormity.

A thin man with long hair and a beard from an El Greco painting was the first to push his food tray back to the door and stare at it until it was taken away. A week later, one of his comrades did the same. And a week later, another. But the first man remained seven days ahead for his appointment with death.

The men wasting in the cells were convinced of the inevitability of death. Their knowledge of the absolute nature of British perfidy made them aware that their demands would not be granted. Famous visitors came and went and promised a solution. But the hunger strikers knew their destination, and after a month it was clear that there was no way back for the first man.

Forty days. Fifty days. Becoming blind and faint, he was sometimes unsure whether he was receiving visions, dreams or visitors. He instructed his sister not to let anyone give him food if in his delirious state he requested it, his bony fingers gripping her arm until she swore a solemn oath. After sixty days, his stomach would be unable to cope with food anyway. On the sixty-sixth day he died, knowing that his death would not save the second man or the third man or the fourth. A million people had died in the Famine without the Brits turning a hair. He had learned this in prison, along with the slow Irish song he hummed to himself while passing into the void.

He had not been particularly senior or gifted or possessed of an awesome military record, although he had been hardy in the way of Catholic boys growing up in mainly Protestant neighbourhoods, something which in 1969 had changed from a mildly disorientating circumstance to a potentially fatal one. His family had gathered what belongings they could and left under the cover of darkness two hours before a mob arrived to burn them out. The boy carried his younger siblings' favourite toys on his back as his parents listened for pursuing footsteps and walked towards a place of greater safety.

From time to time, during the first week, on the seventeenth, the thirty-fifth, the forty-first, and forth-sixth,

Henry thought about the first man and hoped nothing would happen to him. When the man died, Henry realised that the hunger strike could not now be ignored.

After the second death, Cardinal O'Hanlon asked the hunger strikers to stop the fast before anyone else died. Father Lee balled up the pastoral letter before throwing it in a waste-paper basket. The cardinal did not understand. It was not up to the men to end the hunger strike, it was up to the Brits to surrender to the five demands. Father Lee thought about ringing O'Hanlon and appraising him of this fact, but he did not because they had not talked for some time.

As more men died, Father Lee realised that it was his side who would eventually have to give in. When four British soldiers were killed in their armoured car by a rocket launcher, he did not condemn the act from the pulpit. His parishioners lined the porch afterwards to congratulate him on a fine sermon, praising what he had not said rather than what he had.

The fifth man died in the middle of a general election south of the border. Jimmy spent the month campaigning, and realised that while Henry would top the poll again, his vote would not be as big as usual.

In every small village and medium-sized town, in factories, on farms, in ships and outside dole offices black squares of fabric hung. It took just one person to raise a black flag, but Jimmy knew how much approval and collaboration were necessary for the act to be performed. Men and women, young and old, farmers and PAYE workers looked at their feet and shuffled and mumbled as they told Jimmy they could not give Henry their number one this time. They were going to vote for a young man from Belfast who was in his fortieth day of starvation, and probably didn't know where their county was. Jimmy did not try too hard to persuade them otherwise. The votes would return to Henry when these extraordinary times had ended.

In his last week of life, the Belfast man failed to take a seat by only two hundred votes. Henry topped the poll again. Jimmy met Dickie Carberry in the count centre and was amazed at the calm sadness that had taken over the man's voice.

—Two hundred votes, Jimmy. We'll never save his life now.

Carberry and his bitter cohorts had toiled in the shadow of approbation for ten-odd years, loading the communal revulsion at every car bomb, firebomb and mistaken-identity killed on to their shoulders, gathering their unpopularity to their bosoms and repeating their consolatory mantra.

—The people have no right to do wrong.

But recently people had started to approach them in the street and ask them about the health of the hunger strikers. These questions prompted them to talk about saving lives rather than causing death.

Jimmy was a sorcerer of popularity. He could divine it, conjure it up out of nothing and make it mysteriously appreciate in size. He studied its arcana and hunted its sources. The week after the election, he drove around the county to seek the mystical connection between it and the youngster who had died the day before. He found that people disliked the IRA of the machine-gun attacks, the barracks mortar-bombings and the no-warning blasts in London streets because they could not connect them with the past. But they could identify with a beaten and suffering IRA watching helpless as its volunteers died. Because Irish history was a narrative of failure and the love of suffering. The IRA had laid claim to their inheritance in the H-blocks, remaking the line which bound them to Lord Edward

FitzGerald's septic wounds, Robert Emmet laying down his life for the Emerald Isle and Allen, Larkin and O'Brien shouting God Save Ireland high upon the gallows tree.

It worried McKeon that the station's reporters talked to everyone except anyone connected with the starving men. Instead, they made programmes about bomb victims, about the survivors of shootings and with politicians who did not want to see what was happening. His anxiety was assuaged by Niamh and by the news that he was to travel North to cover the first man's funeral.

The professional and sexual spheres became oddly connected the night before his departure. He and Niamh were drinking in a suburban pub when the ballad group played a song written by the dead man. It was a harmless ditty about a poteen maker, but everyone knew the words and sang them as if they contained the essence of the quality needed for bravery in death. That afternoon, the head of News had told McKeon he needed to be briefed before travelling North.

—It's all right. I always do my own research, and anyway I'm pretty familiar with the situation there.

—You need to be briefed. I'm not suggesting this, I'm telling you.

The three men at the briefing made McKeon feel at time as if he was in court on a murder charge, and at others as if he was on a game show where winning the jackpot depended on quick-fire correct answers.

—It's important that we don't give any solace to the fellow travellers of the IRA in this country, and that we get across the fact that this dead man was willing to murder and maim innocent people. It should also be made clear that he was a member of a sinister organisation who threaten us all.

There was the parting shot. Driving North, McKeon

wondered when all had officially ceased to include those who had hung the black flags in the small villages between Dublin and the border.

A pipe band led the mourners to the cemetery, which in twelve years had grown like a shanty town dealing with an unexpected influx from the countryside. People dressed in black to match the clouds, and found their walk mimicking the military march they knew was taking place near the coffin.

Henry had not been in the North since he'd met Rodney Fullerton. He wondered if Fullerton had rejoiced at the death, or if he had been shrewd enough to realise that things would never be the same again because the young men with their shit and starvation had upped the ante and made sure that this story would have an end. There would be some kind of solution.

The failure of the Party and the intrinsic softness of the Tough Guy kept step with him as he marched. They had done nothing except sit around and talk about a United Ireland with an impotent sentimentality which precluded action. The Brits had showed their resolve and depth of feeling by letting their own young men and those of the other side die. This investment was what entitled them to their involvement.

The thought of the first man and the second man dying and of those who would follow them, made him momentarily feel like he had on the day he considered running guns to the fourth green field. Then the memory of Garda Clarke swamped him in confusion and uncertainty.

Father Lee had thought that life in those days could not continue as it always had, that the death of the first man would cause some kind of apocalypse. Now he saw sorrow rather than anger on people's faces. Sorrow, which was directed into the ground and changed nothing. The Iron Lady commanded his reluctant respect for her realisation that nothing had changed. Events did not have to possess immediate metaphorical qualities which transcended their actual reality. To her, ten men dying were ten men dying and nothing else. She did not subscribe to a theory of epiphanies.

On the way up, Jimmy noticed how the road itself underlined the unreality of the whole situation. First you were in the Republic, then you were in the North, then you were in the Republic and then you were in the North again. And all you'd done was travel in a straight line.

The pipe band halted and the shuffling feet came to a stop like a switched-off conveyor belt. A single drumbeat echoed. Jimmy felt it deep inside himself. The media used the quiet commanded by the drumbeat to make reports. French, German, Italian, American, English, Asian and African languages described the scenes of grief at the funeral as something unfeasibly out of the ordinary. Like the Ayatollah's return to Iran, the Soweto uprising or the sight of civilians clinging to the struts of departing American helicopters. They conveyed the otherness of the moment while McKeon stood there with the station's cameras and mikes trained on him and denied that anything strange was happening. Travelling live into the living-rooms of the Republic, he took the strangeness out of it because he knew this was required of him. His country wanted to declare its distance from this territory, this repository of the fault lines and dark secrets of the island. As he finished the report and got a thumbs-up from a cameraman, it struck him that another award might be on the cards.

The strange creature conceived by the death of the first man expressed itself through flame. Buses blazed in the city centre, shops and houses went on fire, people blocked the streets and set their barricades alight. McKeon's road to the border was fringed by burning vehicles. He had been advised to stay put for a couple of days but could not while Niamh was at the other end of the line.

Her absence from home surprised him. He thought he had seen her curtains move and bedroom light flick off as he approached. It is hard to distinguish between apartments from the street, he realised. The fires had lit something inside him, so he went to Nesbitt's pub and watched news footage of a crowd trying to storm the British Embassy just a mile away. A riot broke out when gardai blocked their path and wooden staves, iron spikes and metal barriers flew through the air. McKeon imagined the reporter on the spot intoning himself

—Rational, sane, modern, as he prepared his piece to camera with mayhem panning out all round him.

In the Dodo, Mickey Kelly sat at a table surrounded by young women. None of them talked about the funeral or the riot. Moira Hopkins was sitting in a rattan chair by the bar. McKeon intended to pass her, but he noticed that her eyes had lost the skittery gleam which had lodged there during her pursuit of Kelly, and were again those of the woman who had once brought him home and made him coffee.

—Will you buy a girl a drink?

He did. She had come to say goodbye to Kelly.

—I phoned the station looking for you, but they said you'd be in Belfast for another couple of days.

—I had to come back. It was just . . . the fires. I can't explain.

—I felt sorry when I knew I wouldn't see you before you went.

Moira had given up on the Kelly caper three months

ago and was going to London to work with a radio station. McKeon held her for a couple of seconds longer than expected as she got into the taxi. When the cab left his view, he did not go back into the Dodo but walked as far as Niamh's apartment.

Niamh's conversation sounded borrowed from a made-for-television movie.

—It's over, Seamus.

—How do you mean, it's over?

—I mean it's over, finished, gone, finito, kaput.

It came out of the blue. Like the fires. Like a plank falling from the sky outside the British Embassy to split open the head of an unsuspecting garda.

—It's not you, Seamus, it's me.

—I don't think we're going anywhere, Seamus.

—It's not what I want in my life.

—I haven't been happy lately. *We* haven't been happy lately.

The quotidian language made it hard to register the reality of the event. It was like watching two other people. He begged and cajoled and cried at the foot of her couch for two hours. She was not moved. Acceding to her hundredth request for him to leave, he returned to the Dodo and caught the eye of Sian Guiney as he walked in. Suspicion, investigation, confirmation and commiseration passed between them in a millisecond.

—Why didn't you tell me, Sian? I know you know everything.

—I don't. I just know everything that's not worth knowing.

—Who is he?

—Martin Milne, the film director The English guy. He's making some epic up in the Wicklow Mountains. Lots of swordfighting and cleavage.

—You knew. I know you knew. Why not tell me anything?

—Because you wouldn't have thanked me. You would have hated me.

—But it's the truth.

—It is.

Niamh admitted it was the truth, but expressed disappointment that he had found out. She felt it showed a lack of trust. McKeon apologised.

—He is such a talented man. He's seen so much of the world.

—I love you.

—I find power such a turn-on. He knows all the stars. They've worked for him before and they will again. He's making this film as a little indulgence for himself.

—I love you.

—Seamus, it would never have worked between us. Our worlds are too different.

—I love you.

—I love him.

Sometimes at work in the months that followed, McKeon would pass Niamh in a corridor, but the part of him which might have felt emotion about these meetings was now chained up like playground swings on a Sunday in a Protestant town. He tried to forget the joys of the coupled life, immersing himself in the crowd at Nesbitt's with people like himself who wrote newspaper columns and turned up on radio and television to assure you that Modern Ireland was the best. In a church-gate speech Jimmy had dubbed them

—ABCDE people. What they believe in is Abortion, Buggery, Contracepiton, Divorce and Euthanasia.

But most people called them the Liberals. The Nesbitt's

gang laughed at Henry and Mickey Kelly and even the Tough Guy, calling them dinosaurs and stressing the low esteem in which the Party was held by the general public since they'd lost the recent election. When Henry walked past the place, he looked in the window with a mixture of repulsion and curiosity felt by a religious fanatic travelling through a red-light district.

He arrived home from the Dáil one weekend to find that a young fella had turned up with Dolores, whose 2CV was parked outside the house. Henry could not work out why his daughter drove a car like that, although he was reassured by the fact that Mary made sure all the neighbours knew Dolores was a solicitor. That was a job with plenty of status, even if he wondered at times why she spent so much time defending and worrying about drug addicts, down-and-outs, tinkers and queers.

The abstracted air which she had developed pleased Henry, because he recognised it as an extension of the child she had been. The kind of kid who asked why the grass was green and where Mammy's lap went when she stood up, and who was always the one to fall into a puddle or be knocked down by a bounding dog, not responding with wails or recrimination but with bemused acceptance. Her life now seemed to be conducted with one arm in a coat sleeve and a sandwich in her mouth as she searched for lost items of clothing, scarves, rings and important briefs which would be found just in time for her to make court, and, in the way that she had emerged unscathed from childhood falls, produce brilliant arguments which usually won the day.

Dolores walked into the kitchen to help her mother with the dinner, and left Henry and Mark alone together.

—It's, like, pretty cool, y'know, Mister Caslin.

—Call me Henry. What's like pretty cool?

—Just, you know, everything, Mister Caslin, the entire house type of vibe, yeah, you know.

Henry looked pleadingly at the kitchen door, but Dolores did not come through it.

—What do you do yourself, Mark? Dolores started to tell me, but she didn't get fully round to it.

—I'm involved in a kind of performance sort of thing, we're just, you know, workshopping at the moment.

—How do you mean?

—I'm an actor.

—I'm sure acting is great. I'm a politician.

—Oh, I know. I know. Dolores told me. I mean politics is, like, politics, you know.

—What do you mean, exactly?

—Oh, I mean, you know, like, politics is, I just dunno, have no interest, maybe sometimes it looks like it's all the same, maybe, and not meaning offence to you because Dolores says you're different, but sometimes maybe they all look like they're all out for themselves, man.

—How did you develop such an in-depth knowledge of politics?

—My dad is Minister for Finance.

Dolores confirmed this revelation.

—He's Colm Boucher's son?

—Oh, yeah. He is. But it doesn't mean that much to him. He's not a political animal. He's a very talented actor, Daddy.

During ministerial question time, Colm Boucher would look across at Henry and mouth silent obscenities. He called Henry and Mickey Kelly the Dukes of Hazzard, and regularly bemoaned their lack of third-level education and the fact they must make Ireland a laughing stock in front of more sophisticated European countries. Boucher had more degrees than a thermometer, and an accent which made W. B. Yeats sound like a Cavan cattle jobber. Since the last election, Henry had to look from the opposition benches at the smug fucker promising to tax the farmers, which was very brave of him seeing as there wasn't a single one in his constituency.

—How can you be going out with that yoke's son?

—He's very nice. And his father asked him the same question, except that he doesn't use the word yoke and I'm your daughter. Mark makes me very happy, Daddy. We have a lot in common.

—Like what?

—Like the fact that our fathers do the same job, for a start.

Henry got used to Mark, and prepared for the worst Dearbhla could throw at him.

The sisters were very close because they would never covet the same thing. Dearbhla had gone to college a year later than Dolores and bought her first car two years earlier, a new Mazda which she drove at speeds of close to a hundred miles an hour, shouting out the window at tardy motorists in a voice made Dietrich-husky by forty fags a day. She had risen to a senior position in a management consultancy firm, where she wrote cold-eyed and clear-headed evaluations of state bodies and private companies which resulted in strikes, mass lay-offs and, eventually, improved profits and share prices.

Her young man shook hands and looked serious as if he was applying for a job, making Henry suddenly nostalgic for Mark's wobbling mitt and caroming eyes which slid around in their sockets like mishit balls skittering around a pool table. Garrett looked approvingly round the room at the Paul Henry landscapes, the Tom Nolan gold discs and the animal heads on the wall.

—It's a far cry from the days of the Sunshine Ballroom.

Henry nodded.

—You must have suspected things would go well for you when you had the three ballrooms up and running within months.

—Oh, aye, the Sunshine, the Kon-Tiki and the Goldmine.

—With respect, no. The Sunshine, the Kon-Tiki and the Wildflower. The Goldmine came fourth, some three months after the Wildflower.

After a few seconds' thought, Henry admitted that Garrett was probably correct.

—I know I am. It's very important to get your research done properly in my line of work.

He wasn't a journalist, was he? If he was a journalist he could fuck off out of the house, no matter what Dearbhla said.

—Economics. I'm an economist with the Central Bank.

Over dinner, Garrett brought Henry on a tour of the past, through the ballroom days, the election to the County Council, the first general election, almost frightening his prospective father-in-law with the extent of his knowledge. Henry was outclassed; he only had memory and reality to rely on, while the young lad had facts and figures. Garrett reminded him of a nature programme he'd once seen about a wasp that builds a shelter out of paper.

—What do you think Daddy, isn't he great? Ye had plenty to talk about, said Dearbhla in an unusually pliant voice.

—He's great. He's very, you know, intelligent, said Henry, thinking fondly of the stumbling ticker-tape machine which passed for Mark's conversational facility.

Economists ran in Garrett's family. His father was one, who regularly penned articles warning the Party that the only way to save the country was to carry out spectacular acts of economically stringent electoral suicide. This he called realism.

—Where did you meet him?

—The same place Dolores met Mark, Nesbitt's.

He could not wait for the happy couple to leave. Once again, he needed Mary to put things straight in his head

—When did this happen to our daughters?

—How do you mean, Henry love?

—That they started meeting the likes of that, and hanging around those Dublin Four pubs. With people that aren't like us.

—That's where their friends are, Henry. The people they work with. The people who are doing well for themselves. All that happened was that we did well, and we got them a good education and they got good jobs.

—They've grown away from us.

—Don't be daft. They live their own lives, but they still love the pair of us.

Whatever she said, his children were growing away from him. His daughters would leave him for other men. He and Mary would have to start living exclusively in their own lives now. There would be grandchildren soon, but that would be different. Their parents would be the buffers between them and the dangers of the world.

Momentarily he felt panicked, and wished everything could have stayed like it was. He wished Dolores and Dearbhla and Henry Junior back to the age when he and Mary looked after them and their leaving was unconscionable. But he knew that could not be, because time could not even be stopped, never mind reversed. For the first time he had a feeling that instead of moving away from the beginning, he was moving towards the end. There was a winding down in his life. Excitement, novelty and significance would be ceded to his children. He went downstairs to his bookshelf and took down an old red Bible which had belonged to his grandmother. Inside the cover was a calendar of events in her family's life. The final entry read

—January 4, 1918. Henry died today. He was a decent man and a good husband. Lord have mercy on him.

One day Dearbhla's first child would look at a Bible with his name in it. The next morning he and Mary went to First Mass and prayed for the ability to face up to the changes of life.

—Let's face it, Mary. Our daughters are Dublin Four.

In the heart of the district he bought a massive Georgian pile overlooking the canal. Dolores and Dearbhla took an apartment each, Henry kept one downstairs and tried to let his daughters live their own lives. His neighbours were old money living in houses occupied by their families for more than a hundred years. The fact that they looked down on him filled Henry with perverse delight.

His daughters would sometimes bring him for meals. It amazed him, as it seemed only a few short moments ago that he had been stopping the car on the way home from Irish-dancing lessons to let them buy chips. They, and Mark and Garrett, took him to restaurants where the waiters knew them and no one knew Henry. Sometimes Mary would turn up as a surprise. The girls needed her there to coax him into eating the food. Thai, Indian, Chinese, Greek, Japanese. Initially he would search the menu until he found a steak which could be served with minimum of ethnic input. He progressed to extremes of adventure. Squid, raw fish, octopus, frogs' legs, deer and kid goat.

The fact of his daughters as equals was astounding, Dolores or Dearbhla producing a credit card at the end of the night and brushing off his efforts to pay.

—No, no. We'll pay. Weren't you doing it long enough. The words made him feel sadly resigned to the fact that his daughters would never be fully his again. They belonged to Dublin Four the way their father belonged to the small town and to politics.

Henry Junior belonged nowhere. After scraping into college he had dropped out, hanging around unhappily at home and talking so fiercely about leaving that eventually his father arranged a job for him with the Irish Tourist Board in New York. Henry Junior had been awkward from a boy, and he hummed and hawed about going until Henry cashed in an insurance policy and handed him ten thousand dollars to help him through the first few months.

The money disappeared in weeks, and Henry Junior was pondering life without it when he met Tim Brennan in a downtown Irish bar. Brennan owned one of Ireland's biggest supermarket chains, and told Henry Junior he was on holiday. He phoned a limo which brought them to a cocktail bar where men in white suits moved among potted plants and a pianist played Cole Porter songs. They were sharing a couple of bottles of champagne with two Canadian air hostesses when Henry Junior saw Mickey Kelly walking across the floor with a gang of Irish-American politicos and Kelly saw him back.

—What are you doing in New York, young Caslin?

The air hostesses were all ears.

—Oh, I'm in the film world.

—What's that? A video shop?

Henry Junior saw that Kelly was not pulling his chain out of nastiness, but because he genuinely didn't know how to talk to him as an equal.

—Nah, I'm working in the industry. Duckin' and divin', doin' a few deals. Keepin' the head above water. I got some stuff goin' on.

—Right, said Kelly, taking a large mobile phone out of his pocket and walking away.

The two air hostesses were complimenting Brennan on his tan when he told them about the house in Florida where he spent most summers.

—You just can't spend summers in Ireland. The weather is always autumn there, so autumn is the only time to be in the country. Isn't that right Henry, said Brennan.

Brennan included Henry Junior in all of his sentences, the insistent way he did this briefly making both hostesses look at the younger man as if there might be more to him than they first thought. They decided their initial diagnosis had been correct, and turned their heads synchronously back to Brennan. Their movements had the crash-test-dummy unreality of those performed before take-off. A hand appeared in front of Henry Junior, bearing a mobile phone. Mickey Kelly grinned inimitably from behind a plastic palm tree.

—I have your mother on the other end of the line, Junior.

Henry Junior looked at his companions, trying to make them see that this never normally happened to him, that mother was the code word for someone glamorous, a top film actor, a famous television personality, a drug dealer to the stars. Kelly handed the phone to him.

—Hello.

—Hello, Henry

—Hello.

He repressed the word Mammy, which would normally have followed the greeting. Already he sensed that the air hostesses would not need much prompting to regard him as a comic figure.

—Are you having a nice evening?

—I am, yeah.

Aspiring to a tough yeah. The phone reception so clear that his companions could hear everything his mother said. She was beyond his control.

—Mickey said he met you talking to a couple of women. Are they nice?

—They are, yeah.

Trying to shut out the giggles.

—Wasn't it good of Mickey to phone me?

—It was, yeah.

—Are you minding yourself? I hope you're being very careful over there, I believe it's very rough.

—I can look after myself, Mammy.

—Of course you can, love. I better go. We don't want to be running up Mickey's phone bill. I'll ring you during the week.

The air hostesses didn't even pretend not to be laughing at him. Kelly took back the phone.

—Wasn't that the greatest stroke of luck, bumping into each other like that? Now your mammy knows you're all right.

What were you supposed to do in a situation like that? Tell your mother to fuck off? Would they have found that impressive? It was a pity his father hadn't come to the phone, because he would have told him to fuck off, he would have called him a bastard and a bollocks and a motherfucker and an asshole if that was what they wanted. Because he hated his father, and his father knew this and mentioned it to Mary, who pointed out that he had hated his own father too, when he was growing up.

—Not that I'm saying Henry Junior hates you.

Henry thought back to the day he had brought his father home from the pub. Hate was the right word for what he had felt, but the difference surely was that his father had deserved the hatred. On the other hand, his father had not been the only drunk in the village, and some kids had remained friends with parents who must have been pure nightmares to live with. Henry visited and asked his father to talk to him.

—About what, asked his father.

—About anything you want. About your father, maybe.

Who had been a father of fifteen, had never taken a drink in his life and had a special devotion to St Theresa of Lisieux. He died when a tree he was chopping fell on him refusing with his dying breath the offer of some brandy to ease his final pains.

For the first time Henry heard the cattle-rustling story. Terry Galvin died the month after, and Henry felt proud when his father spat on the coffin, although political expediency forced him to wrestle the old man away and apologise to the mourners. The journey into the past brought Henry closer to his father, but not an inch nearer his son.

In New York, Tim Brennan and Henry Caslin Junior hung out together, not like an old buddy and a younger sidekick, but like two equals. Spending money was a pleasure to Tim. He bought a fifteen-hundred-dollar bottle of wine just because Henry Junior wondered out loud who could afford to spend that kind of money on a drink with their meal, and had stumped up a couple of thousand dollars for front-row seats at the New York Knicks. He used cash as if living in some country where it had been rendered worthless by chronic inflation.

Tim stuck two one-hundred-dollars bills down the cleavage of a tall brunette cigar girl with brown eyes, in a restaurant with a swimming pool on one side and a mambo orchestra floor show on the other. She smiled as he telescoped the notes and eased them down between her jutting breasts, while Henry Junior's eyes followed every millimetre of the descent. He heard the green paper rustle against her sun-tanned skin.

—Jesus.

—I don't think your boss'll get that tip back . . .

—Chloe. You're crazy, guys, you know that.

They met Chloe in the foyer with a red-haired woman, introduced as her flatmate.

—There's nothing flat about her, said Tim as a porter announced he had secured a cab to the hotel.

—Hotel?

—Don't worry, Henry. It's my treat. It'll be your turn the next time, said Tim.

The hotel was one which usually appeared on the television news being mobbed by paparazzi. In the bathroom, Henry Junior pressed his face against the veined black, grey and white marble because he had never seen anything so beautiful. A naked Chloe was on him when he stepped out the door.

She fell asleep soon afterwards, and Henry Junior was careful not to wake her as he slipped out of bed and walked out on to the balcony of his room. The lights of the city grew in number as the night got older. Looking at the sweat-spangled body of the cigar girl lying on top of the blankets, the Rolling Stones mouth logo tattooed on her stomach and breathing the warm thick honey of conditioned air, he told himself that his life was the best. In Rathbawn he had not been appreciated, but here in New York beautiful women appreciated him for himself.

In the morning he asked Chloe if he could see her again.

—Sure you can, son. Just pay me another five hundred dollars. I think your friend said it's your turn next time. See you around.

It is the first time Henry Junior has even thought of the concept of paying for sex, but he becomes familiar with it because Tim cannot relate to anything which he has not bought. It is never Henry Junior's turn to buy women or coke or uppers or downers.

*

Summer arrives, and it is time for Florida. The two men sit in the hotel lobby drinking Tequila Sunrises. Tim hands Henry Junior a magazine and says

—Anything you like.

Henry Junior is not sure whether this is a question or an offer. The magazine is filled with thousands of women and a few men who will do anything. They say this in their advertisements, which are written in a kind of ten-year-old's sex patois reeking of the forbidden. The women look very similar to him. He finds very few of them beautiful, which surprises him because he would have thought beauty to be a prerequisite for the job. There is a hardness about their eyes and, while their mouths pout, there is a suggestion of pain there and the hair, usually blonde, is excessive, like something from a carnival sideshow. They look less like women than a desperate man's fantasy about the female sex. He knows this is the point. They pick a number, ring and wait.

Two hours later, Tim and hi I'm Patti and hi I'm Gina are in a jacuzzi with Henry Junior handing round bottles of champagne and various combinations of pills. Henry feels nervous. When he smiles at Patti she does not smile back. The ad did not say anything about smiles, and exactly what is involved was thrashed out over the phone before the girls, arrived. Tim calls them girls although they are nearer his age than Henry Junior's.

Gina walks over to her coat and extracts a big plastic bag with a tag around the neck. She pours grass on to the table and makes some joints which are overfilled to bursting point, like American sandwiches. Henry Junior tries to see the scene from the outside like he used to do, the hookers, the jacuzzi and the champagne, and think how cool it is. He cannot now. Tim chases Gina across the room, mouthing sexual obscenities. Disgust creeps up on Henry Junior.

It has been a while since Tim mentioned returning to Ireland, but he will have to go back. Every day there is an extra unopened letter market URGENT in the glove compartment of his car. Also, letters in Party envelopes with the same handwriting always on the outside. Henry Junior realises that he will feel betrayed when Tim leaves. Tim and Tina go into the next room. Henry Junior is left alone with Patti, and suddenly feels absolutely terrified. She monotones a pricelist slowly, as if he does not understand the language.

She still does not smile at him. He feels very strange. Her face has turned into a skull with strips of charred flesh hanging from it. She reaches for Henry Junior, her voice booming. He knows that she wants to inflict some sort of harm on him, and that if he does not get out of the jacuzzi now he will die. Gina's face reappears for a second. She looks concerned. The skull returns.

He is in the bathroom. People are trying the door handle. It is them. They have come to kill him and will have the door open in a second. Henry Junior opens the bathroom window and climbs out on to a ledge.

Time seems to be expanding one second and contracting the next. His movements are both urgent and deliberate. He realises that he is naked and looks down at the ground, which makes him laugh because it reminds him of cartoons where characters who are afraid of heights see the street below zooming up at them. Loudspeaker voices are telling him not to do anything stupid. This sets him off into the giggles again. Why would he do anything stupid? He is not a stupid person. It gets dark, and someone has their arms around him and all of a sudden he realises what is happening. He is five years old and having a feverish German-measles nightmare. His mother is comforting him and his father is at the door of the bedroom looking concerned.

At the station house they give Henry Junior an injection

to put him to sleep for a few hours, and go through his belongings to find out who he is. They examine the bag of grass and tablets from the room and speak to Tim Brennan, who they caught fleeing down the fire escape with two half-naked hookers. When Henry Junior wakes up they tell him that he is in trouble and will have to go before the judge next morning.

—You can make one phone call, and it better be a good one.

His mouth feels stuffed with cotton wool and his head is light, but he calls his father's office, exchanging a few pleasantries about the weather with Martina before being put through to Henry.

—Daddy, Daddy, will you just come out and get me.

The call finished, he weeps because he knows he has followed his own road and found it to be the wrong one. He cannot picture a time when he will get back on track. It feels like his life has just ended.

At first, Henry feels tempted to ring the station house back and tell Henry Junior that this is one mess he must sort out himself. Then the sound of Noel McCarrick's arm cracking as it was jammed under a chair comes to mind. The Tough Guy delights in the misfortune of others, confident that what is damaging to anyone else has within it the potential to make him stronger. If he finds out about Henry Junior's arrest, he will make sure that the story is common currency within a day. And he will do so in the knowledge that he is preventing the boy's father from ever becoming Taoiseach.

The unfairness of this situation gives Henry a reel in the head. But he knows that at this moment his survival as a politician is in every bit as much danger as Henry Junior's survival as a man. The country is founded on and obsessed by the family. People will feel some mistake of Henry's has led to his son perching on that window ledge with sex and drugs lurking in the background like two wholly unsuitable friends A man unable to look after his children can hardly be trusted with the care of a country.

—Self-pity is Henry's dominant emotion as he explains the situation to Mary. How could Henry Junior do this to him?

—It's not completely his fault, Henry.

—Well it's hardly my fault. When I get hold of the little frigger. He has no consideration for anyone else.

—If you're just going there to save your own skin, I'd prefer if you left him where he is.

He thought he knew the entire emotional palette which Mary draws from, but he has never heard bitterness in her voice before. She repeats the statement. He realises that there is a connection between her and Henry Junior which he cannot grasp.

—Henry, think of him, think of how he must be feeling. Because you never have before.

—Mary, I don't have time for this.

All these years and no arguments. Now this. Because of useless Henry Junior.

—Henry I'm mad with him too, but you never pass any heed on him. Why do you think he rang you?

—To get him out of trouble.

—I could have organised a solicitor and done all that. He rang you because he thinks you're the best person to do it. He depends on you.

—He shouldn't. He should be independent; I was when I was his age, and a long time before that.

—That's what's wrong, Henry. You think he should be independent because you were. But you know what your father was like, you had to break from him. Henry Junior knows that you're good and that you're kind and that people respect you. How can he be independent of you except to be the opposite?

Henry has no answer to that. He phones Jimmy and tells him they are flying to the States that night. He needs Jimmy very much. Phone calls are also made to a lawyer and to a police chief whose name is in the Party's book of Irish-American contacts. The chief tells him charges can be dropped and publicity headed off at the pass. On the plane, Henry and Jimmy feel as if they are embarking on an adventure. Henry's bag contains a large sum of cash, which will find an appropriate home. He feels proud of the great contribution made by the descendants of Irish emigrants to law-keeping in the States.

And what does he think of his own descendant?

He does not blame him now, because he knows that your own country is where you belong and that outside it all manner of things can happen. Like whatever happened to Jimmy in London, that thing he never talks about. If anything happens abroad you are stranded, cut off from Ireland, dependent on someone else to bring you back.

In the cell, Henry Junior's head is clearing sufficiently for him to know that he is entering a dangerous time. There is another ledge to negotiate, and although it will be his self rather than his body which will be at risk, he knows that the potential for damage will be even greater. Being rescued by his father will return him to a childhood from which there may be no escape. Then it strikes him that there may be something he can offer his father, something which will make this seem like a transaction rather than an act of charity. The envelopes, that stream of missals from the Party. They may be of some significance, because Tim Brennan is not the kind of man to keep unimportant correspondence.

He realises that he is thinking like a Caslin and feels happy. He begins to walk around the cell so he can remember the envelopes, the offer of which is the sole means by which he can retain his manhood. He holds up his hand when Henry walks in, and before his father can say a word, says

—This is important, Daddy. Tim Brennan was arrested with me. Someone from the Party keeps writing to him. It may be important, and now could be the time to put the squeeze on him.

His legs buckle as he feels for the first time the deep glow engendered by the political act. Henry puts his arm around his son, thanks him for the information and points Jimmy in the direction of the next cell.

When Jimmy walks into the cell, Tim Brennan knows straight away that the man is Irish and that this is bad news. He has made a quick deal with the arresting officer, and in fifteen minutes' time will be released without charge. Then he will fly home to Ireland and consign the States to the realm of the past. Now here is someone connecting his real and unreal worlds.

—You bump into all sorts in this spot, Mister Brennan. I'm surprised at you.

—I don't know you, I'm sorry.

—My name is Jimmy Mimnagh. I'm the man who does the work for Henry Caslin. I'm also his best friend and the godfather of the young lad you left out on yon ledge. And I'm not very happy with you.

—Listen, he's old enough to look after himself.

—Listen to me, you slimy Dublin bastard. If you piss me off, this story will be all over the papers at home and your fucking shareholders are not going to be very happy people.

Silence was Brennan's only response when Jimmy mentioned that he had obtained the phone numbers and addresses of the two whores, and was planning to post them to the editor of a signally sleazy Sunday tabloid.

—I'm gong to do all this because you've harmed someone I care a lot about. Unless you can offer me something that would change my mind. And I'm not talking about money.

—I could let you have some documents that might be to your advantage.

—You mean the secret of how they get figs into the fig rolls? When it comes down to it, you're a fucking greengrocer.

—Listen to me.

They flew back to Dublin together. A solicitor supervised the handover of the documents and letters, which would only be made public in the event of Brennan resigning as head of Pricecutter. The enjoyable night Jimmy and Henry had looking through the documents almost made all the trouble worth while. The papers sat in a safety deposit box. Henry was glad to have them, but could not foresee a situation serious enough to demand their use. They would make life uncomfortable for too many people in too many ways. All the same, for the first time he felt proud of his son.

—He did well, the young lad, I'm surprised, Jimmy had said.

—You shouldn't be, it wasn't from the wind he took it.

For months after his return, Henry Junior waited for an omen or sign which would show him where to go next. There was none, so one morning at half seven he drove out to the BB plant. Walking around the factory, he became aware of a strange and almost beautiful purity of function, and told himself that a man who could run this place could do anything. He rang his father and said he wanted to become involved in the business.

—We were hoping you'd maybe want to do something else. Something to do with your college education. I mean,

I started with BB and it's always there for ye, but you know I had no education.

—That didn't do you any harm. I'd like to try it out.

—You know it's not an easy business.

—I know. If it was, you wouldn't have done it.

He studied the mechanics of business, learned how to negotiate with the trade unions, clinch contracts with supermarket chains, conduct product research and development, asked his father for company files and read the history of BB, bought business magazines and combed profiles of captains of industry for factors in common. As his father had once looked for the secret of power, he looked for the secret of business until balance sheets, company accounts and market research became poetry to him. His sisters worried he was becoming too serious. He seemed uninterested in women and their attempts to find him a girlfriend met with indifference.

—You're working too hard, they told him.

Their father did not agree, and, a year and a half after his son's return from the States, retired as Managing Director of BB and appointed Henry Junior as his successor. BB made record profits in Henry Junior's first year in charge, and the employees were awarded a productivity bonus.

—I'd give the fuckers nothing, said Henry.

The new boss spent a couple of hours a week working on the factory floor. His father remained unimpressed when informed that this was the way the Japs did it, and they were leading the world.

Henry Junior built a big house a mile down the road from The Hacienda. Inside it was luxurious and empty and gave the impression of holding its breath as it waited for a second person to give it full life as a home. His lack of a girlfriend meant he was presumed to be in keen pursuit of a wife. He brought the finest-looking women in the county to dinner dances, was charming to them and never looked for a second date. Henry Junior began to assume the mystique of a boxing champ who had retired undefeated at the height of his powers.

When in Dublin he went to Henry's office but his father was rarely there, so he found himself talking to Martina. Sometimes they laughed so much that she switched on the answering machine. One Friday he arrived as she was shutting the office and asked her to come to Nesbitt's for a drink. They found a snug together and she bought the first round, something she always did to give her the opportunity of an early departure if the talk got tedious.

He had not had a drink for a year and a half, but she did not know this so he took a mouthful of Guinness out of manners. The texture and feel of alcohol brought him back to Florida and he began to shake. He steeled himself to finish the pint before telling Martina he had to leave.

A mixed bouquet arrived at her door the next morning, bearing an apology and an invite to dinner that night. Some flowers in the bunch reminded her of Garda Clarke and made her cry. The dinner was hard going too, awakening feelings she had hoped were dead. They spent that night alone in deep regret for the lost opportunities of the evening and the words and emotions which had remained in romantic limbo.

The word romantic occurred to and surprised both of them.

On Henry Junior's days in Dublin, he and Martina would walk to the National Gallery and look at the Irish paintings on the ground floor. Some special pictures they looked at on every visit, as if the paint transmitted a telepathic message uniquely theirs. A picture of a sorcerer in his study. A ragged boy drilling fellow urchins, military-style. Two trick riders in a circus. And, most special of all, an odd picture of a man and his wife, he coloured a peculiar unwholesome blue, she pale white with breasts exposed.

The portrait had a steadying effect on them. It seemed connected with loss. Both man and wife seemed united by want and stared defiantly from the picture as if proud of their state.

When they slipped into a relationship as easily and naturally as if they were getting up in the morning, they stopped identifying with that picture and walked upstairs where Italian and Spanish old masters throbbed with primary colours.

This was how Henry Junior and Martina felt in the summer of 1988. Two locked rooms. Two keys.

— You make me laugh, she said to him.

Puzzled, he protested that he was not funny and rarely made jokes. But what she meant was that he had released her laughter. Because of Henry Junior she began to laugh at television sitcoms, jokes and some of the strange phone calls she received in the office.

He had trudged around BB as if his time in America was the darkest secret in the world. Martina made him laugh at the idea of himself as a repository of dark urges, making him see that he'd been a young eejit for a bit, but this did not mean he had to spend his life flogging himself with a rope of dullness.

The ghost of Garda Clarke was laid in the bed between them. Martina talked about the man, he had been both good and bad before admitting that what she had been toting around was not him but the memorial which had been built at the fatal crossroads.

Their relationship was not a deliberate secret, but remained hidden because it was inconceivable to the friends and relations urging both of them to end their solitude. When Mary asked Henry Junior to bring his new woman in his life home for the weekend, he and Martina packed with the giddy good humour and sang along with the radio on the drive from Dublin, feeling the expectant sly joy of a yeoman about to leap from his priest's disguise in a 1798 ballad.

Mary wondered out loud why Henry Junior had given Martina a lift down. Dolores said that they hung around together a lot. Dearbhla wondered out loud if everyone was in for a bit of a surprise. Henry said he thought they were.

The evening passed by in a ball of confusion and a tangle of embarrassment. At one stage, Henry heard the phone ring and asked Martina to answer it. She demurred before Henry Junior could demur for her. Still no one had noticed Martina's engagement ring. Henry Junior knew it would be noticed when his father followed him to the kitchen, because his mother would look everywhere in the room except into his fiancée's eyes.

—This can't go on, son.

—I'm sorry, but it will. We're having a great time.

—Don't do this to me.

—I'm doing nothing to you. Anyways, you're always saying I'm nearly gone too sensible.

—You used pass some heed on me.

—Not really. Anyways, I used be a bit of a bollocks.

Mary left for the kitchen as Henry returned to the living-room. Passing him on the way like an overeager tag-team wrestler.

—She's wearing an engagement ring.

—She is all right. I kind of noticed that.

—Henry, in fairness, but she's your father's secretary, that's all she's done since she was eighteen. She's done nothing else the past twelve years.

—And what have I done that's so great, Mam, and I'm nearly as old as her, what? What had Daddy or yourself done at that stage? We're only getting going together.

—Henry, you could have your pick of women from the best of families.

—Mammy, don't talk like that or we'll fall out.

At the wedding reception Henry said

—I'm not so much gaining a daughter as losing a secretary.

Martina gave up her job in Dublin to run Henry's constituency office, and when he stepped down from the County Council, she ran in the local elections and topped the poll. At the count centre he congratulated her and asked where her husband was.

—He's at home minding the baby.

On his first granddaughter's first birthday, Henry pushed her pram around the garden of his son's house, turning to the left to talk about business and the right to talk about politics. The Party had returned to power the day before. The Tough Guy had made Henry Director of Elections.

—Get me elected again. Have whatever you fucking want. I know you're the only fucking fucker who can do it.

Henry was deputy leader of the country now. When people congratulated him, he said

—It's a start.

This was the day that Mary stepped out of the shower and examined her breasts. A hard lump about the size of a pea sat in her right breast. She pressed as if she could make it disappear but she could not. She looked at herself and shed a few tears before throwing on her bathrobe and summoning Henry, trying to ward off panic by telling herself that many of those lumps turned out to be benign. The word benign sounded like a soothing term of endearment, which let a child know it was loved and safe.

The lump was malignant. It was removed, and then her

right breast was removed and even then the cancer reached her pancreas.

—I think we're looking at chemotherapy, Missus Caslin. It's going to be difficult, but I think there's a real chance it will make a difference. Otherwise we wouldn't subject you to it.

When they stopped the chemotherapy she would be either cured or doomed.

Difficult.

School examinations are difficult. It is difficult to get across the street when the lights are orange. It is difficult for the Party to win an overall majority. It is difficult to learn French.

Chemotherapy was not difficult. It was some other word still being minted in Hell.

For the first time Henry saw something which seemed beyond endurance, as if a gate had been opened to some terrible world beyond his ken. Mary's face did not look like her any more. Lines spread out on it like cracks in a midwinter puddle.

She would try to talk sometimes and not be able to. Henry just sat there and spoke to her, or looked at her but this too made her tired. He had to learn to judge when she wanted him to go away, because sometimes she was too weak to raise her hand and signal. According to the doctors, she was doing amazingly well. Each day his eyes sprang back from the first sight of her yellow face.

He faced life without Mary for the first time in years. From time to time he had wondered what it would be like to be old and alone if she went before him, viewing this as an interesting abstraction, one of those harmless what ifs that come into a mind drifting off to sleep. Now he knew that his life would be without meaning. Automatically he did the things which kept him connected to the machinery of power, but he knew that if Mary did not get better they would not matter any more.

Letters arrived from all over and he photocopied them and took them home, looking for a door into the inner sanctuary of illness. The letters were mainly written by women, who seemed to regard ill health as a fact of life. They were not resigned to it but it occurred to them as a possibility, and their tone was not the cheated one of the male correspondents. Those who had been sick told Mary that she should embrace the fact that they had lived.

—It's gone, you know, my breast.

Looking at the bandages, he could not think of one word to say. She giggled weakly, the same giggle he remembered from the drapery when he stood there with a line of girls delighting in his discomfort.

—Dolores and Dearbhla were always on to me to come away to one of those topless beaches. I'll have to give up on the idea now.

In the hospital chapel he spoke to God. This was not the time for the complacent formulae of the last fifty-odd years, so Henry talked to God the way people did when they came to Party clinics looking for jobs, a hand out of trouble or some advice. He asked for Mary's life. Underneath the pleading was a threat. If God let Mary die, then Henry Caslin would withdraw his support.

The doctor did not want to call it a miracle, and pointed out that he had counselled optimism over the past few weeks. All clear.

—I've never seen a woman to fight this like your wife. It could reoccur, but I see no reason that it should.

When he had wheeled her as far as the door of the hospital, Mary said she wanted to walk to the car.

—It might be a long walk.

—I know you, Henry Caslin, by hook or by crook, it's parked near the door.

His wife leaned her right arm on his shoulder. The car was only fifty yards away but the walk took five minutes and she flopped down into the front seat as if she would disappear into it. The thinness of her face made her smile look like it might split her mouth. On the way home she sang along to a tape of showband classics in a little voice which dribbled out as though she were a tap ceding the final drops of water in a drought. She slept through most of her first week home, while Henry paced round the house and wondered how anyone could ever inflict harm on another human being when it must cause such pain to others. He became deeply affected by news of the killings in the North.

The crowd at Second Mass on Sunday cheered when they walked in and took their place at the front. When they fell to their knees to pray for special intentions, Henry felt the force of Mary's silent words shake the pew.

They had always been religious, but her time in hospital had left Mary surrounded with the regalia of faith beyond reason. She and Henry cleared underwear from a drawer and installed the relics she had received. A bone from the finger of St Francis of Assisi, a rose petal from the Garden of Gethsemane, wood from the Cross, a piece of cloth from the cloak of Padre Pio. Who was to say?

Preparing for the constituency dinner dance, Henry heard a rustling behind him. Mary was there in a dress he had not seen before, trying to fasten a diamond necklace.

—You're not coming.

—I am.

—Is that a new dress?

—It's Dearbhla's, it's nice, isn't it? There's not enough of me at the moment to fill one of my own. Will you put this necklace on me, my fingers are still a bit slack.

He walked behind his wife and held her for a minute before placing the necklace around her neck, regarding the bones there and the skin stretched over them. And, although she was far thinner than he could have imagined a year ago, this did look like Mary's neck. He could have picked it out if shown a photograph.

—Henry, hurry up, please. We're not having this caper of making up time on the road.

The point of power was that it was supposed to place everything in your life under control. Henry had believed that he could shelter the people he loved behind money and a big house standing like a fortress against the unexpected life, until cancer laughed at him and told him there was chaos which no one could control. Cancer was within everyone and would strike if it wished. Henry wanted to fight back against the forces of death. He studied the papers for evidence of their triumph, the front page telling of their victory in the North, the notices inside the back page telling of their more mundane successes. Was the North as intractable as cancer? Powered by invisible forces which would do as they willed. The fact that he had never saved anyone's life in a world where extinction was everywhere seemed like an indictment. He wondered if it had been a failure of concentration.

It was television which began to undo Father Gerry Lee, beaming the outside world unmediated into the parishes where he had served, showing pictures of English people who had interfered with their own children, and reports from America of priests being jailed for sexual assaults on altar servers. No one liked watching these reports, but in some houses they stirred up memories of hints and stories from the past.

A man watched a television drama about an American orphanage where children had been abused by priests. He began to roar when it ended and put his foot through the television screen. A woman the same age sobbed her way through the programme and dosed herself with sleeping pills when it ended. She hung on to life in hospital and talked in the hope of preventing herself from trying again. In Father Lee's parish, the wounded began to band together outside the orbit of the Church, scared that if he addressed a meeting he could persuade others and maybe even themselves that he was being traduced. He would berate them for the tawdriness of their minds and their naïve susceptibility to conspiracy and whispering campaigns. They met in small houses and told stories to persuade themselves that they were not to blame, finally deciding to talk to the RUC.

Hunter had three files full of information. He informed each victim of this as they gave uneasy evidence. These files traced a long poisonous line of ruined innocence through the years. The families hoped for retribution but despaired of satisfaction. They had taken the power and the love of the Church out from under themselves. Their truth was a difficult one.

His ability to read the moods of his parishioners was one of Father Lee's outstanding qualities, so when the RUC arrived with a warrant for his arrest on charges of sexual assault against minors, he was driving over the border on a back road used by the IRA, cattle smugglers and young lads on their way home from dances who wanted to avoid UDR patrols.

One of Father Lee's heroes had been Father Morse, a Catholic priest pursued by Protestants in seventeenth-century England who had escaped to Europe but then returned to battle the plague and was captured, horribly tortured and executed. The parallels between their stories had inclined Father Lee towards an unprecedented faith in coincidence, as he too was being pursued by Protestants on account of his religion and forced to battle a plague which filled the world with filth, decay and blind panic. The plague of accusation, lies and treachery. Father Lee had enough of guilt, and would not surrender to the pointing fingers of traitors.

In the American-style motel where he first fetched up you could hear the neighbours moving behind the thin walls. Father Lee wore his collar and was greeted heartily in the morning by the owner, who sat at the front desk under a Pallottine Missions calendar. At breakfast he noticed his fellow guests looking strangely at him, snapped off his collar, put it in his bag and drove further south to a town where he rented a room over a pub.

His neighbours there were a lost tribe. Men thrown out by their wives, recovering alcoholics, those struggling to find a space away from the voices in their heads, unmarried mothers like the woman in the room next to him, whom he considered to have far too many male visitors even before the night he found her weeping on the stairs with a handkerchief held to a slightly bleeding mouth. The yellow and purple fossils of old bruises, either blows or bites, soiled her neck.

—Bastards, they're all fucking bastards.

She was scared to go back to her room, so Father Lee brought her to his and offered her a glass of whiskey. She finished the bottle, and by three in the morning was more cheerful.

—I suppose you'd better go back to your room.

—I don't want to.

Her arms were around him. He, recoiled, but fell across the bed.

—You were awful good to me John. Thanks.

She rolled down her trousers before crawling towards him, holding her cleft apart with her fingers.

—Do you like this, John? Have this, John, go on.

The sight filled him with horror. It was nothing he had ever wanted from a female body. He tried to think of his little girls and their tiny perfection and still this hairy, marked, imperfect incision swelled until it made him scream.

Trying to calm himself down, he told the woman that she should pray, that this was no life for her, addressing her as my child, beginning to say the rosary.

—A priest, a priest, oh yeah, I fucking see, I'm not surprised, she said as she gathered her clothes on the way out the door.

All night Father Lee gripped his pillow in terror of her body, and longed for the sweet innocence of the girls and boys he had left behind. The mysteriously remembered cry of a curlew haunted his fitful sleep. In the morning he said his office and realised that he was a martyr like those who had hidden in priest holes or ventured across fields in the dead of night to bear witness to the one true faith at Mass rocks in spite of dungeon, fire and sword.

Blue movies were shown most nights in the pub downstairs, and Father Lee would regard them disinterestedly when cold or loneliness had driven him from his room in the early hours of the morning. Sometimes there were women who though not young enough in reality, achieved the right appearance by careful deployment of school uniforms, teddy bears, hair ribbons, dolls and other paraphernalia. The man with a straggly beard and red eyes engaged him in conversation one morning as the television was turned off.

—I liked that one tonight, John. It was good. Especially that young one at the end. She looked very young, didn't she? How old would you say she was, maybe only fourteen, or what? Did you enjoy it, did you?

—I did. I liked the film with her in it.

—I noticed that about you. You like the ones with the young women in them. It's a pity they're not a bit younger, though. That'd be good, wouldn't it?

—It would be good all right. You don't get to see younger ones though, do you?

—It's good to meet you.

The envelope pushed under his door the next day held magazines which Father Lee perused with nostalgia. He and the man with the beard began to watch the films together. Eschewing the shouting and banter of the other customers, they observed the videos with the patient detachment of critics.

Father Lee was reading his *Imitation of Christ* one night when there came a knock on the door.

—Oh, did you want those magazines back? I'm sorry, I didn't know.

—Whatever you say, say nothing when you talk about you-know-what. Follow me. There's a cab downstairs.

The taxi driver parked the cab and accompanied them to an old house at the very back of a housing estate.

—We always find each other, John.

The videos were cheaply made and often soundless, but Father Lee felt compensated by the joy of finding a group of understanding people before the sight of a squad car parked outside the house a month later propelled him back to his room. He packed his bag and travelled to a monastery where a friend of his was in residence, explaining to the abbot that he needed time alone for meditation and contemplation. His request was granted.

Some of the families were becoming unsure about going to court. Similar cases had been thrown out because the alleged offences had happened so long ago. They talked about moving on and forgetting, not because they wanted to move on and forget but because they did not want to reveal the dripping wounds at the centre of the lives without being sure that Father Lee would definitely be convicted and receive a heavy jail sentence.

Hunter was sure that Father Lee was in the South, safe there in a society run by the Roman Church and where priests had greater power than politicians or policemen. He was not so keen on Northern Catholics, either. They didn't use contraception, so they could spawn enough brats to make a killing off the State and then they didn't look after them properly, leaving them to roam around at the mercy of the likes of Father Lee. This was how he had felt at the start of the investigation before he'd met the families and seen how the eyes were driven back in their head with pain. Whatever religion people were, you couldn't blame their wee kids for meeting the likes of your man. He phoned the Department of Justice in the South and asked if they'd had any complaints about the priest.

—There's a lot of this stuff being reported. I don't know, I think these days you'd want to be careful of patting a child on the head in case you'd be charged with sex abuse.

Hunter gave exact details of what Father Lee had done. There were no head-patting charges.

—Send me the papers. If he's down here, I'll see about getting an extradition warrant ready.

The news of Father Lee's depredations had been personally shattering to his old friend Cardinal O'Hanlon, but there were wider ramifications also. The Church had begun to fight back against the purveyors of contraception, divorce and abortion, but the outcome of the battle remained in the balance. His flock were wavering, but Cardinal O'Hanlon felt he could rally them with assertions that exemplary sexual morality made the Irish different. Cases like Father Lee's could ruin everything. Being perceived as stern or dictatorial did not hurt the Church. But it could not afford to appear hypocritical.

There had always been whispers but admissions of guilt had not been an option, so priests with those tendencies were moved around the country to prevent them from developing attachments to particular children. As if what had happened was a freakish occurrence, and the children involved were not completely free of blame.

The cardinal could not see how the Church could be blamed for the prevalence of these offences. They had warned against the sexualising of the world by the mass media. Was it any wonder that even men of the cloth had begun to be suborned? He had been informed of Father Lee's arrival at the monastery. The man was safe there. There were ways of preventing scandal. Taking away someone's good name was a sin. Logic justified dealing with this situation in secret, and logic had always been one of the cardinal's favourite disciplines.

The sight of water pouring over a crying child's head made McKeon share a communal silent shout of joy before he plunged back into the despair which enveloped him at the sight of ceremonies connected with the married life. The first-born of the station's Industrial Editor was being baptised in the University Church by a priest whose sermon on the evils of the media was greeted by giggles rather than outrage.

People roamed puzzled outside the chapel like American soldiers in 'Nam waiting to be airlifted out of the combat zone. McKeon cadged a lift in a small car with too many passengers.

—Hang on, we'll squeeze in one more. She can go on McKeon's knees.

Why had his generation grown up so young? Was it an ongoing process, which would continue as a geometric progression until two or three generations down the line people spent their years in eternal childhood? His father's generation had worn suits, approached events with a ritual and fitting seriousness and maintained a solemn dignity underwritten by universally acknowledged rules. He, on the other hand, was in a casual jacket and jeans after a ceremony he had been unable to follow, crushed into the back seat of a car with someone the same age as himself about to sit on his knees as if they were sixteen-year-olds on the way to a disco. When the back door opened, there was a shuffling of buttocks across the seat which made no extra space available but did indicate a communal welcome.

—Come in if you're good-looking. Jesus.
—Do I count, Seamus?
—Moira. Fuck's sake.
—That's some answer.

He wanted to tell her she was good-looking, but the car lurched forward and he bit down on his tongue. The journey to the christening party was taken up concentrating on the pain, while a Joni Mitchell tape dispelled the need for conversation.

The wine came from the Lebanon, smelt like pig slurry and tasted deep and earthy, as if it had been extracted from clay or found preserved after a thousand years like bog butter. McKeon chased it down with cheeses of various hues and slimy textures and looked round for Moira, cursing himself for losing sight of her after she had skipped out of the car to plant kisses on the cheeks of the proud mother.

Dylan songs were being played, too many of them about the confusion of love for McKeon's liking so he stepped into the back garden and shinned over the wall, landing himself on the walk by the canal.

He knew the sight of the water should be soothing but it never had been. Patrick Kavanagh had written beautiful words about this very stretch of the canal, but McKeon could not connect them with his own feelings. Perhaps it was a fault in himself. Watching the water, he waited for something to appear. A duck, a swan, even a floating tin can with a brand name visible on the side. Something to read. When he stood in front of landscapes, he looked for human figures no matter how small, and made them the centre of the painting. The water and the sky were maybe what he should have been looking at all along.

Someone slipped as they came down the walk, sending a couple of stones into the water. Moira.

—I shouted over to you, but you didn't hear me. I've been looking for you the whole time at the party. I had to get away from Bob Dylan.

—So. How's life beyond?

Life beyond was grand. She was working in a London radio station, producing a phone-in show with a legendarily rude host.

—Anyone on the scene, or any crack that way?

A couple of brief flings, but nothing that even hinted at permanence. She had resigned herself to living life on her own and bought glossy magazines which made the condition seem if not desirable, then at least bearable.

—And you know, yourself. I mean it's different for you here, I'd say.

The lie crossed his mind before he confessed his lone state.

—If you see any men's magazines over there which make it sound like a good way to be, I'd love to read them.

—You know what we are, Seamus. The pair of us. We're used people. Once we were shiny and new, but we've done everything now, we've had our time on the road and we're wrung out and tired out. No one is ever going to mistake us for new again.

—Well maybe what one used person needs is another used person. I used to look at scrapyards when I was a young lad, mad into cars. When the old models are together they suit each other. They make it look as though it's the cars on the road that are the odd ones out.

—Seamus McKeon, you're trying to chat me up.

—Can I ask you to come home with me tonight? I just want to do it before I get drunk and you get drunk and we persuade ourselves that's why we did it. Because we are going to get drunk.

—We are going to get drunk.

—I've had a good day, you know. I've just made sense of Patrick Kavanagh. Twenty years too late.

—See you at the end of the night.

Dublin parties had a swirl about them which McKeon liked. It was as if you were trapped in an abstract expressionist painting. Time, talk, drink, the whole shebang just careered around you until people got tired and worked out where they wanted to settle. Occasionally out of the corner of his eye he saw Moira rearing up like a figure on a ghost train. They did not look at each other, because they were safe in the knowledge that when the music stopped they would leave together and their friends would look on with expressions suggesting that something not altogether unexpected had happened.

Both of them felt the desire for flight between the hours of four and five in the morning. McKeon killed his by reminding himself that he was at home. Moira remembered she had not got around to booking a hotel room.

—In London, you know, people who worked together all seem to have fallen into the sack with each other at sometime. There's all this easy history between everyone which is a bit disquieting at first.

—And then it's kind of comforting.

—It is. Really.

—You know, your voice sounds very London sometimes.

—I think I'll go back to sleep.

McKeon thought about getting up, but instead watched the red numbers change on the digital clock beside the bed.

He had never slept with a woman for this long without having sex, but knew Moira would make her move in her own good time. The phone rang and the answering machine intercepted the interruptions of the outside world, all the untold stories from the party being choked back into throats when his imprisoned voice came on, all the recriminations, all the queries about behaviour, people looking for reassurance rather than genuine information, all the boasting of telling quips and arguments which the callers had just thought of this morning.

Above all, sentences would wait like blackboards inviting the inscription of the previous night's secrets, sentences containing loaded comments about the hair, conversation and past of Moira Hopkins.

—You know, once I would never have done anything like that.

—Once you weren't interested in me.

—No, once you were my friend, Seamus. It wouldn't have occurred to us. We would have felt this had effected some huge chemical change in our relationship. One that couldn't be reversed.

—And now it hasn't?

—Now it doesn't have to. Maybe there is more to this than sex and loneliness. But that doesn't have to follow automatically.

The next morning Moira flew back. McKeon phoned her at work that afternoon but her answering machine was on, and when it spoke to him five more times in the next week he began to curse a world where human contact could be evaded so easily. She had handed him her card at the airport, and he had not thought to ask for her home number. He limited his phone calls to one a day so as not to appear too keen, but by the end of the week an anxious tone had invaded his voice. He left his number on her machine each time and after the third call asked her to ring him.

—Ring me, he said instead of using the indirect formulation he had employed on the first couple of occasions.

—It would be nice to hear from you.

—If you want to give me a shout . . .

A week after his first call she rang him back, explaining that she had taken the week off after her trip to Dublin and had not checked her messages. It was half eleven. She must have been back in the office for two hours. McKeon felt slightly cheated, as if he had been forced into making an avoidable declaration with his five phone calls. He prevented himself from ringing back that afternoon, though he wanted to very much and the next day was a busy one.

An IRA bomb blew up a crowd of people attending a Remembrance Day service at Enniskillen. People remembered their thoughts from the time of the hunger strike and felt ashamed, as though they had wished for this bombing. The next day McKeon rang Moira and asked if he could come over for the weekend.

—No.

—Oh.

—No, it's not that sort of no. It's just that James is sick and I'm looking after him and I don't want anyone here while he's here. It's just how I feel.

—Oh, I see. I think there's a call on my other line.

—He's going away with his school in a couple of weeks' time, skiing. So if you wanted to come over.

—It's a date.

—I mean, I could end up working a lot that weekend, but I'm sure there's plenty of other things you could do in London.

She did not end up working a lot that weekend and he had not expected her to but he was grateful that she had signposted the escape route in advance.

In London, they walked through parks decorated with uncomfortable benches dedicated to the memory of long-dead philanthropists. They watched a musical where a helicopter landed on stage at the finale. They stepped past inefficient fire-eaters in Covent Garden and listened to the bad-luck story of a wino from Sligo who had danced, drunk and courted in Rathbawn but was unsure which county it was in. They made love for hours with self-consciousness adding to the act instead of detracting from it, as it would have with people who knew each other less.

In the kitchen, Moira sang and McKeon recognised the song as River by Joni Mitchell, which had been playing on the car stereo when she opened the door outside the University Church. He spoke the words of the song slowly to himself as his plane took off into a squid-ink London sky.

On his tenth trip in three months to London, Moira brought him to a party in a Notting Hill flat where an old colleague celebrated the launch of a sex-and-shopping best-seller. The author cornered McKeon early in the evening.

—How long have you been seeing Moira?

—Three months.

—I'm delighted for both of you, especially for her. She's a new woman. I don't suppose it's news to you that she has had the hots for you for the last fifteen years. She told me so tonight.

The party eventually broke up into little cliques interested in sampling a selection of drugs which McKeon did not want to touch, not for moral or health reasons but because he was not sure what was to be snorted, what to be licked and what to be swallowed. He and Moira took a taxi to an Irish restaurant because the idea of one intrigued them. Waiting for the meal, Moira tried to light a cigarette, broke it in half and let one perfect pear-shaped tear tunnel through her make-up.

—I don't like the way you're treating me tonight.

They had never had an argument, and he suddenly realised how rare and precious this was.

—Sorry love, I don't know what you mean.

He had not called her love before. He had called her Moira, and when that sounded too formal constructed little guttural combinations of manly vowels to attract her attention.

—Tonight you're treating me as if you're doing me a favour by going out with me. Completely. I don't want you to do that.

—I don't think I'm doing you a favour by going out with you. This is very important to me.

Listening to himself more clearly than ever before, he still could not hear what he thought should be said. Moira looked at him as though a smaller and quieter voice was trying to make itself heard under his.

—Moira, I love you, I love you, that is what I have to say.

—Seamus, you can't just solve things by saying that. You don't have to say it to me, that's not why I was upset. It's OK.

—No, I love you, I love . . .

The circling motion of his arm seemed to indicate the restaurant, but he meant it to enclose him and her and the whole city and above all the whole three months.

—I love this. I love us. I love you. Can't we try and do something about that?

—What is there to do?

Black rain slanted down when McKeon picked Moira up at Dublin Airport. The weather was the worst of their six months together. Young James fell asleep in the back seat, while Moira talked about being back at the station and asked questions about the old gang and what they thought of her return. McKeon answered for a few minutes until they fell silent, hugging to themselves the language of personal bravery like members of a warrior band who have lopped down a bridge and watched it fall into the river behind them so that retreat is now impossible.

Had McKeon taken up with a teenager, people would have nodded their heads sagely and asked what did you expect from a man of his age? Instead they said

—Marriage, yeah, do you need to?

—Marriage. You're what . . . forty-two? Moira must be forty. Yeah, I suppose.

He had known his friends long enough for their dissembling to be clearer to him than their direct statements, and what they were really saying was

—You're too old for this marriage crack, Seamus. Old, old, old. Why are ye doing it now? Is it not a bit unseemly?

Young James had a gift for asking awkward questions the way others had for healing, second sight or doctoring horses.

—Why are you getting married in a church when neither of you ever goes to Mass?

—Ha, ha, good question, James.

—But why?

Because the faith stayed in the tracks and grooves of your mind, and when you were under pressure from happiness or sadness or uncertainty it came back like a relapse of malaria to a returned missionary. He and Moira told people that since one sacrament, the baptism had brought them together, their decision was made on the grounds of nostalgia. They fooled no one, but nostalgia was the reason they purchased a house by the canal and filled it with five thousand books, twenty years of memories and more love than McKeon had ever imagined possible.

One note jarred and jangled in his head. When Moira talked about the four on-and-off years with Mickey Kelly, she did not deny one iota of the love, the torment or the ecstasy she had felt, even revealing that one night after Kelly had told her he would never leave his wife, she swallowed sleeping pills and washed them down with half a bottle of whiskey.

—What happened?

—Well, obviously I didn't die, love. I just had the worst hangover for three days. I think the whiskey came closest to doing the job.

He wanted her to disown the affair, to explain that she had not been in her right mind, that it had been an aberration, that Kelly had some sinister hold over her, had indulged in some form of blackmail which was what made her sleep with him and spend those nights screaming across the Dodo as the other customers laughed.

Moira considered doing this before deciding that the man she loved was strong enough to bear the truth, even if he thought he was not and flayed himself with visions of her and Kelly in a past which was always more spectacular and more interesting than his life with his wife in the house by the canal.

They both knew that he wanted her to admit to the former existence of a different and lesser Moira, to whom he could make the magnanimous gesture of forgiveness, a gesture which would make him feel superior and sow the seeds of the marriage's destruction. So there was no apology, and her honesty killed his pity and impelled his respect even as his hatred of Kelly grew and became polished like the small stones he had once seen in a French cave, worn away by hundreds of thousands of years of dripping water until they were as clear and hard as pearls.

Understanding James took longer, because McKeon initially suffered the childless man's delusion that all kids are four years of age, leaving him unprepared to deal with a sixteen-year-old whose favourite word was sad, one he frequently applied to McKeon's work as the trio watched the six o'clock news.

—That's a sad story.

—You're sad, Seamus.

—That news is really sad.

Sad meant the lowest of the low, contemptible, piteous, a ridiculous job for a grown man, and only love kept McKeon sitting at the table and listening to a sixteen-year-old belittling his life's work. His paternal urges dwindled rapidly and his jaw began to ache from the set smile with which he reacted to James's comments.

He had thought Moira's love for him would make James love him too. This would have been true had James been a dog. McKeon eventually decided to treat James like any other male adversary, responding to James's comments about his boring TV delivery and conservative taste in clothes with barbs about the teenager's lack of a girlfriend, lunar facial surface and exclusion from the adult world.

Relaxed by a rivalry he could understand, McKeon thought of possible bonding rites between a man and a teenage son and came up with the likes of flying model aeroplanes, watching radio-controlled boats sink in public park ponds and going potholing together. He read American short stories about the joys of cross-generational hunting and realised the buddy points earned by the shooting of a bunny rabbit were hardly worth the trudging through the rain and chances of shooting off your hand while carrying shotguns across gates. His decision was made for him when he found out that James played chess.

—I whupped yo' ass, said McKeon after their first game.

He had taken to mimicking James's attempts at American rap lingo.

—Fuck off, said James, and managed to win the next one.

Chess became their point of contact and, as in all great

affairs, each discovered surprising qualities in the other which had just needed to be awakened by the right partner. At the chessboard the diffident, slackerish James became a mean, competitive fucker with a visceral need to win. James would occasionally wonder who his cerebral opponent was before remembering it was the bogman his mother had unaccountably foisted upon his life.

When the weather was good they brought the board to Stephen's Green, which the black-obsessed James was convinced would be thronged with lightning-fast Jamaican hobo chess geniuses. They played regardless of the absence of these street grandmasters. Best of five. Best of seven. Best of nine. Best of eleven. When they finished, McKeon would hit the pub, but on his own at the bar would feel suddenly cheated, like a man who wakes up alone in bed with just a few mnemonic female pubic hairs for company. He began bringing James with him, and realised that the price for knowing the boy occasionally involved becoming his ally against Moira. The odd sneaked pint, the very odd late trip home for dinner and the purchase of a rap album emblazoned with Parental Guidance stickers didn't bother Moira, as she saw the two men she loved uniting their lives to make her happy.

THE NINETIES

The decade changed, and the Party stayed in government. But just about. The Tough Guy could not gain a clear majority because the public did not trust him, and according to the polls wanted a more loveable Taoiseach, an updated version of the Man With The Pipe. As far as Henry, Mickey Kelly and Jimmy could see this meant they wanted Henry. One of the business magazines had named him best ever Minister for Finance. He'd won the award for best-dressed TD. And most efficient. When your time comes, your time comes. The Tough Guy would have to go for the sake of the Party and country because no one liked him any more, and he had begun to speak in a slow, wasted drone which made it sound like he agreed with them.

Once, challenging the leader of the Party would have been as unthinkable as raising a hand against the God of the Old Testament. The Party founder had been in charge for forty years, leading seven governments before becoming President when he was no longer fit for active politics. Henry had seen him on that presidential campaign, an octogenarian addressing the crowds in Rathbawn like the national spirit come to life. He had been condemned to death in the Easter Rising, fought an economic war with the Brits, kept Ireland neutral in the Second World War and said, 'When I want to know what the Irish people are thinking, I look into my own heart.' He had made it impossible for the electorate to distinguish between country and Party.

And because he had been the greatest of politicians, he had even schooled a successor, passing on to him the exact nature of the secret electoral bond between Party and people. When the successor retired suddenly near the end of the sixties, the Man With The Pipe became the leader of a Party in shock. It was as though we had tired of heroes, Henry thought, and opted for someone whose defining quality was his lack of definition. His very paucity of personality meant that when people looked at him they thought of the old leader instead, and continued to vote for the Party.

All the same, Henry and the others had conspired against him. If asked why, Henry would have answered truthfully, because we could. The Man With The Pipe's overthrow was his own fault. Had he been stronger, no one would have dared to challenge him. Like a householder who does not close windows or bolt doors, his downfall had been partly his own responsibility.

But it had been the Tough Guy who had broken the unwritten rule and challenged the leader. In doing so he had laid the foundations of his own ruin. From now on, every Party leader would be challenged, would spend every day wondering which lieutenant was poised to turn against them.

The Tough Guy might have gone anyway. Henry could not look at him any more without thinking of McCarrick's broken arm, of the bottles on Joan Brosnan's windscreen, of tape machines and buggings and threats and obscenities and bullying, which in the end made him sorry, not for himself or his colleagues but for the country itself. He was a patriot and did not think the nation mean-spirited enough to deserve the Tough Guy as leader.

Kelly thought it was a pity you couldn't replace leaders the way Brutus had but you couldn't, so Henry had to go into a parliamentary party meeting and inform the Tough Guy that he would be standing against him. Several deputies cheered and Henry looked round the room, ticking off the votes he could depend on. The Tough Guy was finished. Henry hoped he might resign and go out with dignity before the next month's ballot. The Tough Guy answered this suggestion *sotto voce*.

—You're not going to win, Caslin, you fucker. You don't fucking want it fucking enough. I fucking need this, and you fucking won't take it fucking off me.

—Do you want to play this fair and square? asked Kelly.

—Because we don't have to, said Jimmy.

—Party leader and Taoiseach are jobs you have to be elected to honourably, said Henry with complete and naive sincerity.

All the bookies made him hot favourite. He did not know what the Tough Guy had been on about. Henry wanted power more than anything except the love and good health of his family.

Except. The fatal except which was not in the Tough Guy's vocabulary when power was mentioned. The letters began to arrive at The Hacienda the next day. Addressed to

—Henry Fart Caslin.

The childishness was what worried Henry. It made it difficult to get inside the mind of the senders of these anonymous epistles filled with foul abuse and written in the same tone, a kind of spite recalling the jabberings of a jilted teenager. All the letters expressed their support for the Tough Guy.

—Dear Arse-bollocks.

—Dear Cunt.

—It's a pity that your wife did not die roaring of cancer, or maybe it was Aids that she had and got it off you.

Razor blades, pieces of glass and dead rats were calmly placed in envelopes and sent to Henry by people whom he knew were members of the Party. The thought made him nauseous. When an important supporter rang to withdraw from the campaign, Henry and Jimmy took a taxi to the man's office, interrupting a meeting to find out what was going on.

—Look Henry, I'm a solicitor and my biggest account is with an insurance company. Without them I'd go under. They've told me if I don't support the Tough Guy they'll take away their business.

—And you don't have any more guts than that?

—Not when it comes to my livelihood, no, Henry. You're OK, you're rich.

Rich enough to withstand the lost orders at BB Baby Foods, though this did not make them any less painful. Jimmy prepared a brief showing which deputies were susceptible to financial pressure, and then watched as one by one they proclaimed their support for the Tough Guy. On the News, McKeon reported that the Tough Guy was launching a spirited comeback against his challenger.

Men in white vans tailed both Dolores and Dearbhla home and warned them that they could easily be taken out. Henry hired a firm of private detectives to keep an eye on his daughters, and when they reported no sightings of the white vans realised the Tough Guy's men had moved on to the daughters of the undecided deputies.

Two more strong supporters appeared on television, begging him to withdraw from the contest. The private detectives told Henry that one man had fallen in love with a call girl and asked her to marry him before she pointed out that he was already hitched to a woman whose family funded his political career. Photos and tapes were in the Tough Guy's possession, as was an affidavit from a rent boy who regularly serviced the second supporter in the Phoenix Park and had been provided with the phone number of a tabloid journalist. Henry's Director of Elections was on the front pages the next day, reported to the Medical Council by a colleague concerned that the man's drinking was affecting his work.

—Mud sticks, said Jimmy, annoyed that Henry would not sanction a trawl through the sex lives of the Tough Guy's supporters, and relieved that Henry Junior had gone as far as America to make an ass of himself.

Kelly stayed loyal. His persona was so bound up with legends of prodigious sexual and alcoholic misdemeanour that the most shocking thing the Tough Guy's people could have done was produce evidence of sobriety and marital fidelity. But he was a rare exception and only the fact that the bookies could not have known how vigorous the Tough Guy's campaign had been left Henry as favourite. On the day of the ballot, he looked at the tops of his former supporters' heads as they scrutinised the ground.

—However this turns out, Henry, no hard feelings; it's been a good tough campaign, said the Tough Guy.

—He's telling you he's fucked you, explained Kelly.

The cheering and jeering of the Tough Guy's supporters outside the meeting lodged in Henry's ears like burning wax. Looking at them, he tried to put faces to the letters and the phone calls and the stalking of his daughters, but gave up because the people all looked normal to him. He had expected some sort of twisted grimaces, and this was why he had lost, because he could not see what the Tough Guy had turned the Party into. On television McKeon employed his usual adulatory clichés about the winner.

—Like a cat with nine political lives . . . his epitaph has yet to be written . . . the wily old warrior . . . the king of survivors.

Kelly and Henry were given half an hour to clear their ministerial offices. When Henry finished packing he drove home to get ready for the funeral of the oldest priest in the county.

There was always an amount of priests at a peer funeral, mainly old stagers viewing the coffin with trepidation and shivering no matter what the weather was like. Henry wondered why someone who had dedicated his life to faith, like Cardinal O'Hanlon, seemed disinclined to view the funeral as being in any way a celebration. The cardinal seemed just as upset by Father O'Reilly's passing as any of the other mourners. The throng of priests made a black cloud which drifted impressively, forebodingly, miserably across the churchyard, their feet seeming to float above the ground.

At the graveside Jimmy was nervous. The Tough Guy was a new man since he'd defeated Henry. On the radio he'd gone on about vanquishing traitors and warning that those who had wanted to split the Party would not be forgiven, even wondering out loud if his rivals were backed by members of the British secret services keen to depose a leader who refused to kowtow to their government.

—Now who is going to listen to that, it's pure daft, Jimmy.

—You've said the odd daft thing yourself in your time, Henry.

—I have, but no one ever believed me.

Snow began to fall as Father O'Reilly's coffin was lowered into the ground. The gravediggers looked ruefully at each other as they realised they would have a bitch of an afternoon trying to chip through the freezing earth. The flakes drifted almost apologetically downwards and melted as they touched the mourners, leaving them with soggy faces which felt as though they were disintegrating. The snow became a dusting on the ground, formed little hillocks on cars and threw a faint smokescreen in front of the people, who looked back at the two men with shovels blowing on their nails and preparing to tuck the dead man out of sight.

The drill was always the same at the funerals; Henry would stand ten yards outside the main gate with Jimmy just behind him. As the people approached, Jimmy stepped into their eye line and gave them the nod, which let them know Henry wanted to shake their hand. Double coverage, the Yanks might have called it.

The first man to emerge from the graveyard looked at Henry's outstretched hand and made a point of ignoring it, walking on to where Party deputies from neighbouring constituencies waited and shaking their hands with unusual vigour. Those deputies smiled smugly at Henry as if they had something to do with this, but he knew they had not. His people could not be intimidated or cajoled. They just knew to back a winner. Party supporters kept walking past Henry until Jimmy was wondering if this was some nightmare where people of all colours and creeds would come out of the churchyard, Pakis and blacks and Spanish, and none of them wanting to shake Henry's hand.

Henry could not put his hand in his pocket because that would be an admission of defeat. He left it out, and the cold turned it pink and then blue. So people could see the hand they were refusing to shake, and that he would leave there for the night if he wanted to. Snow piled up in lumps on his coat and coloured his hair white, but he remained there with Jimmy until everyone had passed through the gate, started cars with difficulty and driven away with their exhausts exhaling long streamers of smoke.

Jimmy took Henry's hand and tucked it back into the pocket of his coat.

—It can't go on like this, you know.

—I know.

—We have to beat the Tough Guy. Whatever way we can, that's all there is to it and all there need be to it.

—You're right. You know what today was, Jimmy? Today is what it's like to be out of favour. Maybe we needed to remember what that's like.

—Aye. But fuck them for giving us the reminder.

—We'll have to go back to Jim's Place.

—We can start tonight.

They were there that night and a month later with Kelly and three young TDs whose first courting experiences had been in discos rather than ballrooms. They reminded Henry of himself at the same age, gamblers backing what looked like the wrong horse if you didn't have the inside track.

Spread on the table were the morning's newspapers, with Tim Brennan's sacking as head of Pricecutter on the front pages. Brennan was only in the front door of his house two seconds when Jimmy phoned to remind him of their old deal.

—It's all the same to you now, Tim.

Everyone held their breath for a few seconds after reading the documents Jimmy handed round. Even Henry. A person who had spent years peering through an observatory telescope and sending radio messages out into the ether would still feel shocked if their predictions of alien life came true. Jimmy remembered how they had once sworn never to use these papers because the risk of damage to the Party was too great, just before Brennan walked in from the kitchen of Jim's Place to explain exactly what they meant.

For years he had paid large sums of money to politicians. The more powerful they were, the better they got paid. His reasons for paying were open to interpretation. Perhaps he hoped the politicians would help his company with changes in tax laws and employment legislation, and ensure that planning laws were not followed to the letter when new shopping centres with Pricecutter as anchor tenant were built. Or perhaps he felt that large, under-the-counter payments to politicans helped the democratic process.

It was all a matter of opinion.

No one had taken more money than the Tough Guy. Even Henry had found this hard to believe until he saw the proof. He had known that the man was ruthless, dishonest and egotistical, and suspected he was stupid. But he would have sworn blind he was really rich. Instead, the island, the wolfhounds, the paintings, the racehorses, all the accoutrements of the lush life had not been paid for by the Tough Guy but by Tim Brennan. The Tough Guy had been like a gossan getting pocket money from his father.

—He's started begging off me lately, said Brennan.

The Tough Guy had become careless enough to call to Brennan's house, promising all kinds of favours if the level of payments was upped. Reality seemed to have escaped on him.

—Sometimes I think he thinks I owe him the money.

No tax had been paid on the money, and some of it had been hidden offshore, but Henry knew that people would not be outraged by this. What would get their goat was the realisation that they had been diddled and that a man whose sublimal slogan was, 'I might be a bollocks but I'm a rich bollocks, and I'll make ye all rich too', was not rich at all, although his status as a bollocks was now without question. Jimmy explained that the Tough Guy would not admit anything, but there were bank records and cheque stubs and a couple of witnesses for starters.

They started small when they rang the journalists. The first names were those of minor politicans from other parties. The Tough Guy was not mentioned by name, but hints were dropped of bigger fish to be fried. In the Dáil, an Independent deputy who had secured election by promising his followers free cable television, asked the Tough Guy if he'd taken any of the Brennan money.

—I am disgusted that the leader of this country would be asked a question like that. I am surprised at you, and shocked by the gall of this imputation.

The deputy would have sat down in a hurry had he not noticed Henry Caslin looking encouragingly at him.

—Are you saying, then, that you didn't take any of that money?

—I am. Categorically.

Henry poured himself a glass of champagne that night, which he looked at and did not drink. The day's events had seemed to demand the pouring.

The Brennan affair was a bit like an early model of the machine-gun. It would probably get the intended target, but might hit a few more besides. Henry checked with Kelly.

—Mickey. Are you going to come up as taking the Brennan money?

—I'm not, Henry. There's no way.

—I don't want to make a liar out of you, so I'll not ask you if you got it.

Tribunals were a fashion in those uneasy years at the start of the new decade. Tribunals and referendums, exemplary vehicles of delay and obfuscation. McKeon saw them as a national declaration of difference from the country above, where people had tried to make things happen and chaos and ruin had resulted.

The Tough Guy announced a tribunal to hear Tim

Brennan's evidence and then, trapped, heard Brennan and his accountant detail how they had handed cheques to him.

At first he skulked around his island like Caliban and denied the charges. When the documentary evidence turned up, he appeared at Dublin Castle and apologised for his bad memory. Back on the island he took to walking at night with his dog, too disheartened to shoot anything. Taking fivers from his pocket, he would set them on fire and mutter that if people could see him now, they'd know he had plenty of money. He shredded files and burned letters but the damage was done. The radio waves from the island carried messages to the Tough Guy's friends in business as he sought to lay down stepping stones for a dignified retreat. A dozen secretaries were instructed to stress just how 'not in' their bosses were. One morning he looked in the mirror and said to himself

—I'm fucked. Those fucking fuckers have me fucking fucked.

Henry just let events happen, keeping mum in the Dáil as the three young deputies spoke about low standards in high places and recapturing the true spirit of the Party. The newspapers said that sixty-seven per cent of the electorate wanted the Tough Guy to be tried for tax evasion. Outside the Dáil they gathered to boo him with all the fervour and courage of schoolchildren taking on a bully with a broken leg. Henry was asked if he thought the Taoiseach should resign.

—I would hope the Irish people would have a leader they could trust. I don't want to bring personalities into this, but nobody is above the law and it disturbs me to see this happening in a country renowned for its honesty.

He and Jimmy had cackled merrily while writing that last bit.

The teeming rain on the day of the Tough Guy's

resignation hid his tears from the cameramen and reporters outside the Dáil. Inside he gripped the platform tightly and quoted poetry incorrectly. The leaders of the other parties agreed it was a sad day for a great man.

—They were very nice about him in the speeches, Jimmy.

—Sure doesn't everyone speak well of the dead, Henry.

The Tough Guy tried to choose his successor, sending against Henry his shuffling, raincoated protégé, the Canny Dub. Henry despised the man whose gait seemed to stem from a desire not to make his leader feel too short. The Canny Dub had left his wife a few years ago, a fact known everywhere but unspoken until Henry commented on television

—It would be good if people knew what house their Taoiseach was going to live in if he's elected, and with whom.

Of course the Liberals regarded this as a cheap shot. Dolores and Dearbhla told him there had been outraged comments in Nesbitt's, and he was not sure that they themselves approved. This prompted some virtuoso self-justification.

Most people had happy marriages, like his with Mary. They and their parents and their parents before them kept the marriage going until they grew old together. In England every second person seemed to be divorced. The Irish had more gumption. More sticking power. This he connected back to a history of famine and subjugation and frequent defeat on the battlefield, which made them learn to stick at things. They hung on and found that a life could be salvaged out of the worst hardships, if you didn't give up and accepted disappointment as part of the bargain. If you wanted to lead the Irish people, you had to show this kind of spirit. Your marriage had to be like everyone else's. This he worked out with the young TD who had encouraged him to mention the Canny Dub's private life in the first place.

—It will send an important signal to people about your attitude to these things.

The young lad was mad on signals. Everything seemed to have a signal. Matters seemingly unconnected were invisibly tied together by semaphore; and what was not said was often the most important part of a statement. The young lad said he should hire advisers who knew how these signals were produced. These people drank in Nesbitt's, and Henry thought they were a gang of hucksters. Hucksters selling nothing. They didn't make anything or write anything or serve anything up. They worked in public relations, and the head honcho of the lot was Sian Guiney, a woman he remembered hanging around the Dodo with Seamus McKeon. She tried to sell him her nothing, offering herself as an adviser, a handler, a spin doctor, someone who could tell him how to get his message across.

—In fairness, love, I was getting messages across at church gates when you were still in nappies.

—But were you getting them across the right way, Henry? For a start, if you call one of these new female journalists love she'll have your guts for garters. And by the way, I'm older than you think. That's PR as well.

—What's wrong with calling a woman love?

—You see? That's one thing I could explain to you. Remember the medium is the message.

He forgot that, but remembered Sian Guiney. Because her product was not quite the nothing it seemed. She took people's fears of how they talked and what they said and magicked them away, her greatness residing in the fact that you felt you'd obtained an unfair advantage by hiring her.

On the big day he woke early in his Dublin Four apartment and looked out at the city.

—Henry, good man, come back to bed. It's six o'clock. Come on, we've got a long day ahead of us.

He liked the way Mary said *we* have a long day ahead of us. Becoming Taoiseach meant more to him if he imagined the job as belonging to both of them. This day would be his best yet. It was as if he was becoming leader of the world. Ireland was enough world for Henry Caslin. On the radio news he was the headline.

—Henry Caslin will today be elected Taoiseach.

The presumptuousness made him shiver. He could be knocked down by a car. He could get a heart attack. The world could end. But he knew it would not, and that his easy win in the Party leadership election made becoming Taoiseach a formality. Kelly had secretly marked everyone's ballot papers, and he and Henry perused the names of their nineteen opponents with political vengeance on their minds.

At twelve o'clock Dolores arrived with Mark, who had gone to the bother of putting on a suit for the occasion.

—Don't worry, Henry. Stage fright, man. Comes to everyone. Think of some Shakespeare.

That bit of advice nearly fucked things altogether.

Kelly arrived to say it was time to shift. At the third go, Henry started his Jag and hit off at a steady forty miles an hour, twenty slower than usual, towards his destiny.

In Belfast someone made a phone call. On the road to Belfast someone else patted a brown envelope in their pocket to make sure it was still there. Father Lee watched the television cameras waiting for Henry, and wondered what it was like to be the centre of so much public attention. McKeon left down the phone and remembered a ballroom dance from long ago. Christy Dockery downed another gin and spat at his television set. Moira Hopkins waited with a microphone and vowed the presence of Mickey Kelly would not affect her. When Henry parked the car she was first to reach him.

—Mister Caslin. How does it feel to be on the verge of the greatest success of your life?

—Sure don't you know as well as me, Moira, congratulations on the new job, it's good to see you back.

Holding his hands up, Henry said he'd answer no more questions till the job was nailed down. Moira cursed the fact that his quote was unusable.

When the tellers announced his victory, Henry felt calm for the first time that day. Hearing shouts, he looked up and saw Jimmy and the rest of the Rathbawn organisation in the visitors' gallery, laughing, crying and clapping each other on the backs in demented fashion.

The Rathbawn people felt like singing, but the county had so few triumphant memories that no song came to mind. Jimmy felt as if he had knowledge of no other emotion but pure happiness. All the years had led to this. Henry as Taoiseach. He yahooed and yelled, catapulting his twisted frame around the gallery to high-five anyone within reach. Even the Ceann Comhairle's voice could not quieten him.

—Could we have some silence, please. The members of the public are reminded that this is not an All-Ireland final.

—No, shouted Jimmy, it's even better, and continued his capering.

The Ceann Comhairle shrugged as if this was all that could be expected, the shrug reminded Henry that his people had always been dismissed because it was known they would never have power.

Now they were in power.

Henry Junior had put three hundred pounds behind the bar in Buswell's. He stood just inside the door with Martina in her new suit with matching gloves, Dolores and Mark, Dearbhla and Garrett. Mary smiled and looked younger than ever. The Rathbawn crew thronged the hotel like an invading army, and looked around wide-eyed as if intending to make off with the fixtures. Jimmy was crying, the happiness inside his face bursting out in sheets of water. Henry took his arm and they walked into the bar, punching the air as if to break through it. They had won.

The Canny Dub was first to be called into Henry's office the next morning.

—I have to tell you there's no place in my Cabinet for you. You're sacked.

The man had expected no different, but still found himself telling Henry this was unfair.

—Listen to me. If you can't do the time, then don't do the crime.

Which was a phrase Henry used on another thirteen Ministers who had made the mistake of backing the wrong horse.

—There's been coups with less changes, quipped Kelly, who was the new Minister for Justice.

Henry's rise to the top persuaded the people of his county to make up for five thousand years of anonymity by celebrating as if 1798, the Fleadh Ceol, a U2 concert and the Eucharistic Congress had arrived together.

Because nothing had ever happened in the county. In school, Henry had written his compositions and done his sums in exercise books which mapped out Ireland's historic and scenic places of interest on the back. His county was a notable blank spot. The inhabitants had been placid in 1641 and unconcerned about flashing their pikes at the rising of the moon in 1798. The county had been quiet in 1916, and the War of Independence there was ignored by historians preferring to concentrate on Cork, Tipperary and Dublin. No provincial title had been won by the county, no native sportsman, artist, writer or politician had ever risen to prominence. No Fleadh Ceol had been held there in the sixties. U2 had never played there. There had been no train crashes, fires or other disasters.

They came into Rathbawn at nine that morning from the farms out in the country, and by half eleven the pubs along Main Street were full, although everyone knew it would be another eight hours before Henry arrived. The people from the town knocked off from their jobs, all kinds of businesses putting up the closed sign until Rathbawn looked like a border village on the day of a hunger-strike funeral. They waited in the pubs for Henry to stand on the gig rig in front of the Imperial Hotel and confirm that the Taoiseach was one of their own.

Pub hierarchy was scrapped for the day. Bars reserved for the Army filled up with solicitors, farmers, doctors and the Army. In the little pub with a shop selling blue mouldy oranges at the front where tinkers got served, the District Justice sat with his back against the bacon slicer talking to a man he'd once convicted for cattle rustling, and shuffled over to make room for Dickie Carberry. Cops drank with robbers, priests with Protestant clergymen and unmarried mothers with Trinity College students whose Rathbawn accents had returned for the day. The Party had always told people they lived in a country without divisions, and Henry's homecoming would for once make that true.

The gig rig had been hired from a promoter of huge rock concerts. It was a long ways from the back of a truck. All sorts of elaborate lights were concealed at the top of it. Henry hoped they would not go off as he spoke, or the whole show would look like *Jesus Christ Superstar*.

Banners. Flags. Singing. He had never got over the strangeness of crowds, and could not see the attraction of belonging to one, carefully making sure to conform to a median level of emotion. In crowds, half the people weren't watching the stage at all, but were instead taking in how the other half reacted. He felt that the crowd would tear Rathbawn Main Street apart if he told them to. The fundamental danger of crowds meant that Ireland was a lucky country to have someone like himself controlling them.

This night was meant to compensate his father for the happy years he had not known. The old man was sitting with Jimmy. Henry led him over to where young waiters were popping corks on bottles of champagne and arranging fresh salmon and lobster on sterling-silver platters. Sian Guiney came over to straighten the Taoiseach's tie. Jimmy's speech reached him from outside.

It was a litany of opposition founded on the virtues that had got Henry from Rathbawn to Leinster House. A listing of the enemies who looked down on the county and the Party. The British, the media, the Liberals, Dublin Four, the Blueshirts. The Prods were in there too, but you couldn't mention them by name any more. Jimmy was speaking about battling against the odds and overcoming the opposition, because a lifetime of political ducking, parrying and hitting back meant they knew about nothing else. But for the first time in his life, Henry was in a place where everyone agreed with him. He was stuck because the oppositional speech was no use any more. Sian tapped him on the shoulder and told him he was on in two minutes.

People were sitting on roofs and packing the top windows of houses whose canny owners had rented out upstairs for the evening. When Henry held up his hand for silence, the gesture worked immediately. The quiet waited and swelled around him as those tens of thousands held their breath.

He had left his notes in the hotel jacks.

The silence only lasted a few seconds, Mary told him afterwards. The crowd had just presumed he was waiting for straggler cheers to die. He felt it as hours, flicking back through showband memories to remember what big acts did when one of the band's mikes failed. Telling a joke was out, and asking for requests was even worse. Finally he remembered a ballroom opening in the only mining village in the country, a spot where the work made people hard and the pay made them bitter. Five minutes into the set the entire stage went dead and Henry expected the crowd to lynch Tom Nolan. The night was saved when Tom took out a megaphone which he sometimes used for a novelty number and started a winning spiel. Henry cleared his throat and got a massive cheer.

—Hello. How are ye?

More words for happy and contented were shouted up than he could have thought of. Mighty. Copacetic. Deadly. Suckin' diesel. Winding on and on as if performed for an inquisitive foreign lexicographer.

—It's great to be back home.

That was all he had needed to say. They cheered for a full ten minutes. Again he raised his hand and the noise stopped.

—Is there anyone here from Kilshalvey?

—Aughnasurn.

—Ennybegs.

—Culmore.

—St Attracta's Park.

—Nevin Drive.

—Cloonbeg.

—Threemilehouse.

He shouted the names of every local parish, townland and street he could think of, and every shout was greeted with raucous and approving roars. He named townlands so small they had never even been mentioned in the *Herald*, and they were cheered the same as all the rest. Henry was turning the local into the epic. Dublin journalists there to record the new Taoiseach's first speech on home ground were pissed off. This was part of the point. Henry was letting them know that this night was not for them, but belonged to the people of this town, this county and this constituency who had written number one beside his name, and in return were being invited to celebrate themselves in front of the biggest crowd they had ever seen.

When he could think of no more place names, he began another list.

—The people who made this night possible.

His family. Jimmy. The activists. The councillors. His running mates. All arriving bashfully beside Henry, because they had been out in the crowd and seen its vast and imposing nature. Picking their steps like cats to avoid the tangled wires on the flatbed surface below them. He hugged Mary and the crowd roared, thinking this was the logical finale.

—And now. One last thing. I'll let ye go then, ye probably have enough of me at this stage.

Thousands of heads shook in simultaneous indignation.

—There's two people I want to thank above everyone else. I owe them a lot more than I can ever repay. My mother and my father.

Henry watched them being helped up to the stage, Jimmy straining that twisted back to get poor Tommy Caslin over the final steps. His mother arrived first, moving with the efficiency she had bequeathed to him along with almost everything else in his character. He was aware of this inheritance, but still searched for links to his father because, like most men, he felt this to be a more fitting connection.

His father approached slowly. Henry loved the man for the concentration in every step. For most of his life Tommy hadn't cared where he fell or even if he stood up at all, but now he rolled his shoulders back, puffed out his massive belly and tried to get his legs to follow the straight line taken by his wife. He looked down as if there was a track he could follow. Like footprints in snow.

Thirty years before he had fallen asleep in a snowdrift two hundred yards from the house, earning himself gangrene in a right leg that was soon replaced by the artificial limb currently exacerbating his navigational problems. Henry waited until his father was five yards away and reached out as the old man began to fall. Tommy put his arms around his son and hauled himself upright.

—I wasn't going to fall this time, Henry.

—I believe you.

The photo of Henry and his father appeared on the front page of every Irish paper the next morning, and also in papers farther afield, where readers knew nothing about Irish politics but understood the esperanto of strong emotion. It looked like an embrace, a strong man hugging his son and letting him know that, though the road ahead would be tough, advice and help would always be forthcoming.

—A chip off the old block, was the headline used by three different papers in three different languages on three different continents.

A spirit of bemusement accompanied McKeon through the corridors of the Imperial. He saw a teenage journalist from the *Herald* boasting to young men about his intimacy with the Caslin circle, and leggy young ones from national papers lapping up stories from the Tourism Committee, the Roads Meeting and the Health Board as if they were getting the inside track on the Cuban Missile Crisis. Rathbawn had turned into Washington for the night. Youngsters from the next county pretended to be from the town, and local people's accents became stronger than ever before.

—I'm from Rathbawn.

—No you're not. You're only letting on. To be cool.

The place had gone mad.

—Bejasus, look who it is, Seamus McKeon.

—Well begod.

—Councillors, how are ye?

The three oldest councillors in the county, among them Christy Dockery, beamed as if they had never said a bad word about Henry Caslin, and talked about the council meetings of the past, recalling what McKeon had worn and how he had walked on his first day in the chamber thirty years before. He had been eighteen years old. McKeon had no old stories to recount because he had been so determined to forget them that on this night he, who was a local and could remember the beginning of Caslin's career, felt like an outsider. Meanwhile journalists down for the day from Dublin were getting stuck into the chat as if they had been all their lives in the town.

The outside had been his chosen destination, but this night he saw what belonging might have been like. Moira was at the bar with Jimmy Mimnagh. Jimmy did a little sidestep to include him in the company.

—Good to see you, young McKeon. We don't see enough of you.

He wanted to ask Jimmy how he and Henry had managed to come so far from the local and still seem connected to it. How they could spend half their time in Dublin and still seem as rooted as the concrete of Rathbawn's main streets. But Jimmy moved away in search of Henry before he could be asked anything. Moira was drunk and McKeon liked this, because she always made drinking seem like a reward she had earned, the way it was supposed to be but rarely was.

—Seamus, I'm having such a great time. Everyone's so lovely and so much fun. You're wrong about Rathbawn, you know, I think it's a brilliant town.

A brilliant town. He hadn't thought it was since discovering there were bigger. But looking around at everyone collapsing into one big maul of mutual love, he thought maybe it could have been one. Given the chance.

In the hotel jacks at three in the morning an old man was tottering around the floor, holding his flute out in front of him like a Buckingham Palace guardsman's rifle. Its impressive size cheered McKeon up and reconciled him briefly to the passing of time. He recognised the old man as the Taoiseach's father.

—Do you see that, young fella, do you see that? Take a good look at it, because only for this boyo, there'd be none of this crack happening tonight.

McKeon agreed that there wouldn't be.

It was said of Henry that he came to power without ever showing why he had wanted it. Nobody remembered any great policies formulated by the new Taoiseach, and he had been responsible for no great ministerial achievements. But to quibble about this was to misunderstand the nature of the Party. The Party existed not to pursue objectives or change society or even manage the country, it existed to win and then exercise power. Henry was Taoiseach because he was able to gain power for himself. Once in, what he wanted to do with it was up to him.

A book about Kennedy's first thousand days in power had made an impression on him some years ago, and left him determined to make an immediate and inimitable mark. The only problem was not knowing what changes he wanted to or could make. His first week as Taoiseach was spent frantically looking for causes or ideas to believe in. Reading the newspaper at breakfast one morning, he felt like someone accidentally coming across a favourite childhood plaything they thought destroyed years ago. Gleefully he showed the article to Mary.

The young columnist said the Brits were to blame for

everything in Irish history. They had been guilty of genocide in the Famine, had inflicted slavery on the Irish people for centuries and committed unparalleled acts of terror in 1798, 1916 and 1921. In the North, they remained a colonial power, and justice there could only be achieved by their immediate withdrawal accompanied by a series of apologies for their historical role as scourges of Ireland.

—Well, Mary, isn't it great that we've moved beyond all that stuff.

—You don't understand. This is important. You should pay heed to this man, what he's saying is all the go now.

—But Mary, aren't you the last twenty years telling me I shouldn't believe this and not to mention Vinegar Hill and Rathbawn's Noble Ten and Kevin Barry in speeches, because that day is gone?

—Well it's back, Henry love. They call it post-colonialism now.

—Is it, not the same stuff the whole time?

—It is, but these lads all have degrees, and they've done studies that have Irish history joined in with all sorts of other countries. It gets taught in universities now and everything.

—So it's all right to think it again, then?

—Yes. The world is changing Henry.

On television he watched change come to countries like Romania, East Germany and Czechoslovakia, which had seemed to be communist in the same way Ireland was an island. It was as if a fundamental religious commandment or immutable scientific law had proved utterly fallacious. The crowds demolishing the Berlin Wall were nearly too much to take in.

Mandela got out of jail and the blacks took power in South Africa; Palestinians and Israelis shook hands on the White House lawn. Wars which had seemed fated to continue for ever stopped, and men who had used guns laid them down and began to talk. The silencing of the guns conferred heroic status on them, making those who had talked instead of fought look anaemic and inauthentic by comparison.

The silencing of the guns in the North, Henry realised, would mean that people in the Republic could have their history back and celebrate their heroes. You could say you were proud to be Irish without being accused of lighting verbal fuses for bombs which collapsed concrete disco ceilings on teenage dancers. He and his advisers studied videotapes on which people responsible for the grossest of savageries against each other now sat down together. Jude Locke was asked to come down to Dublin.

The fact that Locke's life seemed to have been lived on television was one of the reasons he was regarded as a potential miracle worker. Viewers had seen Locke bringing civilians through a sheet of murderous army fire with just a white handkerchief waving over his head to protect him, being dragged through the street by the hair of that same head, being manhandled, mistreated and shouted down by soldiers and policemen in a country where the two seemed indistinguishable. All the time he counselled against violence. Standing by the sites of shootings, bombings and riots, he would explain that the search for peace must go on. Speaking on camera after the murders of his friends, their throats cut, their heads blown off, their remains scattered like pieces of an unfathomable jigsaw, he continued to inveigle against death.

The man's presence in the Taoiseach's office made Henry both awed and envious, giving him the uneasy feeling that Locke was better than him, the bullets and bombs making the Northerner uniquely experienced in the deepest realms of character. Locke showed no signs of agreeing with this. Maintaining his mental equilibrium necessitated the treatment of the primal forces and emotions as almost ordinary.

—Peace is not impossible if we pull together in the search for it. By we, I mean the whole nationalist community both North and South, said Locke. All of us together. The political parties in the South and my party and Sinn Fein in the North.

One set of Taoiseach's and five sets of advisers' jaws dropped. For years the Party had defended itself against the Liberals, who claimed it and the IRA were out of the same bag, and that anyone who sang ballads, wanted a United Ireland and had a shred of regard for the men whom the British had lined up against a wall and shot after those heroes had surrendered to save the civilian population from hardship, was somehow sheltering under an umbrella in these rainiest of times with the men who set up mortars in the fields of South Armagh, left bombs in crowded shopping centres and paraded behind coffins in dark glasses and balaclavas. Now Jude Locke, who had been rendered incapable of saying a wrong word by his sang-froid under baton and boot, was saying the Liberals might have had a point.

—We've got to let Sinn Fein know we will back their objectives if they lay down their guns. That they are not on their own. Henry, you've got to take a risk for peace.

Henry could not argue against that, because he had seen what the loss of a loved one would be like and knew that everyone who died must have been loved by someone, and that in the North people died who should not have. Young guys shot while hanging around in a bookie shop. Workmen on their way home ordered out of a van and gunned down. Customers viewing a football match in a pub made to lie down on the floor before being killed. All mourned. Locke was saying these extinctions might not have to continue, and one hundred and fifty needless mournings a year could be averted. Thousands of lovers and parents and siblings would escape misery. What could Henry do except whatever Locke wanted?

It was also likely that anyone taking part in this preemptive strike against the funeral processions of the future would earn a prominent place in the history books.

The combination of sadness for others and hopes for himself made Henry agree to the meeting near the border. Inside the farmhouse, Locke waited with the two men whose speeches exhorted the nationalist people to fight the foe. They now assured Henry that what they really wanted was peace.

—Peace with honour.

—Peace with justice.

Not once did Burns or McConville say the word without the embellishments and emphases which made it palatable to them. Peace was not an absolute to them. That was Henry's first lesson.

His second was that Burns and McConville were only tenuously connected to Dickie Carberry or the Southern men with names in Irish who had run the IRA in those last visible days before booby-trapped cars and bloody bank raids had forced them from view, and sundered the romantic line stretching from the Boys of Wexford to Padraig Pearse to Sean South of Garryowen to the present.

The rhetoric of green field and Caitlin Ni Houlihan had been supplanted by the language of modern political struggle. Volunteers had been led to jail by stories of Plunkett, Pearse and Tone, but once there had discovered the primers of Marighela, Fanon and Che. To Henry, the professionalism of the new men in charge rendered them both dangerous and pragmatic. They would not be fooled, but could be persuaded.

Not merely professional, but Northern as well. Their distrust of the South reminded Henry of Rodney Fullerton.

They used the phrase the South instead of the Republic, and expressed for their paramilitary adversaries a kind of respect not extended to anyone below the border. Burns and McConville spoke of their seriousness of purpose, their belief in efficiency, their outspoken nature, their inability to tell a lie, their impatience with calumny, flimflam and beating around the bush and their black humour, stressing the Northernness of these virtues with a pride Fullerton could not have surpassed.

When they spoke about a ceasefire, Locke insisted they were serious, and that an end to their struggle could be achieved if the British accepted that these men had to be included in any talks on the future of the North. A different future, which would mean no armoured cars and no barbed wire and no young lads from Bolton, Newcastle and Wigan searching shoppers in the streets of Irish towns and no shopping centres in Bolton, Newcastle and Wigan being searched for bombs planted by young men destined to spend years in English jails.

—It doesn't have to go on the way it has, Henry, said Locke.

The contradiction at the heart of the plan haunted him. Burns and McConville made it clear that any ceasefire depended on the Brits talking to Sinn Fein and carrying out whatever was agreed between them. Yet they did not trust the Brits, and made constant reference to the lying, cheating, brutality and ill will which were second nature to the colonial oppressor. They expected the worst from the Brits, and the ceasefire was based on expecting the best. They planned to sit down with people who could not be trusted, talk with people who never said what they meant and agree with people who always broke treaties and went back on their word.

Henry agreed with this plan because Locke said it made

sense. He believed the moments of danger must have revealed to Locke how it could all be solved, how the circle could be squared and the opposites attracted. He now knew that allowing the problem to remain intractable was an unaffordable luxury.

—If Seamus McKeon gets hold of this he'll play puck with it, said Henry to his advisers on the way back to Dublin, at the same time as McKeon answered the phone in RTE.

—Hello, is this Seamus McKeon?

—It is indeed. How are you doing?

—Never mind that. I've got a story for you. One you should be interested in. Take this seriously now, mind.

—All right. Can you tell me, now, what your story is about?

It was twenty-five to six on a Friday. McKeon's finger dangled over the phone, ready to send the caller into oblivion so it could help the rest of his hand lower pints in Ciss Madden's. A year later, when his story had changed so many lives, he wondered how things might have turned out had he cut the caller off.

—Listen to me. This is serious business. It's about a priest called Father Gerry Lee, he's stationed in West Belfast but he's been in the South as well. Father Lee has been abusing children for I don't know how long, but I'd suspect thirty-odd years, twenty-odd anyways. I've read up on these boys, they start early and they don't ever stop. He's fucked hundreds of kids both ways, he fucked them and they're fucked now.

These stories were beginning to make the news. Only last week Cardinal O'Hanlon had complained that the use of the term 'paedophile priest' was proof of anti-religious bias among journalists, when McKeon knew all it proved was their love of alliteration in headlines. Child abuse was not something you wanted to do a programme on. No thanks would be forthcoming.

—Father Lee is under investigation by the RUC, and if he returns to the North he will be arrested. However, I believe he is in the South hiding out, which may or may not be where you come in. By the way, you know this Father Lee character, Seamus.

—I don't think I do.

—He served in your home parish for a couple of years, Rathbawn, when you were a wee lad in your first job.

McKeon remembered the night of the fund-raising dance. He thought of the photo being taken for the *Herald*. Father Gerry Lee. A nice geezer, a great money-raiser for the parish, involved in all sorts of activities, very good with the kids ... everyone said that ... how good he was with kids. He loved them.

—You know this is slander, and I couldn't repeat it. There probably isn't a word of truth in what you're saying.

—I have your attention now. I'd say, and it's a wild guess, that Father Lee left Rathbawn in a hurry. Am I right?

He'd left suddenly for America. That proved nothing. Although it had been strange how quickly he had departed. But you would have known if he'd been a pervert. He was a decent man who enjoyed his pint and a game of football. Why did McKeon keep thinking of seeing Father Lee with children?

—Listen, you should check this information, don't take my word on it.

—I'm not.

—Good thing too. It's no wonder you've won so many awards. I'm sure he's hiding out in the South, and I'm sure he's fucked kids there, probably he has in your home town.

Have you got a biro? I'll give you a list of names and addresses of people in West Belfast who can confirm what I say.

By the time the caller hung up, McKeon had already decided to head to Belfast at the weekend, telling himself he was going North to expose a falsehood.

They'd stopped bombing the famous hotel some time ago. In the cocktail bar McKeon met a woman from Sinn Fein and told her why he was in town. It was her manor, he explained, so it was only proper to let her know. He had hoped she would say the story was complete shite, but instead she told McKeon her people wanted nothing to do with this.

—It's up to you what you want to make of it, McKeon. We're keeping out of it. Do you want a few bits on British Army dirty tricks, some counter-insurgency stuff?

—You know they won't be used.

—I'm not sure this will be either. Even if it is true. And we're definitely keeping out of it.

The area was familiar to him from his reports on the electoral rise of Sinn Fein, which had been hampered by the fact that the station would not let him interview anyone who had voted for them. It was not prime journalistic territory. He knocked on the door of the first house on the list. A Staffordshire bull terrier grinned gormlessly out the front window, slid off his perch and headed for the hall. The door was opened a chink by a woman with a fag in her mouth, the smoke making McKeon's eyes water as he prepared for the fuck-off.

—Are you Margaret McQuillan?

—Who wants to know?

—I'm Seamus McKeon from RTE. I want to ask you a couple of questions concerning Father Gerry Lee.

The chain was taken off and the Staff bull got kicked into the kitchen. Margaret McQuillan wore the expression of a criminal recaptured after a long siege who is relieved it's all over but aware that what follows might not be any better. In the front room a little kid was sitting in a make of wooden playpen not seen in the shops any more.

—Thanks for coming. We'd been hoping someone would. I'll go around to a couple of the other houses.

McKeon regarded the dog warily until the woman came back with a photograph of a priest beside two children on the steps of a church.

—Confirmation. One of those kids is me.

He recognised Father Lee, and a showband tune from a night long ago whistled around the edges of his thoughts.

—And the other one is dead. Killed himself when he was seventeen. He couldn't cope. Father Lee did desperate things to us later that day. We never told anyone for a long time, but we knew people were looking and wondering what was wrong with us that he picked us out. It wasn't him they blamed.

The dirt of the room, the unwashed smell of the baby and the antidepressant look of the woman made McKeon feel trapped. The child began to cry.

—Listen, I've come out of my way to meet you. Just tell me first, is there any proof, or am I wasting my time?

—Oh, there's proof all right. It depends, though, on what you would call proof. What is proof to you?'

—Documentary evidence. Hard facts.

—Hard facts. Aye, the facts are hard all right. They're wild hard altogether. Call back here at seven o'clock. I'll have the others then. Hear the stories and see if you believe.

When he heard the stories he did believe. Because this could not be made up. Imagination could not generate these acts performed against five- and six-year-olds, on teenage boys, teenage girls. Perpetrated by a man who became more clearly defined as the victims told their stories in an odd, amalgam language, the tongue of pain intermingling with others. The lingua franca of denial. The argot learned from social workers. And the whole repetitive testimony demanded by a man in uniform asking them to go over it again so he could be absolutely sure of the facts. A man named Hunter.

McKeon phoned Moira to say he would not be back for a few days.

—Your voice sounds strange, love.

—Ah, no, it shouldn't, not really. I just want to clear up a few things.

In his office, Hunter made dismissive comments about the Free State and told McKeon that the BBC was the world's best broadcaster. RTE, he confided, seemed to him a Third World station. The hard Orange mask disappeared when McKeon asked him about the stories. Hunter seemed grateful to share the burden of his knowledge, and handed McKeon files containing stories both familiar and unfamiliar. The unfamiliar detailed the affliction of a new generation by Father Lee. Medical evidence. Hard facts. Documentary evidence.

—Someone rang me in Dublin. Tipped me off about Father Lee.

—It wasn't me. I would have no interest in ringing your station. I cannot see what good it would do. You Romans would never say anything bad about a priest.

That night McKeon stayed awake and pondered the mysterious journalistic rules defining what was and what was not a story. The President cutting tape outside a community centre only used for playing badminton could be converted into a story by custom, despite the fact that no one outside the relevant village was interested. And sometimes, as in this case, graver happenings did not quite seem to qualify as news. McKeon begged Father Lee's victims to understand this.

—There are no charges. No one knows where he is. And this is not an uncommon crime. We can't just focus on it just because he's a priest. That wouldn't be fair.

They looked at him as if nothing better had been expected. He resented this.

—I need an angle.

He stressed that something else was needed to make their story sufficiently interesting. A hard-faced man in a wheelchair blocked his path to the car.

—What do you mean, angle?

Patrick Armstrong wheeled his chair against McKeon's shin.

—What makes this different? I'm very sorry for your troubles and all that, but it's just another crime.

—You don't want to report it because he's a priest.

McKeon explained that this was not the case. He was known for his willingness to take on the Church, to confront them on mixed schooling, on contraception, on vasectomies, on adoption rights. All his colleagues regarded him as the scourge of the bishops.

—You're scared of them. You haven't the guts. When was the last time you took them on?

Involuntarily McKeon thought of a story about the objections of an elderly Munster curate to the siting of a nudist beach in his parish. Armstrong continued to repeat the word 'scared' as McKeon started the car.

Scared. He was not scared of the Church. The self-justifying mantra became jumbled in his mind.

—I am not scared of the Church.

—The Church is not scared of me. The Church is not scared of me.

How could the Church not be scared of McKeon? Did he not take them on at every opportunity? Yet why on earth would they be scared? Had it not all been a skirmish against the Church on their terms? He had thought a condom held aloft on camera was a weapon to damage the Hierarchy, when all it had been was a prop in a show. The Church needed the media as a tame enemy, and journalists needed the Church to prove their bravery. But the battle had been fought with blanks.

When he received the next phone call, McKeon recognised Armstrong's voice immediately.

—You've got to ask yourself the questions first, Seamus, before you put them to anyone else. You've got to see why they have to be put.

—I don't know where this is going, Patrick.

—You know that's wrong. That makes you worse than Father Lee, you know, Seamus. Because I don't think he knew he was doing wrong. In fact, a lot of people are worse than him. Because they had the knowledge. Ask yourself: who else only a priest could get close to other people's children at all hours of the day? Ask yourself: how could the Church not know about thirty years of this, when they know about every little detail of everyone's lives?

That was the angle. Without proof that the Church had been complicit in Father Lee's actions, there was just a heap of wood with no spark to make a fire. And he did not believe that the Church would actively collaborate with evil because he had been brought up a Catholic. He could rail and rebel against the Church without losing belief in its purity of motivation.

Anyway, the Father Lee story was too frightening to take on for one major reason. Because the priest had murdered childhood. McKeon even felt his own being encroached upon. He looked at young girls and boys in a new light and saw that for some people they were sex objects. Everywhere he saw danger for children, cringing at their innocence in parks and playgrounds where an escape from rape was a matter of luck. He thought of his own defenceless and unknowing seven-year-old self. There was no reason he had not lived a life like Patrick Armstrong's. He could have come close to it and would never know how close. This new knowledge was hateful to him.

Every week Armstrong would ring and insist that Father Lee was being sheltered by the Church in the South.

—Nobody's doing enough, Seamus. The Free State cops won't do anything.

—They really can't do anything. Nobody's reported him down here.

—How do you know?

—Listen, if he's convicted I'll run the story. That's all I can promise. Then it will be a real story.

The possibility of a ceasefire inspired Henry mentally to compose chapters of an autobiography entitled, *Henry Caslin – Man of Change*. His sense that the time was ripe for progress led him to a decision which finally validated the amazing life and times of Senator Martin Kingston.

His status as Ireland's first televised homosexual had earned Senator Kingston more than his fair share of spit in the face, excrement in the post and bricks through the window, but nothing could persuade him from his path. Even when the gay community centre he had founded was burned to the ground, he just stood in the ruins, sifting ashes through his hands and pondering his next challenge to invisibility.

People eventually became quite fond of the senator, as time transformed him into an orchidaceous and oddly reassuring feature of national life. What made him acceptable was his difference, the fact of his being a scholar, a connoisseur of wide-brimmed hats, a lederhosen-wearing cyclist, a high-pitched speaker of the vowel and consonant sounds of a departed ascendancy and a performer of a one-man show excerpting the fruitiest bits from the Wilde canon. He showed that homosexuals were exotic, flamboyant and immediately identifiable. They were nobody like the plain people of Ireland or their sons or anyone they knew. They were not builders or guards, teachers or bank officials, priests or farmers.

Dolores informed Henry that Senator Kingston was camp. The phrase made Henry think of the tinkers, prompting the reflection that more than one minority might pledge their vote in return for a few favours. His announcement of the forthcoming decriminalisation of homosexuality earned him two kisses on the cheek from the senator, who led a parade of followers in singing celebratory Judy Garland numbers through the streets of the capital the following day. Henry explained his decision to the Party Women's Committee, whom he felt would snigger less than the male TDs.

—I'm not comfortable with the idea of homosexuality, but in this modern society, there are people who lead the kinds of lifestyles that we'd find very strange. And we have to put up with that. I saw some strange things when I was in showbiz, and we all have to accept that things are changing. Homosexuals have their own world and we have ours.

The showband days. Never mind Tom Nolan, it was the other lads that tore the arse out of it. Straights was what Kingston called them. Little did he know. Some of the hoors were so twisted you could have opened a bottle of wine with them.

One lad, a Monaghan farmer's son, slept every night on a mattress stuffed with the pubic hair of groupies. Another had eight children by eight different women, each met at a Caslin ballroom opening and all in their teens when he poled them. Straight, don't make me laugh.

When the senator suggested a meeting with the clientele

of Dublin's main gay bar to cement the good impression created by decriminalisation, Henry was all for it. Politics. You did the favour and reminded people that they owed. But Sian Guiney told Henry the Canny Dub and his followers would use the visit against him. And he knew himself that some voters thought shaking hands with queers could give you Aids. Someone had to go, but no Minister fancied a photo of themselves surrounded by a bunch of pansies going through letterboxes the morning of the next election.

—Jimmy, just do this one thing for me: meet up with Kingston and see this crowd. I know it'll be strange for you, but I sort of promised him someone important. You never know, you might get on grand. None of them are married, either.

The welcoming committee was told that Senator Mimnagh was the Taoiseach's right-hand man, but regrettably of a generation and geographical provenance which meant the Ship would shock him. It shocked him all right.

Unbelievable. Completely unbelievable. Jimmy could hardly make sense of what he saw. What was the world coming to when a place like this existed?

The bars of his memory were not like this. He looked for the self-hatred, the feelings of being hunted, the dampness on the walls fostered by a hundred frustrated exhalations, the apology for existence implicit in the gestures, the depressions, the guilt. All had gone. Not completely, but almost enough. Whoops and catcalls flounced around the bar, the sound of people taking their definition by their enemies, turning it inside out and pitching it right back, macho poses done with a wink. Kingston protectively shielded Jimmy while Jimmy luxuriated in the sights, the noises, the smells.

Happiness had been added. Jimmy remembered the Black Gull in London's East End as different to other pubs because it lacked joy. It was no pub for young men even in one another's arms, but here in the Ship bucks smooched and kissed and swayed with their lips on each other's lips, their hands on each other's arses and their looks at the crotches of passers-by bold and flirtatious. Their bodies seemed borrowed from a sculptor's studio. Black women singing over pounding music had replaced tinkling pianos and tepid Noel Coward impersonations. Jimmy wanted to travel back in time to the Black Gull, bearing witness to the ecstasy to come. Senator Kingston introduced him to men, and a couple of women with cropped hair, who spoke of their gratitude to the Taoiseach. Now was the time to stick the knife in and remind them how their community should vote, but he couldn't be bothered.

The senator was sorry to see a man so gobsmacked by a first visit to a gay bar.

Jimmy was so happy he didn't know whether he was coming or going. And he loved the manners of the lads who still did the flirting thing with an ugly oul fucker like himself. Kingston came into his line of sight. Could he not stay out of the way even for a minute?

—Senator Mimnagh, it's great that you've turned up here. I'd say it's been a bit of an eye-opener for you.

—It certainly has, said Jimmy.

The nineties were a lot better than the fifties. But the fifties might have been a lot better than the fifties, too. He had tried to blot them out, worried that in between all the guilt, pain and conscience there had been fun as well. Now he was not sure. His eyes were occupied by the dancers, but his ears strayed to the two guys down the bar because of their accents. Their voices moved with the same rhythm, put the same emphases on the same letters and enunciated the same slang, same cant, same lingo as his did. They could have been him. If he had been born later he could have been here with them, but he felt happy rather than bitter, the happiness going back all those years and touching the young man he had once been, telling him he belonged and was not a loner or eccentric.

—I am a homosexual, Jimmy said to himself for the first time.

Looking round the pub again he caught the eye of a suddenly understanding Kingston, who wagged a finger playfully. Jimmy mirrored the gesture before closing his eyes and seeing himself and Guy passing through the thick drapes of time, walking on to the dancefloor of the Ship, throwing their hands in the air, adding their voices to this carnal choir, singing

—High energy, your love is lifting me, high energy, your love is lifting me high.

Senator Kingston reported to the Taoiseach that he had sent the ideal man to the Ship, and though Henry felt this was an exaggeration, he decided to reward Jimmy for his success on such a tricky mission.

In the North, rumours of a ceasefire grew. All sides waited for an announcement, but in the meantime life and death went on much as before.

An RUC patrol is moving through the streets of a market town, listening to the sound of *Coronation Street* from the living-rooms of houses, when another familiar noise prompts five dives to the ground. The shots come out of the dark and continue for a couple of minutes. When they stop there is no sound, not even of fleeing gunmen, as if the shots have resulted from a chemical reaction between patrol and night. The constables cannot hear *Coronation Street* any more. They listen to the noise of the blood in their ears, that seashell sound letting them know they still exist and have not gone into the silent blackness.

*

The man locking up his bicycle repair shop is embarrassed by his difficulty in closing the shutters. When he sees someone approaching, he searches for a smart quip to cover his awkwardness before noticing the pistol in the man's hand. The trigger is pulled but there is no explosion, and the gunman bangs his weapon on the ground, tries to shoot again and then says 'shit,' as if he has stepped on a sharp object, before running off.

The shopkeeper's heart pounds as he thanks God for a truly miraculous escape. He is aware of the reliability of that make, as he has used it to blow the brains out of four Catholics at similarly close range. He does not know why the IRA came for him tonight. His last killing was four years ago, though he would have no qualms about shooting more Taigs if it was necessary. The shutter goes down at the tenth attempt.

The house-proud streak in Clinton McCain makes him unhappy about the two circles in his double-glazed front windows. His recently acquired hearing difficulties explain why he did not register the shots as he tidied the garden shed. He is not in the least frightened. His wife might have been, but she is dead two years of a heart attack. The shooting was amateurish, almost ritual. They were not sufficiently bothered to make sure. He knows what happens when they make sure since the booby-trapping of his son's car ten years ago, leading to the identification which Clinton could not make. Powerless, he was forced to yield to the superiority of dental records.

His son had been in the UDR, though he had not shown the same flair as Clinton. The elder McCain had revelled in the black comedy of the B Special life in those glory days when it seemed nothing would change. Tormenting his neighbours, intercepting people he had known all his life and requesting proof of identity, asking them where they were going, holding them up at checkpoints so they would be good and late for the Ulster final, making their sons walk barefoot through mucky fields as they headed home from dances the other side of the border. The Clinton McCain cabaret. Reading his Bible, he remembers how the Pharaoh's pride caused the extirpation of the first-born. The only satisfaction he draws from his survival is that it denies the enemy the joy of his death.

These neighbourly patterns of dispute, blame and revenge mean nothing to Private John Burke as he walks across the road at a checkpoint outside a town he had not heard of six weeks previously. He is thinking of a present list for a marriage which would have taken place two months later, had a sniper's bullet not entered the back of his head and exited at his right eye, killing him immediately. The sniper raises his fist and celebrates silently before proceeding to a waiting car and the admiration of the driver.

Private John Burke, Orsett Road, Grays, Essex, RM17 5EX, ceases to exist at 11.52 p.m. on a Tuesday night. Eight minutes before the ceasefire.

Peace breaks out the next morning. The IRA announces the suspension of military operations. Henry is not sure this means they will stop killing, and is aware that there will be no halt to the punishment beatings, protection rackets, kneecappings and other perversions growing symbiotically on the armed struggle. But it is hard to be unhappy on the morning of a ceasefire. The word hope is ubiquitous, poetry is quoted and the television news shows Troubles footage as if it now belongs to history. As if one announcement, following a recognised code word, has wiped out the past.

The code word had always preceded news of death. Acknowledgement of responsibility for a bombing, the position of an informer's body, the beginning of a hunger strike. Now a uniform precursor of dread has become the harbinger of the ultimate good news.

South of the border, the ceasefire liberates the feelings hidden in the thatch when the masonry began to collapse and the ambulances rush towards the flames in the other kingdom. Plunkett, Pearse and Tone can be thought of without a wince. The verdict has been overturned. They have been cleared.

Henry feels proud as he stands in front of government buildings with Jude Locke and Charlie Burns. They are harking back to . . . to when? To before the Troubles. No, because then there had been no real links between North and South, no sense of a united Catholic front like this one. Before 1922? No link there, either. The photo of their meeting evokes nostalgia for a past that never was. The Holy Trinity. Henry Caslin, leader of the Republic, Jude Locke, leader of the Northern Catholics, Charlie Burns, leader of . . . what, exactly? Perhaps some tradition. Maybe the ghosts of Father John Murphy, O'Donovan Rossa, John Mitchel. He suggests some historical avatar of revolution come to life. All the opprobrium shovelled over him and his men over the past twenty years has melted away, silenced like the guns.

Soon after the ceasefire, the Republic's soccer team wins a World Cup match, sparking extraordinary celebration in that country and among the Northern Catholics, who give the team their allegiance. The Northern celebrations are of necessity more circumspect. The Catholics cannot take over the streets and drink cans of beer in fountains or drive their cars down the main thoroughfare in Belfast, hanging out of the doors and windows, smiling and joking with journalists and photographers recording a moment of unequivocal national joy.

All the same, their jubilation is noticed by men who brood and make phone calls, gathering a group who travel beyond the city, past the small towns, off the main roads, into the countryside of isolated bungalows and inflammatory GAA pitches standing mutely insolent by the roadside. They laugh and joke on the way, not mentioning their journey's purpose until they arrive outside a pub whose customers are discussing the wonderful possibility of Ireland winning the World Cup. Leaving the car at a quarter past eleven, the five men check their weapons and pull balaclavas over their faces.

The owner of Tom's Bar tells his customers the next pint will be the last one.

No one understands why the men in masks have burst into the pub until they start firing. The place is too small for alcoves and partitions, so the customers are easy targets. The men empty their guns into them, their aim slightly affected by drink. Mirrors behind the bar, the television and the cash register are all pocked with bullet holes. The attackers flee with the sound of moaning and death in their ears, their leader staying for a minute to reload, picking his targets more carefully this time, luxuriating in the pathetic spectacle of the other side crawling, cowering, dying. Later, in their drinking club, the fact of twelve dead Taigs leaves the jubilant gunmen in awe of their own power.

The following day their organisation declares its own ceasefire, and now they too are men of peace.

If asked why he led the gang to Tom's Bar, Floyd McCausland would probably mumble something about feeling that the Protestants were losing out, that their way of life was threatened, that they were a people under siege. In the world of peace he will need such justifications. The casual word of hate which earns respect in the drinking club will not suffice, and he will have to learn political-speak, culling it from clips of his paramilitary rivals on the News. But he knows that what brought him to that remote country pub was the agony he felt watching Ireland win as he imagined the build-up of unrestrained Fenian joy. He has committed the ultimate act of football hooliganism.

Henry may struggle to understand Charlie Burns, but he cannot begin to imagine what drives Floyd McCausland.

The announcement of the second ceasefire heaps petrol on to the blaze of hope. Everyone holds their breath for a week. No one is killed. The grim reaper seems to have gone on strike. The News is imbued with a strange sense of absence. A young man decided this was an opportune time to drive to Belfast.

The young man's unstinting devotion to the Church overrode any other consideration. Father Ulick Connaughton was able, dedicated, highly intelligent and someone Cardinal O'Hanlon hoped never to see again when his task was done. The young priest was a product of his times, a disturbing fact when the Church's power lay largely in its timelessness. The Church of Father Connaughton, and of the other bright new stars in the hierarchical firmament, was a Church of reaction, a ministry of combat, conflict and confrontation.

Cardinal O'Hanlon did not wholly blame them for this. They had been forced into the posture by a modern world determined to trample on all religious values. Nevertheless it troubled him that Father Connaughton was driven by negatives. His stated reasons for joining the Church all contained the word 'against'. He was against sexual promiscuity, against abortion, against euthanasia, against a valueless contemporary society. He never mentioned the glory of God or the mystery of the sacraments. His outlook was, in fact, a secular one.

In Father Connaughton's pockets were two brown envelopes, one containing several thousand pounds in cash and the other twenty-four photocopies of a letter from a solicitor with a senior position in a secret Catholic organisation. The letter offered a settlement in respect of the Father Lee affair. Important conditions were attached.

The gas in the first house he visited had been cut off. A Staffordshire bull terrier growled at Father Ulick as he took note of other unopened bills lying beside an off-the-hook phone.

—I think those are very generous cash terms, Miss McQuillan.

—The Church should have done something about that fella. Ye must have known what was going on.

—There is no question of our being aware of what was going on. We deny that totally. And we are very sorry about what has happened. That is why I am here on behalf of the Church. We await your response. No money can compensate you for what you have suffered, I know that. I think the conditions attached to the settlement are very generous, as well.

No media interviews by anyone who receives money. In fact, although he knew there was no appropriate legal formula, Father Connaughton hinted that an interview by any victim would result in everyone else losing their money.

—Father Lee will still go to court, won't he? He'll still be convicted?

—That's up to the RUC, although I should point out that a court case involving Father Lee might delay the payment of monies. As far as I'm aware, anyway, no one knows where he is. It's doubtful if he would be convicted in any case, as most of the offences took place so long ago that evidence could be ruled inadmissible. I must stress that I'm only speculating.

Father Connaughton gave the same spiel at the end of each visit.

—The Church does not have to do this at all. This is a

gesture out of the goodness of our heart. Under canon law, we bear no responsibility for Father Lee.

Canon law. Father Connaughton loved canon law, its mystery, its order, its inscrutability and its complications. Most of all he loved the way it could be mentioned when the Church's authority was challenged. It was infinitely preferable to Scripture. The devil could cite Scripture for his own purposes, but he could not cite canon law. It was the ideal legal code, known only to those who invoked it.

—I would like you to have this money to tide you over for the time being. As an expression of how seriously we are taking this case.

Not many of the people he was dealing with were in a position to refuse money, and Father Connaughton did not see why they should. In fact the whole hullabaloo puzzled him. He could not understand why child sex abuse left the Church paralysed with fear, as though it had revealed the essence of evil. In America he had seen the greatest depravity of all. Abortion. Yet people were free to speak on television and write in newspapers that women should be allowed to kill their babies. No one spoke or wrote in favour of child abuse. Father Connaughton did not think they should, but at least the sufferers remained alive. No one made pay-offs to the victims of the abortionists. He had pointed out the incongruity of this to the cardinal, but was not listened to.

Some of the victims refused the money, and let him know that should he remove the settlement offer from the envelope, they would tear the sheets of paper into little pieces and sprinkle them over his head like confetti. They did not want to settle on the Church's terms. Even his reasonable argument that, in the absence of Father Lee, no other solution was possible did not seem to impress them. The drunk in the wheelchair did not bluster or threaten or ask in a belligerent manner why the Church had not tackled Father Lee long ago. He seemed delighted with the settlement. Father Connaughton felt relieved as he enumerated the advantages of a speedy wrap-up of the affair. His relief meant that he had no objections to answering a couple of polite questions.

—The Church knows all about what Father Lee did?

—Oh, well, there's a certain knowledge there. We want to help people overcome the pain they felt and say they still feel.

—This sort of proves in a kind of way, doesn't it, that the Church knew about him years ago, and that they know the RUC are looking for him.

—I suppose so. But what we are interested in is coming to a settlement which will take account of your pain.

Armstrong rang McKeon the second Father Connaughton pulled the front door after him.

—Jimmy, I'm nominating you to the Senate. Senator Mimnagh, doesn't it have a nice ring to it. A bit of the oul assonance they used talk about in English class. The big time, boy.

Finally Jimmy was a member of the parliamentary party, someone who could attend meetings in his own right. Henry realised this was the first gift he had ever given the man. The thought of all Jimmy had given him made him feel embarrassed. In his first interviews as Taoiseach, he had constantly stressed that his own hard work had brought him to the top. Soon the phone records for Henry's office showed Jimmy's number eclipsed by those of Martina Caslin and Sian Guiney.

His time in Rathbawn had lent Jimmy a reputation as the mastermind behind Henry, and the embodiment of a rural political tradition of native cunning regarded in the capital as both impenetrable and invincible. His utterances restricted to the County Council, he had become legendary in the manner of a great musician whose only recordings are on ancient acetate, or a famous writer who has left a handful of works. Once in the Senate, he was reduced to a little man with a red face and badly fitting suit, whose contributions were only notable for unintentional surrealism.

—The turf in Rathbawn bog is unfit for human consumption.

—The quality of the water in my county is so bad that people have to boil it before they can make a cup of tea.

—There's been a lot of talk about the poor condition of public urinals, but the arsenals are in an even worse state.

The laughter every time he stood up eventually decided him against making speeches, and he began to favour the complicitous company of the no-hopers who made up the majority of his colleagues. But because it was not in him to be lazy, he would ring Martina in the constituency office twice a day and ask if all was running smoothly. Twice a day she would tell him it was. A less busy woman might have detected what lay behind Jimmy's question, and from time to time asked for help.

—How are things going in the Senate, Jimmy?

—Fine, Henry. Great. Everything is going fierce well.

Henry would have spotted the lie from anyone else, but it did not occur to him that Jimmy would struggle with something as easy as a job in the Senate. He told his mentor that as long as Henry was Taoiseach, Jimmy would remain a senator.

Between Rathbawn and Kilnatty that night Jimmy lost control of his car, which tumbled through a frosty field before coming to a halt on its back with the wheels still spinning. Walking away with a sprained ankle, he ticked off the crash as his twenty-seventh.

His cars had flown over gates and fences, and through

fields containing a wide variety of crops and beasts. He had crashed into the backs of lorries, vans and tractors, drifted off into a pleasant sleep and woken up with the car upside down on the motorway out of Dublin at five in the morning, slewed off the road at a Galway seaside resort, the car crashing across rocks until it lay by the ocean with puzzled seagulls regarding Jimmy's climb through the passenger door window. The thought of harm coming to himself or anyone else on the road had long since been banished from his mind.

On Ash Wednesday he drank from eleven to eleven in the Imperial, taking solace in the presence of familiar faces in the bar, the black smudges on their foreheads showing that not everything was changing. At five past eleven he began to drive the three miles home. A mile out the road, the car behind him flashed its lights. Another car joined it. They both wanted him to stop. He pulled in to the side of the road, parking diagonally a few inches away from a telegraph pole.

—Mister Mimnagh, we have formed the impression that you are driving with an excess amount of alcohol in your blood. We would like you to blow into this bag.

The crystals turned green just before Jimmy got sick on them. When the cops asked him to accompany them to the station, he realised something was up.

Normally the cops were friendly when they pulled him, telling him he looked wobbly and to mind himself the rest of the way home, or following him out to the house, beeping the horn in friendly fashion when they saw him moor safely. On occasion they pointed out that he was too drunk to drive and left him out to the house in the squad car. The next morning he would pick up the keys at the station and leave a bottle of whiskey with the desk sergeant.

There were no friendly beeps of the horn this night. The cops looked slightly troubled. Jimmy gave a urine sample and was left home by the same lads, who the next week gave him a lift to the courthouse where, at half past ten, he was convicted of drink-driving and banned from the road for twelve months.

He had been unable to get hold of Henry, and when he called Mickey Kelly was told nothing could be done. The rules seemed to have been changed without his knowledge. The Minister for Justice telling him he could not fix a simple drink-driving case, where was the justice in that? Kelly repeated that there was nothing he could do. Maybe Henry, he said, and left it at that.

It was half eleven before Henry took any phone messages. He did not want to hear what Jimmy said in case it dissuaded him from the decision Henry had made after the last crash. The decision to tell the Rathbawn traffic cops to make sure Jimmy was put off the road so his friends had one less reason to worry at night.

If Henry had explained this to Jimmy, everything might have turned out differently, but he could not explain because he had acted for Jimmy's own good, and the knowledge that you were unable to act in your own best interests was not something to be divulged by your best friend.

After the verdict, Jimmy did not take his usual place at the Imperial bar. Instead he retired to drink a bottle of whiskey in a snug so he could avoid being pitied by people he employed for one pound fifty an hour. The voices of one of the traffic cops and the young journalist from the *Herald* wafted towards him from the bar.

—I heard Caslin set him up. I heard he asked ye to bag Mimnagh, said the journalist.

—He did, said the guard, but I'll say nothing else.

—And do you know why I think he did it? I think he was worried that Jimmy was going to kill someone. I think he was worried this might reflect on him.

—I'm saying nothing.

—I think poor oul Jimmy has become an embassassment to his old friend the Taoiseach.

In the snug, Jimmy crouched like a hunted fox, waiting for discovery and shameful death. When the voices stopped he crept out, ordered another bottle of whiskey and got a taxi home.

At first he berated himself for being an embarrassment to Herny, but the whiskey made the story clearer and revealed its implications. This slight could not pass un-avenged, not because of personal pique but because of the laws which ruled their lives, the hard codes of pragmatism where friends were favoured, enemies destroyed and insults remembered. He could not let Henry get away with this. It would not be fair to either of them. Henry knew the story.

If you can't do the time, then don't do the crime.

The phrase repeated in his mind through the next day, and meant he did not say a word at the County Council meeting until he was jolted back into the familiar local world by a Party councillor who had the bad grace to raise a matter on Any Other Business as everyone else was putting their coats on.

—Mister Chairman, I'd like to bring everyone's atten-tion to the problems which the people in Colmcille Park are having with the, how do we say it, the travelling folk.

A tennis court had been used as a cockfighting stand and horse paddock, scrap metal had been piled outside front doors, greyhounds allowed to run free. One traveller family had responded to financial difficulties by cutting up the stairs in their house and selling them to a timber merchant.

—How long can this go on, Mister Chairman?

Jimmy polished the weapons of his own destruction as

keenly as any tinker's sharpening stone would have, handing them to himself with a cheery there you are, boss.

—I take Mister Colleran's point, but perhaps we as a council could do more for the travelling community. A lot of them wouldn't be used to living in houses. We could, how would you say it, house-train them. Help them in skills like putting on the kettle or switching on the gas or cleaning the house. If we work with them, then they might be able to live like normal people.

When a fleshy young woman with red hair in a long plait appeared on the RTE news with the Market Square in Rathbawn as a backdrop the next day, he felt the familiar joy of seeing an acquaintance on television. Now what was her name again?

—Nora Lawrence, I'm the Chairperson of the Rathbawn Travellers' Women's Group, and I think it's a pure disgrace what Jimmy Mimnagh said. It's a pure insult to us travellers. House-training is a way you'd be going on about animals, and I never seen no traveller woman that wasn't able to clean the house.

—You're not very happy then, Missus Lawrence.

—I am not. We want Jimmy Mimnagh to say he's sorry. We want an apology for him making a laugh and a mock of the travellers in this town.

The first four calls on Jimmy's answering machine told him fair play, good man, sound skin, up ya boy ya and it's about time the knackers, the gyppos, the minks, the itinerants were told where they stand, were put in their box, had manners put on them, were let know the score. This had not been his intention, but the response heartened him. The fifth call was from Henry, who wanted him in Dublin pronto.

—They're looking for an apology, said Henry.

Jimmy nodded. A stack of national and local newspaper

headlines had colonised Henry's desk. He looked at the headlines.

—Trainer wanted for Rathbawn's tinkers, said the *Herald*.

—Mimnagh's forthright comments on traveller situation draw stern response from local travellers' group, said the *Irish Times*.

—Tink again Jimmy, said the *Sun*.

On the way to Dublin, he had heard Nora Lawrence on three radio stations. Going on as if she was someone important, when he knew well what she was. Hadn't himself and Henry got her parents a house when they were on the side of the road in the freezing cold and hadn't a pot to piss in?

—It's a disgrace, Henry, the tinkers going on like this. Jesus, at least in the old days they'd be glad for a bit of oul food or some old clothes, and they'd call you sir to your face at least, whatever they were saying behind your back, and if they were on your land you could have an oul blast at them with the shotgun and they'd move off without making too much of a fuss. But now suddenly today they're on about their rights. Rights, did you ever hear the bate of it, of course it's not themselves that thought of it in the first place, it's those social workers that they have, that have the head rose on them, as if they had rights, them and their training workshops as if you could train them to do anything or as if anyone would give a tinker a job. Would you listen to them, going on and on on the fucking News and saying that they're a minority and they have rights. They're not a minority, Henry, they're tinkers, the same as they always have been.

—I want you to make an apology, Jimmy, and I want you to make it today. As soon as you can put something together.

—That's a good one, Henry. You hoor, you had me going for a second.

—I'm serious, Jimmy. I know you meant nothing by what you said but you have to apologise. That's all that's to it.

The phone rang. Locke was on the line to explain how things were going with the sinister confrères of Burns and McConville. The Chief of Staff. The Army Council. The Quartermaster. Henry waved Jimmy out of the office without explaining why the apology had become necessary.

A lift up to Dublin in Martina's BMW and a quick tour of the Taoiseach's office should have been enough to keep Nora Lawrence happy. Only it hadn't been.

—You were very good to us, Mister Caslin. There's a lot of us settled in Rathbawn.

—I always made sure ye were looked after. I remember your mother well. I got her that house and helped her out with the rent at the start.

—She always spoke well of you, Mister Caslin. We used say a little prayer for you before we went to bed at night. There's not a traveller in the town that doesn't vote for the Party, Mister Caslin.

—Your votes are very special to me.

—They're the same votes as anyone else's. One vote each. Over a thousand votes. Always for yourself. We're your voters, Mister Caslin, only it goes the two ways, you see. You're our TD as well. So you have to do the right thing by us. We want Councillor Mimnagh to say he was sorry for what he said or we'll have a demonstration outside the Dáil. We'll go home then and think about who we're voting for.

—I don't know if I can tell Councillor Mimnagh what to say.

—I know. You can.

He looked in the woman's eyes. She had been born in a house and lived in one all her life, but she still had that look, forged from hundreds of years of living off their wits which told you they knew exactly how the cards were falling, how strong you were and how much they could get away with. It was the way they looked if you tried to outsmart them on a horse deal or find the queen in a three-card trick. All you could do was shrug your shoulders and let them know they'd won. He told Martina to give Nora a couple of days' work a week in the office. She was one for the future.

Christy Dockery had told him he was foolish to look for the tinkers' vote because they would feel they had a right to respect from the Party. Back then the mere recognition of their existence had been enough for them. Now Henry had backed down in front of a tinker woman who had done to the pride of his best friend what her mother had done to the windows of Rathbawn at a horse fair long ago. He could almost hear the crash and see the shine of the sun on the glinting petrol cans as Biddy Stokes shattered the windows on the settled street, laughing as she went.

Jimmy's colleagues hung their heads in sympathy when his apology was read out. He kept telling himself there was now documentary proof that Henry thought his best friend was lower than a gyp. Words repeated in his head. That is it. That is it. That is it No more. Revenge. Soon.

Henry could not read these thoughts because he had become part of history. For six months he had met with Jude Locke and also with Charlie Burns, and finally the two men from the country above came up with a document setting out conditions for entering talks. Henry perused the document and advisers confirmed his dark suspicions. The requests were perfectly reasonable: Locke was a genius and

Burns was not a fanatic. He backed the document and let the British know the shooting might stop if they did the same. The Brits said they were interested in this idea. The ceasefires had been called and everyone was waiting for the talks to start.

It had not been a simple process. Sometimes the aspiration to peace had seemed impossible, and the killing likely to go on for ever. Like the morning Locke rang Henry and told him to turn on the television news. Armstrong's men had planted a bomb in the heart of a Protestant district, and nine people out grocery shopping had been killed along with the bomber. Locke said it was important to maintain a united front, his voice sounding as if all the sadness he had seen was conspiring to weigh him down, as if his famous hope was wavering. Keeling in the force of the blast which had brought walls and a roof down on the heads of Saturday-morning shoppers.

—Is that it, then? asked Henry.

—No, said Locke, it just proves how important it is to stop it all. But there's one very big problem I have to warn you about. The man who blew up the shop was killed in the explosion, and Burns says he's going to carry his coffin. He says he has to. He says his people expect him to.

A firestorm broke in Locke's direction, but he withstood it even as the photo of Burns carrying the atomised remains of the bomber were flashed round the world as a reproach to anyone who dared think there could be a solution in the North.

Henry understood that firestorm because that morning he too had cursed Burns for his sentimental belief in gesture. The week after the ceasefire he saw the same sentimentality strut the streets. He had presumed that people would celebrate peace by going to a football match, having a meal, visiting the seaside, seizing the new normality and forgetting the dark doings of the past. Burns's people did the opposite. They swam in that past as if wishing to summon it back with their freedom carnivals, demonstrations and street theatre about women banging dustbin lids on the ground to warn of approaching British soldiers. The people on the other side were preparing for a summer of commemorating a battle won by a Dutch general three hundred years before. Henry marvelled at the durability of ill will.

Peace or no peace, no one wanted to let things lie. The past was a compendium of events and ideas which proved the justice of your cause and the decrepitude of your opponent's. Memory was not that long in the Party. During the Civil War, Free State troops had tied nine Republican prisoners to a landmine which they then detonated. One man survived and became a Party TD, within ten years sitting in the Dáil opposite friends of the men who had bound him. Things were different in the South.

Locke always insisted on the similarities between nationalist people North and South. One of their secret meetings had coincided with a rare victory for Celtic over Rangers. Henry, Locke and Burns jumped with joy simultaneously when the final whistle blew. Burns seemed happiest of all.

—Let's face it, Henry. We should be on the same side, getting what we want by peaceful means. You're up for the nationalists, the British are up for the Unionists, don't give me this neutrality shit. If we all say what we really want and are honest about that, then things can be solved.

Henry knew he understood Burns better than he could a Protestant politician. A fortnight after the ceasefire he visited him, their handshake prompting a mass whirr of camera motors and a run on the use of the word historic by reporters. Burns gestured grandiloquently at the crowd, in a manner which Henry suspected had been learned from a textbook for revolutionary leaders.

—Look at them, Henry, my people. These are the citizens who have been utterly demonised by everyone, not least by those you represent.

Nodding, Henry allowed Burns to make his point, and met nice men and nice women and the word demonised was used a few more times, and Henry would have felt fantastic if he could have told himself that they were exactly the same people in Rathbawn, and had not deserved one bad line of press ever.

But that night in bed he could not stop thinking about a piece of news film from a few years back, shot during an awful week of killings and cortèges and coffins borne on shoulders. Burns had been one of the pallbearers when a car drove right into the middle of a funeral procession.

The two men in the car were British soldiers, but it was the next day before that was generally known. The men who surrounded the vehicle may have found out earlier. The film showed the driver and passenger trying to escape, perhaps attempting to explain that they had made a mistake as they began to realise their fate. The crowd swarmed over the car, one man furiously wielding a wheelbrace as if trying to beat some dark demon back to Hell. The two men were dragged away. You could feel their fear from watching the film, a small and pathetic emotion beside the fury of the mob.

The next pictures had been taken from a helicopter, and showed the soldiers being dragged to nearby wasteground. It was left to the following day's newspapers to reveal that the men had been stripped, beaten, tortured and dispatched with shots to the head by the IRA. But all that information seemed to be contained in the film, as if somehow transmitted by the aerial view of the crowd moving remorselessly towards a satisfying closure. Photos showed the men's bruised and bloodied bodies lying horribly naked on the football pitch.

The memory of the film made Henry realise that his and

Burns's people were not the same. He cannot picture his constituents participating in such a rite, although he knows Burns would accuse him of demonisation if he said this. But what happened to the two men seemed somehow demonic. Years of death and fruitless hatred had to affect the man beating the car roof with a wheelbrace. He might have turned out like someone from Rathbawn given different circumstances, but he had not, and there was no point pretending otherwise.

An average of thirteen people a month had been murdered in the North lately. When the first month of peace went by, Henry thought to himself that thirteen people had already been saved. Some days he counted thirteen people on the street and imagined the loss they would have been to the world. Peace had arrived and had begun to prepare a page in the history books for him.

Mickey Kelly's unhappiness was contemporaneous with that of Jimmy Mimnagh, and later Henry would wonder if Kelly's condition had hoovered up all available compassion and concern, blinding everyone to Jimmy's feelings.

The first sign that anything was wrong came one Wednesday, when Henry phoned Kelly's office and asked where he was. Henry recognised the pause from Kelly's assistant as a weighing up of the pros and cons of candour. The woman was not naturally dishonest, but working for Kelly had provided a high-powered tutorial in dissembling, deception and downright treachery.

—He's gone to Lough Derg, Taoiseach.

Mickey Kelly on a religious retreat at Lough Derg. That was definitely a lie.

It was not.

At Lough Derg, Kelly shuffled round in a circle and recited prayers from a black-bound missal. He had not eaten or slept in twenty-four hours, and offered his discomfort up to God before climbing Croaghpatrick and then taking to the skies in search of the Kingdom of Heaven, first visiting Lourdes and Fatima before travelling further into the interior of mysticism, reaching Compostela, Garabandal, even Medjugorje and other sites the Church could not bring itself to anoint with the chrism of approval. In his head were the singing and wailing voices of young Medjugorjan visionaries, and the Spanish girls from Garabandal who had seen the Blessed Virgin. He dreamed of the Angel of Mercy leading Bernadette's feet where flowed the deep torrent Our Lady to greet, and saw the sun dance in the sky over Medjugorje. At each stop he saw the familiar faces of the terminally ill on a last desperate voyage.

He returned sunburned, changed and with a special devotion to Our Lady, whose virginal purity embodied all that was good in and unattainable by women. Back on home soil he continued his explorations, leaving his driver reading the sports pages in the state car while he looked at grottos inhabited by moving statues, walked through fields where Our Lady had recently appeared, handled rosary beads which had dropped blood, examined stigmata on the hands of healers and heard the postmistress on a windswept island speak in tongues. Each experience deepened his new-found belief.

The gossips said Kelly was mentally ill. The man had always said his favourite part of Mass was the display of young ones' arses when they knelt down for Communion, and now he was walking around with a gigantic holy ring on the middle finger of his right hand and saying 'God bless' all the time. He had even started to walk in the treading-water style used by the Pope on foreign visits. It was this walk that brought him purposefully into Henry's office the day he returned from Fatima.

—What do you mean, you're going to resign? Sit down

there, Mickey, like a good chap, and don't be giving me heart attacks.

—I have to resign from your government. It's nothing against you, Henry, but I feel we are no longer providing a moral lead for the people.

Henry felt like he was on *You've Been Framed*, and wanted to mouth an obscenity so someone would jump out of a filing cabinet and say we had you going there, Henry, didn't we, before the situation degenerated into a matey welter of laughter, tears and playful shakings of the fist.

—How do you mean, Mickey . . . exactly?

—Making sodomy legal, Henry, is an offence against God, and I cannot be part of a government which offends the Almighty.

Henry sniffed the air surreptitiously. No, Kelly hadn't been drinking.

—Ah, come on now, Mickey. I'm no fonder of the homos than you are, but sure what harm can it do? They're at it anyway, and it wasn't as if it was really illegal. The guards have better things to do than go around arresting lads for riding each other.

—It is abhorrent in God's sight, Henry. It is unnatural, and He destroyed the cities of Sodom and Gomorrah for their citizens' indulgence in such vice. They have called down a plague on themselves, and tolerating them places us all at risk.

Henry was fucked if he was going to let his most powerful ally leave the Cabinet because he seemed to have swapped souls with Ian Paisley. He suggested a drink in Buswell's.

—I don't drink any more, Henry, I'm a changed man.

Some of the biblical sonorities leached away from Mickey's speech as, over minerals, he agreed to withdraw his resignation before suddenly looking troubled again.

—It's just that they say you're going to legalise abortion. For a start.

Henry knew who they were. The lay warriors who had seen a threat to the Church's hegemony before the clergy had. Many of them reborn on traffic-cluttered roads during the papal visit. The reason for the Pope's visit revealed to them as they sat in traffic jams. Some seven then and some seventy, but the pictures in their minds the same. Graven images of Columbanus, St Gall, Colmcille, St Fiachra, the Irish missionaries who had travelled out from the island in the Dark Ages, saving civilisation. Ireland had once been a beacon of hope in a godless and brutish world. It could be again. They would make it so.

Their first mission had been to make abortion illegal. It was illegal already, but that was not the point. Before he saw the vigils and the pickets and read the letters to the newspapers, Henry had not thought much about abortion. He knew it was the murder of a defenceless, unborn child and could not be condoned, and he did not need to be told this by the men and women who stood in his way as he left the office and handed him leaflets containing photos of aborted foetuses in rubbish bins and plastic bags. Abortion was made doubly illegal.

They now seemed to be part of Kelly's life. Because he was too much of a politican to believe in conversion without motivation, Henry made it his business to find out the reasons for the man's religious rebirth.

The Minister for Justice had returned from three days of sex and white wine in Corfu, with a young model who picked up wealthy older men and underwear contracts with equal aplomb, to find his wife sitting in their hall surrounded by boxes, crates and black bin bags. She told him the marriage was over just before removal men arrived to bring her belongings to the house of Kelly's Special Branch bodyguard.

—It's the first affair I've ever had, Mickey. How many is it for you? I can tell you it's thirty-six because I've known about every one.

He forswore all adulteries and carousing and told his wife that things could go back to how they had been once.

—They can for you, but not for me.

Drink could not erase the thoughts of his thinner, happier wife with another man. Prayer and thoughts of Our Lady, whose purity was the supreme virtue, did.

At Lough Derg he walked beside a holy well and muttered prayers for the dead. A tall grey-haired man with an oddly familiar face joined him.

—Minister.

—I am not a Minister when I am here. I am just plain Mickey Kelly, a sinner.

—My belief too. My name is Mark Fleming, I am one of the senior civil servants in your new Department. It is marvellous to see you here.

Together they circled the well, praying to God as if beseeching Him to ward off something lying in the dark waters all about.

On Monday Fleming returned to his station, a mahogany desk that had been in the Department of Justice since the state's foundation. Every morning he examined the grain of the wood and marvelled at its intricate, subtle beauty. He was a man who noticed such things.

This eye for detail was only one of the qualities which made him an ideal senior civil servant. Also there were his teetotal status, his punctuality, his lack of levity and his devotion to making sure the paperwork in the Department was attended to with dispatch and energy. Warrants did not pile up and cases were not delayed if Mark Fleming had anything to do with it.

—I have done the state some service.

The quote from *Othello* was a favourite. Hard work at

his Christian Brothers School had earned him first place in the civil service entrance examinations. Forty-five years of service had seen him to a position of seniority from which he would retire in two years. Checking the day's post, he was only slightly distracted by the thought of the extradition warrant bearing the signature of RUC Inspector Clive Hunter, which four weeks previously he had taken and locked in the bottom drawer.

Hunter's wife had worried about his trip South for the angling competition on Lough Mask. There was a ceasefire, but not all IRA units recognised it. The Provos were well capable of turning up on railway platforms to shoot young squaddies home on leave. Shooting a senior RUC man as he waited for a twitch on the line would hardly be beyond them. But the waters of the South's fishing lakes killed thoughts of murder. He never felt safer than when by the Mask, Lough Moy, Lough Conn, Lough Arrow or Lough Gara. Death was far from his thoughts when two burly men clapped him on the shoulder in the hotel bar after the prize-giving.

—Inspector Clive Hunter, RUC Belfast, we presume?

Hunter nodded.

—Could you come with us outside? It would be better not to do this in the bar.

They brought him to a blue sports car in the hotel car park and offered him a cigarette. He accepted, and passed a comment on the beauty of both weather and countryside.

—We were wondering, could you do us a favour?

—Willie Kilcullen told us you might be able to. Sergeant Kilcullen.

Sergeant Willie Kilcullen. Coarse and game angler, and expert speedboat pilot. Hunter's nemesis in many a fishing tourney. A good chap.

—We work at the same caper as Willie.

This Southern bullshit drove him mad. Why could they not just say they were policemen, instead of talking out the sides of their mouths as if ashamed? It was the attitude of a servile people. Eight hundred years saying yes sir and no sir to lords and landlords.

—There's a little favour we'd like to ask you.

The brother of one of the gardai had broken an opponent's jaw in a pub brawl, and as he had been previously bound to the peace would face a spell in Mountjoy Prison if found guilty. His police connections would make his time in jail very difficult. Hunter gave an empathetic shudder of ecumenical solidarity.

—The thing is, like, that your man he clattered is a salesman. He'll be in Belfast the day before the trial. If he got held there for twenty-four hours then he'd miss the trial, and the brother would be away with it. You see the crack?

Hunter assured them that he saw the crack. The two Free State cops assured him of a favour in return. He mentioned casually that if they found Father Gerry Lee, they could consider the debt wiped out.

Not that he expected much. He only arrested the salesman because he was in a good mood after his fishing trip, and knew policemen should stick together against civilians. The Free Staters were always assuring the RUC of their full cooperation in security matters, even though the most they achieved was occasionally to unearth six ancient mortars, three flintlocks and some halberds which had last been used at the Battle of Ballinamuck. This the Garda Síochána called a triumph.

Six days later, Hunter received a phone call telling him that Father Lee was in Balcrotty Abbey in the South, and would be for some time. He sent the extradition warrant to Dublin. Three months passed, and nothing happened. When he rang Mark Fleming in the Department of Justice, he was told the warrant seemed to be lost. Hunter travelled South and handed the documentation over in person. Now Fleming was talking about an unavoidable delay.

The delay puzzled Hunter, only because he did not know about Mark Fleming's relationship with God, one rooted in genealogy rather than theology. His father had been sacristan of an inner-city church, and received a minor papal honour shortly before his death. His mother attended Mass every day and knitted vestments for the local clergy. Brothers, sisters and cousins were camp followers of the big battalions of the Church, ringing bells, ferrying offertory gifts, serving Communion, reading at Mass. His own devotion was of the highest order, and he read the Gospels through once a month. They taught him compassion. He had not taken a drink since his wife left him, and now his evenings were spent in soup kitchens on the quays, shelters for the homeless and ruined housing estates, which would have struck fear into anyone unaware of the greater dangers overcome by Elijah and Samuel, Moses and Job. He contributed handsomely to charity and visited cancer patients, drug addicts, even those dying of the new disease he regarded as a divine punishment, a judgement he kept to himself.

As a young man he had been scared of the nullity of death, but now he worried about adequately repaying Jesus for the gift of eternal life, trying to replicate the Saviour's pain by flagellating himself in the evening until he bled, following the example of the penitent Matt Talbot by wearing under his clothes chains which bit into the flesh.

The crimes of Father Gerry Lee made Fleming pray that the victims would find peace and the perpetrator divine forgiveness. He reviled these acts against children, the most precious of Jesus' followers.

But.

He was no hermit. He did not spend his life on a pillar in the desert, but in an office with a computer and a fax and a home with television and newspapers. He wondered if the revelation of Father Lee's crimes would damage the belief of the faithful and rang his spiritual adviser, a man connected with secret organisations whose links to the Church were unclear. The adviser told him the warrant should not be seen by anyone else. Fleming set aside a place in the bottom drawer.

A new year began with Father Lee no closer to justice, and Hunter protesting until the Minister for Justice was forced to ask Fleming why the warrant had not been acted on. The civil servant reminded Kelly of the solace and comfort he derived from the Church. Would he do anything to damage it?

Kelly shook his head, and when told the warrant would sit in limbo rather than ascending to the eye of the Director of Public Prosecutions, smiled in the knowledge that he was giving something back.

McKeon continued to work on the story, listening to his tapes, reading the handwritten notes, the typed pages, the sudden thoughts which had come to him in pubs, in the car, in restaurants, and were written on the backs of beermats, on tissues, on Post-Its, on parking tickets, railway tickets, left-luggage tickets, and had once been scratched into the table in his study with a knife when the house was biroless and the thought fleeting.

By writing and rewriting, he was trying to make the testaments take on the shape of a story where a trail could be discerned, a path on which he could follow Father Lee. Everywhere the man had left a monument which would remain until his victims and their children and the children after them were buried and forgotten. Maybe even then

Father Lee would live on as inspiration for some dark despoiling myth of unknown origin.

The priest had touched the Church as well as McKeon. Armstrong's story about the settlement offers made that clear. McKeon rang to confirm the truth of the account, the tremor in the voices telling him that some people had found the power of that money almost too much to withstand.

He looked at old local papers in the National Library, finding an unbearable pathos in the welcomings of Father Lee to so many parishes. The priest's features thickened as the transfers became more common, but the smile remained the same, saying trust me, trust me, sometimes even catching McKeon unawares until he found himself thinking, yes, I trust you. He looked at old copies of the *Herald*, thinking of his father working there until ink settled in every pore of his hands like love had in his marriage. The paper informed its readers of Father Lee's departure to America. Upstate New York.

In the town of Schuylersburg Falls, two hours from New York, people were mowing their lawns, washing their cars and raking leaves as if caught in some leadenly ironic heavy-metal video parody of Middle America. The man he had phoned from Kennedy met him at the hotel.

—You've got a pretty appropriate name, Mister McKeon.

—Why's that?

—Seamus. You know, like a detective, a shamus.

McKeon had not heard the word before. Father Pavese spoke of municipal history as they passed a strip of motels oddly out of keeping with the rest of the town. The young priest had responded to McKeon's advertisement seeking information about Father Lee's time in Schuylersburg Falls.

—Are you not a bit young to remember him?

—Believe me, Mister McKeon, I am the best person to help you on this one.

They sat in the van outside a bar slumped between the town diner and a record store full of white kids buying rap records about ghetto life. Advertisements for seven different kinds of beer flashed in the window.

—You've been very helpful, Father Pavese. I'm surprised.

—We're not all bad, Mister McKeon. The abuse issue blew up here a few years before it did in Ireland, so we've had time to find ways of dealing with it. This is a litigious country, it's just too damn expensive to ignore any more.

In the darkened bar, two men were playing pool in time to hoarse metal laments for and paeans to long-legged ladies, mean city boulevards and your own set of wheels. A big man, maybe about three hundred pounds, six foot six, was scooping popcorn into a white cardboard receptacle. He had tattoos on his lower arms and patches of babyish pale skin on his biceps, where tributes to past loves and enthusiasms had been scraped off. Ten empty beer bottles sat in front of him. Two men at the bar recalled a beer-can shooting contest from the night before. The big man looked McKeon in the eye and flexed his hands as if measuring them against the newcomer's neck.

—How are you doin', Father Pavese?

—How about you, Burt? This man here is the reporter from Ireland I was telling you about.

—Maybe we better move away from the bar. We can sit by the jukebox. I might get to crying, which happens sometimes when I tell this story, and then I might think someone sees me, and it ain't that I get embarrassed by that but that I get angry and I'm likely to smash the place apart, and the owner's a good friend, a real good friend.

Father Pavese ordered three beers as Burt's voice began connecting this town with the war-torn city on the other side of the world and the small towns and villages in the country below.

—My father was Irish. He was a good man, liked maybe a few too many beers, but he was a pretty regular blue-collar guy. He had faith in the Church and when I was eight he told me he'd be real happy if I wanted to be an altar boy. I thought it sounded pretty cool. The next day he came home from the sawmill with a box under his arm. He said it was a surprise for me. I opened the box. This red and white altar boy's outfit. I kind of felt like he'd brought home the sun for me. My mother was Italian. She's dead now.

Tears flowed down the big man's face like coins from a Las Vegas slot machine surrendering a jackpot when he recounted what had happened with Father Lee in the sacristy. He looked straight at McKeon, defying him to mock, to run away, to notice, to do anything which could be construed as an insult to those tears. Burt walked his eight-year-old self from the altar to the sacristy and held him there. The eight-year-old had been trying to escape for thirty years, and McKeon saw that every day Burt wanted to let him but could not. Every day he watched himself looking at the sacristy clock as a grown man threw the altar boy's vestments over his head and whispered endearments and threats in the same accent as Burt's father.

—It was the best thing I ever got, that altar boy's outfit. I still remember how it felt in my hands. Do you remember yours, Seamus, Father Pavese?

—Yeah.

—Yeah.

A fight was breaking out in the bar when the two men sat into the pick-up.

—An eight-year-old altar boy, for fuck's sake, Father.

—I know what you're thinking, and I know how you look at this, Seamus, but I'm not going to apologise to you and I'm not going to be ashamed that I spread the Word of God.

Shame being something Pavese knew about, because he too had been handed an altar boy's outfit at the start of the seventies by a father who was also a regular blue-collar guy. Regular except for his predilection for abusing his children, which ended when Pavese's elder brother cracked his skull with a tyre iron.

—And there's not a day goes by but I don't wonder where I'd be if he'd continued for another couple of years. Maybe I'd still be a priest, because everyone who is abused is not ruined. I don't know why I'm not, but there are other people who've come through as well.

In a sports bar with a hundred and twenty-eight televisions hanging from the roof like avalanche-inclined snow over a cliff, they met a man who had raised four sons and three daughters with his high-school sweetheart. He had served as an altar boy for Father Lee. In an Irish bar run by Italians, a barmaid told her story as giant Riverdancers cavorted over her head. Every evening for a week Father Pavese would arrive at the hotel accompanied by men and women who remembered Father Lee and asked urgently where he was now and what he looked like and if he had stopped. Before McKeon could answer the last question, they would always say no, of course he hasn't, he can't stop, that's the way he is. Always in the room were the names of the absent. Wendy. Jason. Bob. Jessica. Suicides, deaths from the needle and the damage done or too many bourbons, too many Scotches, too many beers. Cries for help and notice which had slipped one grade too far mixed with deliberate searches for extinction and an escape from nightmares.

The names of the dead and the words of their friends were punched on to reams of typing paper by McKeon.

What was he typing?

A history of Father Gerry Lee. An ecclesiastical biography. A pathology of evil licenced, unchecked and ignored. A babel of disbelieving voices. Fragments of poems from counselling groups. A charge sheet. A calendar with pages being discarded as the day of reckoning approached. McKeon's story, too, the story of his obsession, his alchemical transmutation of pain, confusion and shame into one honed cry for justice.

When he scripted a documentary on Father Lee, the aesthetic considerations were as necessary as they were obscene. He knew a badly made programme about authentic suffering and pain was still a bad programme no one would watch. It would not do justice to the stories.

He took the script to the man at the station who could give him the go-ahead. It arrived back on his desk with the pages barely cut. When he collared the man he was told that people were not interested in this kind of story. McKeon did not believe him. He knew that the public's prurience could be counted on even if their moral outrage was a more elusive quarry. Perhaps he had not angled the script correctly, had allowed the obsession to dull the professional instincts of thirty years.

That night, he and Moira watched a documentary about the sadistic treatment of children in an orphanage run by nuns. Radio callers the next morning were outraged that such awful allegations had been levelled against the Church. When the station interviewed the nun who had run the orphanage, McKeon saw how she was lit, how the camera pitied her, how the questions were not questions at all but openings for justification, for pleas for understanding, for implications that the children had been embittered by their lowly status. He watched the distortion with professional admiration and understood how things were. He rang one of the Northern stations.

They were interested but said the programme could not be transmitted until Father Lee was convicted. In the absence of a trial, it might be regarded as libellous. Screened during a trial, it would be seen as positively contemptuous and might enable the priest to escape justice for good. Still they gave McKeon the money and the crew he needed. The letters, words and numbers of the script began to take shape as a programme, a process which seemed intrinsically false. The mere hour and a half available meant that the mass of letters, tapes and memories had to be edited into coherent form, as if Father Lee's story had a clear narrative structure, when in reality it made no sense at all.

He did not know if the programme would ever be shown.

Watching the final cut, McKeon marvelled at the way he had presented the evidence, the anger he showed and the power with which he made his case against Father Lee, and the Church which had licenced his crimes. He wanted viewers to share his outrage and obsession, but also to admire his skill. Because he was a journalist. He was not a social worker, a policeman or a priest. He was a journalist, thought about the story as a journalist and would tell it as a journalist. He could not change his nature either.

McKeon too had used the victims. Their suffering had become a valuable commodity. Without it the programme could not have been made, and this opportunity to boost his reputation would not have arisen. He consoled himself with the thought that once he would have pretended not to know this.

—Tonight we look at the story of how one man blighted the lives of children over a thirty-year period, and how he used the shelter of the Catholic Church to evade justice. This is the harrowing story of Father Gerry Lee.

Cut to a figure in silhouette, the voice distorted electronically.

—There's not a day goes by that I don't think of Father Gerry Lee . . . and what he done to me . . . when I was six years old.

Tears. McKeon had chosen that piece because the tears were the saddest, the most choking, the most accusing and demanded the audience's attention, making them feel that to change channels would be to connive with Father Lee.

The tape was wrapped up and left at the Northern station. When he returned to Dublin, there was a message from someone he had not spoken to in years. He rang back straight away.

—Seamus, we've got a fantastic story for you.

He rang Moira and said he would be home late. She told him to be careful.

The man who had rung sat at the head of the table in the eating house where Henry Caslin was rumoured to have plotted the demise of both the Man With The Pipe and the Tough Guy. Nothing changes, McKeon thought. Twenty-five years on, Myles Duff is still doing the Special Branch cloak-and-dagger routine and I'm still responding to it. Duff introduced the other men at the table. A former newspaper editor who dabbled in politics, a young man making a name as a post-colonial commentator and a tall bloke whom McKeon guessed was English from the public-schoolboy shine off his face and his way of regarding everyone else with a mixture of intense concentration and absolute boredom.

—Do you know what MI5 is? asked the Englishman.

—Is it a sort of car, asked McKeon, irritated at the presumption of ignorance inherent in the question.

The Englishman clucked. Duff whispered something to

him. The newspaper editor asked for drink and found there was none to be had. The post-colonialist made an encircling gesture with his hand to show everyone was in this together and there was no need for anyone to fall out. All friends here. Duff began to tell the Englishman's story, stopping to let him interject occasionally.

The Englishman had been an officer in British Army Intelligence, one of its top operatives south of the border. He had set up the Dublin bombing, organised a couple of bank robberies and run a network of covert operatives. He was also responsible for smear campaigns against Irish politicians, the Tough Guy in particular. McKeon's antennae went up at this point. A need to see where the story was leading made him pay very close attention. He could see the others mistaking this for interest in the story itself.

—I left Intelligence because I was disenchanted with the amount of dirty tricks we were involved in.

—I thought you left because you were nabbed for a bank robbery in Manchester.

Duff intervened.

—He was framed for that robbery, Seamus. By MI5.

The two newspaper journalists nodded as if this was beyond dispute.

—I retain a great many contacts in Intelligence, and have recently become aware of a plot to destabilise the government of Henry Caslin. Caslin had been involved in brokering the IRA ceasefire, which is anathema to British Army elements who wish to push on for a full military victory. They are aiming to bring Caslin down by implicating his Cabinet in a major legal scandal.

So much of this stuff had turned out to be true in the seventies. A lot of it had been false, too. The twilight zone was the worst. Bank robbers who may or may not have been working for Military Intelligence, ditto journalists, ditto ambassadors. You had to listen because you just did not know. McKeon suspended his scepticism for a moment.

—Why have you come to me about it?

—Because you're the best journalist in the station. The one I trust, said Duff.

If it had been left at that, McKeon would have listened because he was in the mood for conspiracy theory. The former editor interrupted.

—We think it's important that you know what's going on. Because you've been in contact with this man.

A picture of Hunter was dropped on the table. McKeon agreed that he had met the man. To say he knew him was stretching it, and seemed to carry an implication not yet apparent.

—This man is an MI5 operative. He is in charge of the operation to destabilise Caslin. A priest has been accused of sexual offences against children, witnesses have been bribed and suborned into giving statements against him.

—Father Gerry Lee, said McKeon, the realisation of what was behind this meeting suddenly sickening him.

—We know you know his name. MI5 have been behind the case. They want to use it as a weapon to weaken both the Catholic Church and the Irish government.

They looked at McKeon like dogs who have brought a stick back from a great distance and expect to be petted and praised. Except for Duff, who could see that he was not biting. They had blown it somehow, or more likely it had always been a desperate and useless gambit.

—You're all religious men, aren't you, said McKeon.

—I don't see what that has to do with anything, said the former editor.

A resigned Duff turned away. The young columnist leaned across the table until McKeon could feel his breath.

—If you give succour to the enemies of our country then

you are an enemy of our country. Think of what the foreign press are going to make of this case.

—Why does it always have to be the Brits to blame?

—It has to be because it is.

—Fuck you, you'll let a nationalist priest be hounded by the B Specials, said the former editor.

—This has nothing to do with the Brits, said McKeon, and I want to go home.

—Yes it has, said the columnist. Have you heard of Tawana Brawley? She was a black girl in New York who was raped and beaten by white men.

—And she was found out as a liar.

—Yes, but if that terrible thing did not happen to her, something had to be awfully wrong to make her claim it did. She was a black woman in a white society, injustice had been done to her since the day she was born. The Brits are to blame because of the last eight hundred years. Everything evil, everything wrong in this country is their fault, whether they are directly responsible for it or not.

—Gents, good night and fuck off, said McKeon.

At home he realised that he should have asked how the Father Gerry Lee case could possibly destabilise the Caslin government, before remembering that someone had been sitting in the booth behind the four men. The face had not been visible but he had glimpsed a hand requesting a menu, a hand which bore the huge, ornate and absolutely unique holy ring worn by the Minister for Justice, Mickey Kelly.

Crossing the border at Blacklion, Father Lee noticed with satisfaction the scaling down of security since the ceasefires. Before, young British soldiers ran alongside your car, swerving in and out as if about to attack. Now there were just the sensors which registered him as the property of the Northern Irish state.

At a checkpoint on the outskirts of Belfast, Hunter

tapped on the front window of Father Lee's car and informed him that he was under arrest for sexually assaulting a number of minors. It felt like an exact repeat of his last arrest, except that Hunter had put on a little weight and the RUC men with him were different. Father Lee was comforted by the thought of the possible fate of the previous acolytes.

Why would they not leave him alone? They had arrested him once before. Surely that was enough. Were they not tired of this? He was tired. He was getting old, the war was nearly over and surely the B Specials could forget the old grudges now. There was no need to keep punishing him for the past.

He did not have enough life left to serve any sentence, right any wrong or tender any compensation. At the monastery, he had read that a thickening of the arteries was a common cause of death in men his age. At night he thought he could hear them thickening. A noise like fur collecting on a water pipe. The noise of the machine of himself running down. The music of corporeal morality. And as his arteries hardened, his mind softened. His analytical, rationalising mind was remorselessly draining away into the blackness of the unused brain, that secret chasm which used age to pull the rest of the mind in and make itself whole.

Father Lee's solicitor decided not to allow his client to speak in court, because the man did not seem to believe he had done anything wrong and just spoke of tickling, a bit of fun and games, horseplay. The priest said he would apologise if he had done something wrong, but, having done nothing wrong, to express regret would be dishonest. Dishonesty was an especially pernicious and demoralising sin, Father Lee pointed out, before lecturing the solicitor on the need for ethics in the legal profession.

The faces outside the courthouse were like those dead

from the catacombs come to accuse Nero and Diocletian in the afterlife. Father Lee recoiled at the sight of his accusers and the paralysing hatred in their eyes. Spit rained down on him as he was led handcuffed to trial. He tried to remember his Office as he ran the gauntlet of jeers, leers and tears. This parade of raw emotion could not be good for the souls of these people. Where was their forgiveness, their charity? For whatever he was supposed to have done.

The trial of Father Gerry Lee was also more than that. McKeon watched the crowds outside the courthouse increase, heard the abuse roared at Father Lee, saw the RUC battle to keep back the onlookers. Twice women broke through the cordon, but on reaching Father Lee could only stand and weep. The priest had put his hand out to comfort one, and she had attacked the air as if trying to escape from a coffin. The Church itself was on trial, and all the other Father Lees who had been sheltered.

Outside the courthouse McKeon spoke to the victims. He was aware that the term victims bore a certain pejorative weight, but could not think of a better word to describe them. Survivors was apposite, but their victimhood continued to strike him as more obvious than their survival. They paced the street outside, smoking cigarettes, biting nails down below the quick, seeking McKeon's assurance that a guilty verdict would be delivered.

It was obvious that some of them wanted to kill the priest, and that given a guaranteed escape from detection most of them would have done it. All this ritual, all the my lords, the swearing on a holy book which the defendant probably knew better than anyone else in the courtroom, all the wigs, the paperwork, the calling to order, the shushing of the crowd, all the apparatus of civilised society did not change the fact that people were there for revenge. It would have been more honest to throw Father Lee into the street and let them tear him to pieces.

Ten years had never seemed such a short and insignificant time to McKeon as it did when pronounced as sentence on Father Lee. The priest was taken to the prison van. He waved to the crowd, the door shut and none of them ever saw him again.

Papers on both sides of the border printed the photo of Father Lee waving from the van, an old man without an ounce of repentance, his face full of contempt and spite and defiance. McKeon used the picture as a publicity shot for the documentary because Father Lee looked the part. The viewers could feel they would not have allowed him near their children. He looks like a child molester, they would say, can't you see the badness in him?

In the programme he would use a photo from the files of the Schuylersburg Falls newspaper. Father Lee in his prime. A fine, tall, handsome man with a shock of blond hair and an engaging smile which would have made anyone want to be his friend. McKeon did not want this picture used in advance publicity in case it discouraged people from watching the documentary. Because the man in that photograph did not look like a child molester, and that meant they could look like anyone, like someone you thought was a good person and whose company you enjoyed. McKeon himself was unsettled by this.

Around the corner from the courthouse the prison van stopped at traffic lights. A couple of straggling shouts caught Father Lee's ear as he looked through the mesh on the window and realised how fond he was of this city, despite all its faults.

He saw her.

A little blondey girl. She must have been about eight. Carrying roller skates in one hand. The other hand extending a thumb into her mouth. How beautiful she was. In a little orange t-shirt, her little white arms beginning to display tiny brown splotches of tan. Splotches. Of tan. And on her legs too, because they were bare. Her legs were bare from the knee down. And above the knee she wore those tight shorts. Tight because she wanted people to look and see how tight they were at the crotch. He watched her walk across the road with her little bum hugged by those shorts, the way she hugged to herself the knowledge she and Father Lee shared, that she knew how the men looked at her and how Father Lee was looking at her now, as he thought how he would give anything to be that girl's friend, just to be her friend and talk to her and hug her and cuddle her, have a bit of fun, both of them enjoying this game and laughing about it, tickling each other, and then he would ask her to take her clothes off, no, he would take them off for her because that was what she wanted and then . . .

The girl disappeared. Father Lee wondered where she had gone before realising he was lying on the floor of the van with his mouth bleeding and one of the B Specials looking at him.

—You dirty bastard, you dirty fucking bastard, stay there until we get to the prison. Just stay there, don't look out the fucking windows.

The man seemed in a terrible panic, so Father Lee did what he was told despite the discomfort for a man his age in lying on the floor of a van. When he heard the prison gates close behind them, it struck him that he would never see the outside world again. The prospect filled him with unexpected relief.

The documentary began at half nine in the evening, and during the first commercial break people rang friends and neighbours and insisted that they watch McKeon.

In the beginning. Patrick Armstrong in his wheelchair.

Silhouetted. Telling how a man had stolen his childhood and how every night he saw this man in his dreams.

Followed by another silhouette. A woman. To show the inclusive nature of the evil described. The woman breaks down and cries. The camera and microphone are left on and her tears slowly faded out as a crucifix and biblical quotation come up on screen.

—Whoso shall offend one of these little ones which believe in me, it were better for him that a millstone were hanged around his neck and that he were drowned in the depth of the sea. *Matthew 18:6.*

A sorrowful hymn. The music fades and is overcome by the sound of people shouting in anger and thumping the sides of a prison van. Then the camera freezes for ever the face of Father Gerry Lee addressing a grin to the television audience. McKeon's voice begins the story.

—This is the story of Father Gerry Lee, a man who stole the innocence of hundreds of children. It is also the story of how he was allowed to do this by the Catholic Church. This is a tale of the destruction of childhood and also of a search for justice.

Nobody watching the programme moves until the first commercial break. A huge surge of power as viewers rush to make calming cups of tea overloads one sub-station, blacking out towns where people continue discussing what they have just seen as they search for candles and matches.

In the second half of the programme there is more of McKeon and less of the taped remembrances. The tapes now bear the voices of bishops from Father Lee's old dioceses. McKeon argues that these men must have known about the priest's misdemeanours, and over a picture of the young Father Lee throwing a football to some American teenagers, the audience hear the bishops disclaim any responsibility though not denying knowledge. They mumble, shuffle and invoke canon law with a certainty that infuriated McKeon. He was surprised how well this fury came across. Moira had squeezed his hand as the tapes became part of a shared televisual history as strong as any folk memory.

—So ... Bishop ... with all due respect ... what you are saying to me is that you could not have stopped Father Lee from committing these abuses.

—I am telling you that under canon law, he could not have been disciplined by me at that time.

—Bishop ... should it not have been incumbent on you to inform the police of Father Lee's activities? Should you not have tried to ensure that he would not have access to young children? I believe you recommended him for a post as Chaplain at a children's home.

—That is correct. But under canon law he was not my responsibility once he had left the diocese.

—Bishop ... I find it hard to believe, and I think people will find it hard to believe ...

What had set the bishop off? Was it the mention of people? The idea of being subject to public scrutiny? McKeon did not know. He had not seen the bishop's reaction coming, and it was still a surprise when he watched it on television.

—Mister McKeon, I have outlined my position under canon law. How dare you question my authority. How dare you. How dare you imply that the Church is culpable in this matter. I do not propose to endure this line of questioning from the likes of you.

—Bishop ... please.

—How dare you, Mister McKeon.

The sound of the receiver being slammed down. The buzz of a dead line. The silence sounding louder than the conversation, as if McKeon had somehow enhanced it. But he had not. That was just how people heard it.

How dare you. The viewers listened to those three

words and winced, repeating them and reacting with a visceral power they would not have thought themselves capable of.

How dare you. The contempt, the impatience, the presumption in those three words were not addressed to Seamus McKeon but to everyone who watched. The bishop dismissed their intellects, their lives, their right to ask about Father Gerry Lee. The disembodied voice told them the Church did not care what they thought. They should just shut up, put their money in the collection plate and bow to the power of canon law.

The three words activated dormant memories of stories heard at school, advice about which priests to avoid, tales about orphanages and reformatories and other scandals not remotely connected to Father Lee. The size of bishops' palaces. The excoriating of loose women from church altars. The fact that the relations of priests got good educations and that the rise in the minimum sum for Sunday collection seemed connected with this. The sadism of the Christian Brothers. They heard the bishop tell them he did not care what they thought about these things either.

In the closing minutes of the programme, McKeon asked calm questions in a cool voice and made it clear he had no vendetta against the Church, somewhat dishonestly giving the impression that its welfare was of paramount importance to him.

—You have heard some of the victims of Father Lee's abuse claim that they were offered compensation by the Church. This begs the question, as the Church was aware of the abuse, why did it continue to shelter Father Lee?

Watching, he steeled himself for the final lines.

—RUC sources said that Father Lee could have been brought to justice much earlier, had an extradition warrant which they sent to the Irish Department of Justice been acted on. They say they have made repeated requests for

Father Lee's extradition, and have been fobbed off with unconvincing excuses. If this is true, the Department and the government have questions to answer about the Father Gerry Lee affair.

A traumatised audience disregarded political allegiance and nodded their heads as one. McKeon had skilfully avoided crucifixion on the cross of partisanship. He was not displeased by the fact that Henry Caslin looked set to be holding the shitty end of the stick for a couple of days.

Cardinal O'Hanlon watched McKeon outline the case with the gloom of a burglar watching forensic evidence melt away an alibi. The phone call from his unfavourite bishop was little consolation.

—Cardinal, did you see that programme? People are going to be absolutely outraged.

The cardinal wondered aloud why the bishop's tone was so gleeful about this indisputable fact.

—Did you not see that McKeon taped our phone conversation unknown to me? That's against all ethics. People will be disgusted with him. We have them now.

—Maybe we do, Jerome.

He envied the innocence of the bishops, who assured him they would crush McKeon when in fact the days of crushing were as good as gone. The bishop who shouted How Dare You might as well have gone into every church in the country and ordered half the congregation never to come to Mass again.

On the late News, an RUC man named Hunter said he thought the extradition warrant had been deliberately lost, and that strings had been pulled to help Father Lee evade justice. Another log on the fire.

*

Henry had sat with Mary and watched McKeon unspool the story. He did not know what good it did to talk about such terrible things, but he could not stop watching. He also felt sorrow for the victims and outrage at the fact that Father Lee had escaped justice for so long before McKeon, by mentioning the warrant, the Department of Justice and the government, transformed Henry from a concerned viewer to a protagonist. The phone rang and he let it ring. Seven different messages told him the opposition wanted an emergency debate tomorrow in the Dáil, to find out if Father Lee had been shielded by someone in a high place. The opposition stressed that their intervention was prompted solely by concern for the nation's children.

Henry did not believe that McKeon was telling the truth, but did not know why the man would lie. He hoped Kelly would give him an explanation when he answered the phone.

— Mickey, were you watching the television?

— I was, Henry. It's pure lies. I never heard tell of this document, or saw sight nor sign of it.

— That's grand, Mickey. I'll tell the Dáil that.

Horror put its hand through Henry's ribcage and grabbed his heart. Something in Kelly's voice told you when he was lying, and it was there now. He put the phone down and rang Jimmy for the first time in five weeks.

During that time Henry had been hanging around with Sian Guiney, with posses of advisers, with his Ministers. Yet when he scented real trouble it was Jimmy he rang. Jimmy felt this increased the insult, and would have told Henry to fuck off had he not noticed something vulnerable in his voice which suggested a potential opportunity for revenge.

That night seemed especially black, as if the dark was a

positive entity rather than just the absence of light. It was thick, black treacle, a fog of tears, a gloom which might choose never to lift. These kind of feelings were unusual for Henry. Jimmy saw that he was shaking.

The Taoiseach greeted the men on guard and walked across the theshold, marching purposefully towards the office of the Minister for Justice. He requested the key of the office from a security man who complied instantly. Henry entered and flicked on the lights. Jimmy told the guard he might want to take a walk down the corridor.

Henry rummaged through the files on Kelly's desk and asked Jimmy to check the filing cabinets. They were joined in a search which would do no good whatever the result. A positive result would make them accessories, a negative leave them still on the outside.

Notes, files, letters of petition. In different circumstances the familiar paraphernalia would have made Henry nostalgic. He did not have time now, and instructed Jimmy to break open the drawers of the Minister's desk. Henry knew Kelly would keep anything important close to him, but loyalty made him check the obvious hiding place last. When Jimmy handed him the extradition warrant, Henry held it at arm's length as though it were poisoned. There was no going back now.

It was beginning to get light outside, and cars had begun the recolonisation of the streets, the sound of their engines not yet sufficient to mask the drumbeat of Kelly's footsteps making their way towards the office. Outrage had been the Minister's original choice of weapon, but he and Fleming were disarmed by the sight of Henry holding the warrant. The Taoiseach and his most trusted Minister looked at each other in silence for a minute.

—We have to talk, they both said at the same time.

Normally Jimmy would have told Henry to cut himself loose and blame the Minister because that was the only way to survive this. But now he wanted to give Henry the worst possible advice, so he suggested letting Kelly explain.

—I know what this looks like, Henry.

—It's not what it looks like that bothers me, Mickey, It's what it is.

In the past Henry and Jimmy had walked away, cutting people loose with the ruthlessness of castaways on an undersized raft. The till-fingerers, the crooked land re-zoners, the junketeers had all been shucked off before they could impede Henry's progress up the ladder. Jimmy felt the memory of those people in the room like a suit of armour around Kelly. To cut Kelly loose, to do what was wise, Henry needed Jimmy's encouragement. And he was not going to get it.

The civil servant exercised his power like mood music as Kelly explained why the warrant should remain hidden. There were so many good reasons.

—It doesn't matter now, Henry. Father Lee is in prison. That warrant will not add to anything.

—You saw what he did to those children, and you still let him stay free.

—He's probably not guilty at all. It's a disgrace to see the leader of a Republican party, of a Republican country condemning a man of the cloth on the say-so of the RUC, a bunch of Orange go-boys like them. I've heard it's all an MI5 plot to attack the Church and the Party.

—That's nonsense, Mickey, and the worst thing is that you know it is.

So many good reasons.

—The Church is under fire from them. The Liberals, the Dublin Fours, the trendies, the crowd who laugh at us and try to bring down the Party. Do you think they'll thank you if you get the Church into more bother? When they've finished off the Church, they'll come for the Party.

So many good reasons.

—People will be lost without the Church, Henry. Don't you be causing damage to them. Do you remember when Mary had, you know, when she was sick? Prayer kept you sane, Henry. I remember you telling me that you owed God something when she recovered. Well, now you can protect his one true Church from harm.

So many good reasons.

—Henry, we are friends these thirty years, we fought on the same side, where is your loyalty, Henry, that you will ruin me for the sake of someone like Seamus McKeon? Because make no mistake, McKeon is no angel, Henry. He's done this to make a name for himself and because he has it in for me because of his wife and myself back in the days when I knew no better. Don't give him the satisfaction, Henry. How can you choose him ahead of me?

It was Anyways time. The moment hallowed in the Party when Anyways would act as the overture to the clinching argument. Jimmy knew that there was no appropriate Anyways line in this situation, but he kept quiet.

—Anyways, Henry. Think of this politically, of the damage it will do the Party. The Party is what we are about. Think of the solace it will give to our enemies if I am denounced by my own leader.

—We must hang together or we will hang separately, said Henry, quoting the Tough Guy.

—Exactly. Henry, all you have to do is go into the Dáil and say there has been a thorough search of Department of Justice files and that there is no record of such a warrant being received.

It was that easy to Kelly. He was not thinking about God any more, but about the old belief in the Party that everything could be denied because political wrongdoing was remarkably resistant to indisputable proof. Even if everyone knew you were guilty, it was up to the other side to force your resignation, and this they could not do unless your own people turned on you like they had done to the Tough Guy. Henry realised how few people actually knew where the warrant was.

—I'll think about this, Mickey. I'm not promising anything.

—Thank you very much, Henry. I won't forget this.

When Mary opened the door to Henry, she saw pain bursting through the skin of his face and distorting it almost beyond recognition. Henry reversed the sequence in which Kelly had presented his arguments, in case their persuasive power derived from the original order. Mary's eyes still signalled agreement with the pragmatic reason, the Party reason and the Anyways line. Tomorrow he would have to lie to the Dáil. His only consolation was Mary's agreement with the necessity of this course of action.

The next morning Sian Guiney's thoughts kept coming back to a Yank secret service man she had met in New York. He had claimed intimate knowledge of matters apocalyptic, and explained that when nuclear attack seemed imminent, the US forces would go on immediate alert, the controllers at missile bases starting countdowns, the pilots of the big fighters and bombers scrambling, the President and his closest aides leaving on Air Force One for a bunker which would serve as command centre. This state of emergency was called Def Con One. Sian imagined the panic, the sense of movement and the buzz, but what had excited her most of all was that a select few would control information about the situation. Now her very own Def Con One was taking shape in the Taoiseach's office.

—I have a speech here, Henry. I've been working on it all night. I think it covers all the questions raised by McKeon's documentary.

—I don't want your speech, Sian. I'll speak my own mind. Everything is going to be all right.

How was she expected to deal with the problem if she was kept outside it? If your husband had a serious heart condition, would you perform cardiac surgery yourself while the doctor looked on? She felt like throttling the Taoiseach.

—Everything is going to be all right.

He repeated it, not like a mantra, because they were supposed to improve things, but like a dirge. Again he insisted on writing his own statement. Her hands twitched alarmingly under the table.

As she had watched the previous night's programme, pity had turned to outrage as McKeon detailed how the Church had covered up for Father Lee before turning to chilling when she heard him suggest a political equivalent. Mentally she constructed the chain of command, her oldest political friend Mickey Kelly and her best current client Henry Caslin. She could not believe that they would have colluded in the escape from justice of a man who had raped little kids. She wanted to hear Henry absolutely dismiss McKeon's suggestion and phrased her question accordingly.

—Henry, there's no way that McKeon is correct in implying that we had that warrant and didn't act on it in order to protect Father Lee, is there? I mean, I'm sure there's not.

The Def Con One answer.

—I'll be saying that to the best of my knowledge and the knowledge of the Minister for Justice, we did not receive the warrant.

The words I'll be saying told her the allegation was true. She realised that Def Con One would be less fun than she had imagined. Henry headed for the Dáil chamber like a man walking down Death Row.

The inquisition began with a question from the leader of the opposition. In the gallery McKeon marvelled at how well Henry answered. He was certain the man was at best dissembling and at worst lying, but might still get away with it. Henry's career had been built on the unlikely, and he led a party which regarded escape as the ultimate virtue. Its founders had famously escaped from imprisonment by the British, and later, during the Civil War, by their former comrades. Elusiveness in tight corners had taken on the status of a principle for the Party. Henry was calm, as if back fielding queries about the ballroom business.

—All the Department of Justice officials have been questioned, and the gardai are satisfied with their answers.

The leader of the opposition was followed by the leaders of the smaller parties. All united in their desire to put the Taoiseach on the canvas. As if it had come down to the Party against everyone else. This made Henry feel strangely satisfied, like a paranoid finally seeing his worse fears confirmed. Twice before he had seen a Party leader wobble on his pedestal like a huge statue of a dead communist about to be tumbled into the dust. Those days had dawned for the Man With The Pipe and the Tough Guy, and they had not survived them. In his head he chanted the favourite hymns of his youth as he continued to answer questions.

The RUC had told journalists that the warrant had been sent, and the gardai said they believed them. The previous night's radio chat shows repeated McKeon's allegations, and turned up scores of people who had been sexually abused, many by priests. The voices continued the next morning until it seemed to Henry that everyone in the country who had ever been interfered with was blaming his government. A psychologist might have explained to him that he was providing a useful focus for their anger.

There was nothing he could do. Facts were no use, and

logic did not matter a damn. Pointing out it was not the Party's fault that people had been abused would have sounded insensitive. But as the questions continued, people began to look at each other and silently suggest that the Taoiseach was playing a blinder which would enable him to survive this terrible day and use it in the future as proof of his coolness under pressure. Henry explained again that everyone possible had been questioned and that there was no record of this warrant arriving in Dublin. As he left the chamber, Sian clapped him on the back.

—Maybe we might ride this out, Henry. It's only a maybe, but at least it's that.

The reporters were convinced Henry had talked his way out of the woods. In the lobby people still talked of McKeon getting an award, but the praise was tempered with whispers about his naivety in trying to connect the story to the government. He had been guilty of overkill, had not been happy with the human interest and tragedy, had imposed a political dimension because he considered himself a political journalist. The warrant had disappeared because of incompetence rather than corruption.

Mickey Kelly, who had gone into the chamber with a face as white as a marble Virgin Mary, had revived magnificently. He stared across at McKeon and made gestures suggestive of the twisting of a noose. Caslin, oddly enough, did not seem to be that happy, and McKeon took some comfort from this. He wondered for a second where Jimmy Mimnagh was before remembering that the little man had been superceded by Sian Guiney.

A Dáil messenger handed him an envelope which he opened and then quickly stuffed into his pocket. In the car he read it again and again. The letter was written on the notepaper of a well-known Dublin hotel.

Mister McKeon,

If you call to this hotel tonight at ten o'clock, then there will be a package at reception for you which will reveal the complete truth about how Father Gerry Lee was protected by the Department of Justice.

No signature.

At half nine he left the house, having waited to watch Moira interview a farmer whose cattle had been poisoned by a chemical factory. Sometimes she was just brilliant, and he hoped everyone realised how very often that sometimes was.

He walked in through the revolving door of the hotel, said hello to a porter and went to reception, where he picked up a white envelope amateurishly bound at the top with brown masking tape, which looked as though someone had used their teeth to remove it from the roll. He did not want to open the package in front of Moira, so he drove south. Past the station, looking behind half-heartedly but knowing he was not being tailed because this was not Caslin's style but the Tough Guy's. McKeon wondered who would take over from Henry. Perhaps someone to the country's detriment, North and South. He did not care. The story was what mattered.

The twenty-four-hour McDonald's was full of shouting Spanish students. Opening the package proved difficult for McKeon and the Spaniards spotted this and laughed before continuing their cacophony. There was no note with the contents, and nothing to tell him who had sent it. Just copies of warrants with a note saying when they had been received by the Department of Justice. A year ago and six months ago. A memo from a civil servant named Fleming advising Kelly to keep stonewalling, and to stick to the story of the warrants not being received in Dublin. In time, he noted, it might be possible to place a question mark over the credibility of the RUC.

Treachery all neatly done up in a Department of Justice folder. Spread on the plastic table was the political death of Henry Caslin, the fall of the government and the personal ruin of Mark Fleming, Mickey Kelly and perhaps a few others besides. He thought of Kelly's noose gesture that afternoon, and how fitting it now seemed. McKeon had never pegged Caslin as a man who would leave himself open to betrayal, but perhaps power engendered bad habits. When he got home he woke Moira up and showed her the evidence.

—Holy fucking Jesus, she said, and gripped the side of the bed.

During her time in England, she had picked up the gagging 'a' which they used as second letter and dynamo in the word fucking.

Jimmy had copied the documents after Henry asked him to stay in Kelly's office and root around for further information. Supplanted as an advisor by Sian Guiney, made to apologise to the gyps as if he was no one, humiliated by his appointment to the Senate and banned from the road by express order of the man whose career he had created, Jimmy no longer took pleasure in Henry's successes. Henry as Taoiseach without Jimmy at his side was meaningless. He had to learn that.

The morning after he dropped off the package, Jimmy went to an early house in a cobblestoned street which had once fed and watered men from the nearby meat market. The barman turned on the radio news when Jimmy asked him to. McKeon was announcing a press conference later that day at which new information about the Father Lee case would be disclosed.

*

The word was that the press conference would be something special, but the trappings of the occasion were no different than usual. The scattering of microphones in front of the speakers, the numberless glasses of water, the ancient and meaningless antiphons.

—Testing, testing, one two three.

—Testing, testing one, testing one two.

The long wait. The buzz. The abstract and abstracted racket of a roomful of expectant curiosity into which would walk the man with the story. This was the ritual.

The waning of the Church had not left people short of ritual. They had the Press Conference, the Radio Phone-in, the Film Premiere, the Vigil for Peace, the Greenpeace Protest, the Student March, the Pro-Life Demonstration, the Radio Two Roadshow. All with their own codes and patterns of behaviour, mysterious to the outsider and comforting to the participants, making them feel closer to the strange and distant forces orchestrating their lives. Sometimes there seemed to be nothing but ritual.

Flashbulbs went off as McKeon walked up to the mike. The cameramen and reporters were pressed so close together their movements had to be made as one. Holding up the documents, McKeon explained what they were and what they indicated. The response was so loud he had to sit down. A couple of questions followed, but the faces of the reporters told him there would not be much grilling. The warrants and the memo said enough in themselves.

Reporters from Irish and British television stations were speaking to camera, people with radio mikes contacted their studios, journalists made hurried calls on mobile phones. The sounds of English, French, German, Swedish and Italian voices bespoke an interest in the story wider than had been expected by its author. The different modes of speech overlapped until the small room sounded like an interactive museum of news-speak. The measured military

Oxbridge tones of the English broadsheet, the elliptical meanderings of the American papers, the languid self-importance of the Irish quality daily. The definite tone of the tabloids conveyed the essential message to their news desks in concise, simple and fitting language.

Henry Caslin is fucked.

The same conclusion had been reached by the man himself once the station announced that normal programming would be disrupted by the conference. This harbinger of the extraordinary meant that people left the fields, nipped out of offices or parked their vans and cars in front of pubs where they watched McKeon, and afterwards agreed with complete strangers that the Taoiseach was a liar. The object of their outrage and his wife watched the conference in the kitchen of The Hacienda.

—Did you hear him, Mary? Talking about children. Saying he had to do this because the welfare of our children is too important to be the subject of political chicanery. You know I worship children. You know I never did one thing to harm any child.

And he had not. But that was not the point. Mary left the phone off the hook and watched the answering machine fill up with calls inside fifteen minutes. She pictured the journalist's cars setting off eagerly for Rathbawn like competitors in a treasure hunt. No one at that press conference knew about the money Henry had raised for Rathbawn Leisure Complex, about the people he had housed, the families he had helped, his drainage scheme which meant farmers in the North of the county no longer had to use boats to get around their land three months of the year, the football teams he sponsored, the industries he had enticed to the town. All they knew was that they had caught Henry and did not have to respect him any more. Tears plopped into Mary's cup. Henry held her till the front door rang to announce Dolores's arrival.

Dearbhla arrived fifteen minutes later. Henry played with his two granddaughters, simulacra of their mothers at the same age. Dolores's Winnie fell over and smiled a lot, the plasters on her legs changing location and size so often that her mother joked she was trying to find which style suited her best. Dearbhla's Emma had displayed an unerring ability to hammer the right pegs into the right holes at nursery school, began to read at three and had disquieted Henry at the age of seven by outlining the disadvantages of National Wage Agreements.

Friends began to call to the house, and Mary ushered them out the back to sit on the boards covering the swimming pool. Henry remained indoors, conscious that out there were long lenses ready to capture any expression on his face and convert it into disinterest, insouciance, vengefulness, sorrow or whatever emotion the news desks deemed correct.

When Sian Guiney arrived he brought her into the library. She sat facing Henry. He was flanked by Mary, Dolores and Dearbhla, and explained that his family had to hear what Sian was going to say.

—Or else they'll try and cheer me up by pretending I mustn't have understood you.

Sian said Henry knew himself what had to be done. He nodded and shook off a couple of indignant nos from his daughters. Mary walked over to Sian, put her hand on her shoulder and walked out the door with her daughters. Henry heard his wife quiver as she greeted some new arrivals.

—I'm going to have to send out a press release saying that you'll be making an important announcement to the Dáil tomorrow. Is that OK, Henry?

—It's OK, Sian. It is.

He was so calm that for a second she wondered if he realised what the announcement was going to be.

—It's all right, Sian. I'll have to go, I know that. Take the evening off, go back to Dublin and have a bit of dinner. I'd like to write this speech myself.

On the dual carriageway into the city, Sian had the windscreen wipers switched on before she realised it was tears that were blurring her vision. She pulled into a hotel car park and listened to Henry's enemies on the radio.

On the back of an envelope Henry scribbled a few key words for the next day. Too much or too little to memorise might make him break down. As a youngster, he had been beguiled by visions of gallant defeat, imagining himself composed and dignified in the face of unavoidable disaster. He knew all the great exits, the fine last stands. But he was not going to go like unbowed Liam Lynch, continuing the Civil War in the Knockmealdown mountains with a dwindling band of fighters, or fearless Cathal Brugha charging out the front door of Hamman's Hotel with both guns blazing. He was like Wolfe Tone, a man with his dreams in tatters cutting his throat with a rusty blade.

He wished he was a man who drank.

Martina and Henry Junior arrived back from skiing in Andorra. Henry apologised for ruining their holiday. He knew it was few they took.

—Ah, daddy . . . stop, please.

His son turned away as if suffering a seizure. His daughter-in-law hugged him, a message pulsing through her arms and back that all sorrow was surmountable. In time.

—I'll stand down as TD at the next election, Martina. Come in this day week, there's some stuff I want to give you. It's as well to start making sure now that you get the nomination.

The absence of Jimmy increased Henry's sense of desolation. He presumed that seeing all they had worked for destroyed had sent him on the skite. He wanted to know Jimmy was safe, that the news had not proved too much for him to handle.

People with drinks in their hands were watching the six o'clock News when Henry walked into the living-room. The tail-end of murmured imprecations told him McKeon had just left the screen. The Canny Dub appeared at the head of a phalanx of senior Party figures. Someone asked Henry if he wanted the television switched off. He shook his head. Everyone wants to see their own funeral. He felt like an Indian widow watching her neighbours collecting firewood.

—I would, ah, obviously, ah, be concerned about standards in public life, said the Canny Dub.

—What about your fucking mistress, you Dublin cunt?

—Dearbhla, be quiet like a good girl.

—Sorry, Daddy.

—It appears that the Dáil was misled, and I think someone needs to bring the Party back to the standards of openness and accountability for which it has always been noted. I will be talking to some of my ministerial colleagues, and discussing the possibility of moving a vote of no confidence against the leader.

Men cursed, women shushed and somebody threw a wine glass against the wall. Henry marvelled at how few of his followers recognised the rules of the game they had played this twenty-odd years. It was always your own side that gave it to you. He had shafted two leaders himself, after all. You couldn't blame people for taking their chance. All this standards stuff was nonsense, high-moral-tone hypocrisy sculpted to please the likes of McKeon, who had never engaged with the real world of politics and seen how it was driven by different imperatives than that of the ideal world they compared it to. But if that was what the Canny Dub wanted to use, let him.

Moira Hopkins appeared on screen, asking people in Rathbawn what they thought of the Taoiseach now. Henry thought the question made him sound like a convicted murderer. His enemies scarified him, Christy Dockery lurching towards the camera on a blackthorn stick, the implacability of his hatred making him look 3-D. Erstwhile friends dissembled, saying it seemed to be a sorry affair and that they would reserve judgement until all the facts were available. Nora Lawrence came on and Henry braced himself. You could do anything for the tinkers and it was the same thanks you'd get.

—He always done a lot for the travellers in this town, in this county and I'll tell you this, that when no one else wanted to know us Henry Caslin did, and he's a decent man and we'll pass no heed on the blackguarding going on because we don't forget a good turn nor a bad.

It was the early hours of the morning before he finally broke down in tears at the unfairness of a lifetime's work being undone by one second of bad judgement.

—Henry Caslin is today expected to announce his resignation as Taoiseach.

Television was always right, and Henry was not surprised that morning when the Canny Dub shouldered his way past Sian Guiney, accompanied by two men who had been fired the last time they had stood in the Taoiseach's office. They did not have to wait for an invite any more.

—We've come for your fucking head, Henry. We want you fucking gone this evening. You know no one will support you. They think you've made the whole Party look like liars.

The Canny Dub's delivery suggested several trial runs in front of the bathroom mirror.

—I'm resigning in an hour's time. Don't you know that?

—We've come for your fucking head. We want you to know that, and we want everyone to know it was us who gave you the boot.

The Canny Dub came across as a low-definition TV movie version of the Tough Guy. His strength lay in his weakness. It was conceivable that no one would ever feel sufficient dislike to dispose of him.

Henry could hear the baiting from the smaller parties on the opposition benches when he stood up. The main opposition party's glee was more subdued. They knew what it was like to lose power. All the barracking, the jibes and the demands for resignation did was remind him that he had often heard worse at the church gate. He began his small speech.

—I would like to inform the Dáil that I have decided to resign as Taoiseach, due to recent media revelations which have made it impossible for me to continue. I will also be resigning as leader of the Party. Yesterday I informed the Dáil that there was no record of an extradition warrant dealing with Father Gerard Lee having been received by the Department of Justice. I am now satisfied that this information was incorrect, and that I misled the Dáil. There was no intention on my part to do so, but I accept full responsibility for so doing. I should have known about the existence of the warrant.

With the irritation of a hung-over teacher, he noticed people shifting around in their seats and talking to each other. They had heard he was going and that was enough for them, but he would continue speaking. He deserved that much.

—I regret having to step down as Taoiseach. I have always endeavoured to do my best for my country, and have been proud to serve its people. I do not think I have done a bad job, and in some areas I hope I have left behind a better situation than I inherited. I have been blessed with a fine team of Ministers whose help has been invaluable to me. I have also enjoyed crossing swords with the members on the opposition benches. I will miss the repartee and I will miss the responsibility.

He made to sit down, and then remembered his intended finish.

—I would like to say a special word of thanks to my wife Mary. Being the wife of a Taoiseach exerts pressures of its own. She has been a tower of strength . . . she will always be a tower of strength.

There was silence for a full five seconds after he sat down.

In days to come, the leader of the opposition would call for judicial enquiries, tribunals and think-tanks to work out why the Party seemed unfit to govern the country. On this day he contented himself with tributes to Henry. This amused Martina no end.

—Do you know what your father should say, Henry? That seeing as your man thinks so highly of him, he's changed his mind and he's staying on.

Nobody noticed Henry slipping away afterwards. The talk in the lobby was of his successor. Reporters from seven different countries heard the Canny Dub describe himself as a man born to rule. Sian Guiney told everyone the Taoiseach had left the building.

Heading west, ten minutes short of clearing the capital, Henry felt an irresistible urge to stop the car. He parked in a lay-by near a filling station, got out and walked along a grass verge to see where he was now.

He was in the suburbs. Looking at what had defeated him. Everyone told him that elections these days were decided in the suburbs. There were no voting patterns here and no traditions. People changed their vote every month here, and without them you could not win power.

He had done wrong. He could accept that. But once he could have survived by brazening it out. You could not do that any more because of the suburbs. The inhabitants had too much time to themselves in these lonely places. Time to indulge egotism and the pathological taking of offence, and confuse these conditions with morality. On their beloved phone-in shows, the smallest of feuds, the most trivial of topics, all the detritus of daily life were addressed in a language of gravity and hurt which demanded the recognition that there were no longer any laughing matters.

—I would feel that I am certainly owed an apology.

—I cannot overemphasise how hurt I am by the whole affair.

—This is a matter I would find very difficult to forgive.

And what they were talking about was their neighbour holding on to a garden rake for two months, the fact that there was a one-pound-twenty-five-pence booking charge for concert tickets, or that their National School dance troupe had been excluded from a pantomime.

The close communities of countryside and small town were dying, and these places were taking over. They had no centres, no binding forces but the voices on television and radio. When the Arms Trial could have torn the country apart, the Man With The Pipe sat down on an old armchair and spoke to the whole country on television like he was addressing a GAA meeting in the parish hall, explaining patiently what was going on because he was confident he and the voters shared a common language. If they thought about it, he said, there was no need for him to go. Wasn't he doing his best?

You could not speak like that any more. It was not the Taoiseach people listened to.

He continued along the grass verge, watching the cars whizzing by, before the realisation of what exactly had happened to him stopped him stock-still.

He had become a man of no consequence.

His entry in the history books would be cross-referenced with disrepute, incompetence and failure.

And the North would not save him. Even if peace did hold, it would no longer be his peace.

Futility shrouded those great moments of his life. The striving at school, the decoration of the dancehalls, the sound of Mary's shoes squeaking across the lino to meet him for the first time. He had imagined that happy memories would lift a person at their lowest ebb, but what happened was that misery dragged them down to pointlessness along with everything else.

His breath seemed to catch in his throat. He felt a sharp pain in his chest and his head span. He worried that he might disappear completely from the earth, but managed to shuffle another few yards along the verge. The dark was a cool and comforting half-tone in the shade of the concrete pillars supporting the motorway bridge. He leaned against one of the pillars. Two young lads got off their bikes and walked over to him.

—Are you all right, mister?

—Are you OK, do you want us to call a doctor?

He said he was sound, and slowly walked back to the car, thanking them profusely.

They had not even recognised him. Though they were voting age and identifiable as decent by their concern for him, they did not know the leader of their country. All his time in politics made not a blind bit of difference to youngsters like them.

The car radio announced his demise as Taoiseach. He

had become just another man in his sixties sitting lonely in a car. A man with nothing going for him. An old man.

McKeon made breakfast for Moira that morning. She was working on the News, but he had a day off. He ate muesli and drank orange juice. Since getting married he had begun to look after himself. The urge for self-preservation notwithstanding, it took someone else's love and worry to make you look after yourself properly. He went out for an *Irish Times*. The shopkeeper complimented him on the programme. They both agreed that Henry Caslin had to go. You couldn't run a country in this manner.

On the answering machine, foreign broadcasters requested interviews about the current crisis. Crisis, thought McKeon, what crisis? I've never had a better week in my life. At noon Patrick Armstrong rang.

—Are you having a party or something?

No something about it, Seamus. We're having a party for you and the programme and that evil-collared cunt Lee. And because Caslin is gone, that's great news too.

—How come?

He asked the question a second time. Armstrong took his time answering it. McKeon pictured him groping a woman and handing her a beer to be going on with while he talked on the phone. Poor broken Armstrong and his dead legs.

—He had to go, Seamus. He's the proper sacrifice. This is the revenge of the children for everything that's happened. All these hundreds of years. What Father Lee was doing was against nature. Everyone knew it was going on. You never heard of anyone being arrested for it, it was let happen like it was kind of normal, like it needed to happen to some people to keep the rest safe. Like in fucking *King Kong*, where they give up one beautiful wee black girl the odd time to keep the monster happy out there in the jungle.

Have no sympathy for Caslin, he's one of the people that let it happen . . . Seamus, could you ring me back, something's just come up.

Giggles and the sound of a ring-pull snapping and beer foaming. McKeon almost had the phone down when he heard Armstrong shouting.

—Seamus, Seamus, you should be proud of yourself. You did it for us. To us, you know, you're a fucking hero.

A round of applause from the other side of the border.

By half eight he was sitting at his favourite table in his favourite restaurant with his favourite person, who was telling him about her vox pops in Rathbawn and how some tinker woman had stood up for Caslin. There was still enough Rathbawn in McKeon for him to enter this on Henry's debit side.

This dinner for two would cost three hundred pounds. His father and mother had probably not spent that much on meals out in their lives. He loved this place. Impossible tastes, spotlessness and servility in a room his parents could not have imagined. Pâté de foie gras. Quails' eggs. Bottles of wine costing eighty-five quid. Truffles. Caviar. Mousseline of guinea fowl. You could eat the whole world in here if you came often enough.

—You did it for us.

—You're a fucking hero.

He wondered if they were right, and a second later wondered if they could have been more wrong. He does not have a clue why he made the programme, and, job done, questions the reasons which had seemed so obvious.

What are the reasons? The memory of his father tipping his cap in the *Herald*; his revenge on Mickey Kelly for his treatment of Moira; his revenge on Moira because maybe he has never forgiven her for those nights in the Dodo when she was someone for everyone to laugh at, and maybe he laughed too and he is taking revenge on himself as well.

Perhaps he is jealous of Henry Caslin, whose achievements are almost a personal affront to McKeon. Perhaps all these reasons combined and forced him to make the programme, the pure motive of outrage in reality playing an infinitesimal part. Perhaps this was obvious to the discerning viewer, and will eventually be made known to everyone.

The racing of these thoughts he tries to retard with wine, and glasses of it disappear into him like morning tumblers of water down a hung-over throat. Moira tries to get him to slow down. McKeon can see that he appears drunk but he feels sober, his mind filled with a horrifying, irreducible clarity.

He knows he will not be able to sleep tonight.

Moira insists on driving home, and looks strangely at him as he wrestles her for the keys before collapsing against the side of the car as if the air has been let out of him. They have just walked in the door of the house when he insists on leaving. There is somewhere he has to be, but as he says this he realises he does not know where this place is. He feels he must have known a second ago and is trying to rewind his thought processes when he realises that the car keys are in his hand. At the front door, Moira stands in his way.

—You're not driving, Seamus, you're far too drunk. What is wrong with you?

—What is wrong with me, ha ha ha.

His voice surprises him because it does not seem to be his. He has to get out of the house.

—Moira, get out of the way. I'm warning you.

He wishes he could get back to the start of the evening. In a minute he will wish to get back to the start of his life.

—Seamus, love, come on, get up those stairs to bed.

—Don't call me love.

There is something he has to find. He is the man who has brought down the Taoiseach. He gets the door half open but Moira is pushing him back with all her might, the effort causing a blue vein to pop up at the side of her forehead. He has to get out of the house.

Slowly, as in an action replay, he sees himself strike Moira across the face. She drops her hands in complete surprise. He strikes her again, as if to confirm to them both that the first blow happened. She staggers back into the hall and looks at him. Appalled. They both are. His hand is stinging. She feels her jaw. There are terrible tears in her eyes of a kind he had sworn to protect her from. He has seen these tears before, and they were of terrible despair and a knowledge that life would never be fair to her. They had disappeared after the marriage.

—I love you, Moira, he says, and walks towards her.

She shrinks back. He has never struck Moira before, but this knowledge is not reflected in her face. She is looking at him as if surprised he has not tried to kill her. As if he does this all the time, and she has expected this moment from that day at the christening party beside the canal just two hundred yards away. He sees something white on the floor and thinks for a second that it is one of her teeth, but it is an earring which has come loose.

McKeon hurries out the door. He knows that his marriage has, from the moment he swung his panicky hand, changed irrevocably.

On the road to Rathbawn he remembers what he is looking for. A photo taken in a dancehall thirty years before of Father Gerry Lee, Henry Caslin, Jimmy Mimnagh and Seamus McKeon. He knows it must be in the huge dusty archaeological boxes that are the *Herald* photo files.

The wine tells him that possessing this photo will help him understand why all this happened.

At dinner he remembered how, in the *Herald*, he had helped a woman in the front office proof-read advertisements. She had special difficulty deciphering the spidery scrawl of Jimmy Mimnagh's notices to Party members. McKeon was able to read it. It was an idiosyncratic script, identical to the one on the hotel notepaper directing him towards the warrants.

On the way down he stops at Mother Hubbard's truckers' restaurant and rings the young reporter from the *Herald*. There is the usual delay as the lad struggles to make the hall phone box in time. He can tell the youngster is thinking how wonderful to be McKeon, the man who broke the big story. Once McKeon had wanted to be the him he was now. When he became that person he discovered that there were no mysterious gear changes in life. A streamlined rut is still a rut.

Jimmy had lain all day in a hotel bedroom, lacking even the energy to drink, letting his phone ring out until he was woken at half eleven and picked up the receiver in a state of dozy surprise. He had never heard Mary in a panic before.

—Jimmy, Henry is gone missing. I'm pure out of my mind with worry. He left Dublin and he should have been home hours ago. Jimmy, you've got to find him. I've tried every hotel in the city looking for you.

He pulled his creaking frame together, draped the clothes over it as if dressing a scarecrow and headed west. The radio was running a profile of the Canny Dub entitled *The Man Who would be King*. History was moving on, and Jimmy was taking a taxi through the dark. Him and the driver and the full realisation of what he had done.

After all those years, those meetings, that tramping around the countryside, the seams, the whole crack, he has destroyed his own life's work because of feeling insulted and unwanted. Without even talking to Henry about it. Now everything they had achieved might as well never have been.

During his incarceration, Father Lee has said Mass twice a day. It was a consolation. The little radio in his cell tells him Henry Caslin has resigned as Taoiseach. He is sorry about that. The Brits had feared Caslin, and now they would be happy.

He was allowed to hear the confessions of other prisoners segregated for their own safety. Rapists mainly, and men who had committed particularly brutal murders. Even they moralised to him about the sacred nature of childhood and the evil of his actions.

This morning he takes for confession a young man who had informed against his INLA colleagues in the hope of a deal with the state which never transpired. He is just thinking how edgy the youngster was when he feels a fierce pain in his right eye. The man stabs him as hard as the blunt pencil will allow before trying to plunge it into Father Lee's ear. The warders arrive and as he is stretchered away, Father Lee hears his assailant being bounced off the walls. Two warders accompany him in the ambulance.

—Seemingly you'll live, Father. More's the pity, says the first warder.

—Do you see what's going on in the South, what a fucking mess, says the second warder.

Then Father Lee does not hear any more. His ears are filled with the sound of a curlew's cry. He remembers.

It is a cold evening. The six-year-old boy and the man walk home with the noise of a single curlew filling the air around them. The man grabs the boy and bundles him into the shed, holding the youngster between the legs and ripping off his clothes. The man's hand smells of the hide of wet cows.

—If you say anything, I'll kill you. Be a good lad and nothing will happen to you. But if you say anything, I'll give you away to the tinkers, I will, Gerry.

Almost disinterestedly, Father Lee wonders where his father, Martin, an otherwise kind man who always sat in the front seat at Mass, and would walk two miles in the rain to chop wood for an elderly neighbour, got the ideas for the buggery, the masturbation, the forced sex with the other children and so on. His imagination? Or his own experience? As he drifts off to sleep, rocked by speed bumps, Father Lee thinks of the Jesuit maxim.

—Give me the boy and I will give you the man.

McKeon was back in the *Herald* newsroom. Thirty years after it had all begun. Rifling through folders, cardboard containers and old chocolate boxes stuffed with photographs. His progress like the history of the county told in rapid time-lapse. The snapshots like geological layers.

At the top, the confident nineties with Henry Caslin handing the keys of an IDA advance factory to an American industrialist, who swore his computer firm would soon employ six hundred people. The dour mid-eighties, a picture of young Rathbawn men and women at Knock Airport as they came home for Christmas. The mid-seventies, a hundred cars in a line outside a Texaco garage, a couple of motorists looking at the sign telling them they can buy just one gallon of petrol. The early seventies, a happy, drunken, flarey-trousered crowd at the Rathbawn Folk Festival, money in their pockets, convinced they were home from England to stay. The funeral of Larry Lynn, men in black berets firing a twenty-one-gun tribute over his coffin.

Veterans of the War of Independence taking the salute from the Army on the fiftieth anniversary of the Easter Rising. The first ever photos in the *Herald*, from the early sixties, of a group of dancers performing for a reporter from the infant national television station. No photos from the dank and desperate forgotten land of the fifties. And no sign of the photo he had come for. He realised now it did not matter very much. The door behind him opened to admit Jimmy Mimnagh.

—You have some cheek coming in here, McKeon.

—You can't talk to me about cheek, Jimmy, said McKeon.

Jimmy acknowledged the truth of the statement with a slight heron-like dip of the head and invited McKeon to give him a lift.

—I've something I want to show you. And by the way, I suppose you'd like a look at this before we go.

The photograph. McKeon could see that Jimmy had dusted it but there was still a thin veneer of grime giving it the look of a shot taken through a window. Gerry McDonagh, dead now, had stamped his name on the back. The surface of the photo rippled like waves but had not yet torn.

One of McKeon's arms was severed by the left edge of the photo. Beside him, Henry Caslin smiled his famous smile and dominated the picture to such an extent that he seemed like a hologram floating above the surface. His right arm was around the shoulder of Father Gerry Lee, who appeared to shrink away from the camera. Beside Father Lee, Jimmy Mimnagh's eyes were going both ways with drink but one of them managed to gaze at Caslin as if he was afraid the man would bolt from the building and never be seen again.

McKeon wondered how he had remembered the shot so exactly. This piece of paper was significant now because of all that had happened, but a month ago it had just been another photograph. He might have forgotten it even existed, but he had not. Had he somehow known all those years ago the importance it would one day take on?

The photograph showed Henry Caslin and Jimmy Mimnagh on the night they became friends, such friends that Jimmy would dedicate his life to the cause of making Henry Taoiseach before taking his gift back. Father Gerry Lee had given Jimmy the means of betraying Henry, and Seamus McKeon had completed the betrayal. They had come together again, far more closely than in the photograph. Back then, proximity had been all that united them.

Anyone looking at the photograph might have seen it as proof of a connection between the four men which made the Father Lee affair understandable and sinister. But there was no connection. Maybe the photo proved the strange synchronous workings of coincidence. Or just the fact that in a small country, love and power and betrayal are contained in small circles intimately and extensively connected.

They stopped the car at the head of the Canal Line. The Royal Canal had once run right into the heart of Rathbawn, bringing barges and boats into the middle of the town. Jimmy and Henry had led the fight in the mid-sixties to have the harbour concreted over. A Party bigwig wanted to build twenty-four houses there. Jimmy pointed out that no one used the canal except outsiders. They won the fight. Now the houses were derelict, the developer was in jail and the Canal Line had become a lonely walk overgrown with grass and weeds, a venue for cider parties, sexual trysts between the desperate, cockfights, dogfights and bare-knuckle boxing bouts to crown the King of the Tinkers. It was quiet now as Jimmy and McKeon walked along till they came to a little turlough down the hill from the old GAA ground. Water stored in the grass dampened their socks before they reached the remains of the handball alley where the Brits Out logo was weathering the years far better than the front wall that bore it.

A man was sitting near the right side wall, staring ahead as the wind blew papers and leaves around the muddy surface. He was talking to himself, reciting the same words over and over. Jimmy began to cry, but Henry showed no sign of noticing, not even when the two men arrived beside him.

—We did this, Seamus. We did this.

Jimmy sat down beside Henry, who still continued to stare ahead and repeat the words. McKeon drew closer and tried to make out what was being said. When he did, he realised that it made no sense at all. The former Taoiseach kept asking the wind

—Who stole the sheep, who stole the sheep, who stole the sheep.